HOT-FOOT THROUGH THE HIGHLANDS

Also by Alan Plowright

Plowright Follows Wainwright

HOT-FOOT THROUGH THE HIGHLANDS

Alan Plowright

Moorfield Press

First published in Great Britain
by
Moorfield Press 1997

Copyright © Alan Plowright 1997

Filmset by
Highlight Type Bureau Ltd, Bradford, West Yorkshire
Printed in England by
The Amadeus Press Ltd, Huddersfield, West Yorkshire

A CIP catalogue record for this book is available from the British Library

ISBN O 9530 1191 7

The moral right of the author has been asserted

Cover photograph (Glen Tilt): Alan Plowright
Other photographs: Alan Plowright
Maps and Illustrations: John W.Holroyd

ITINERARY

1. **DEESIDE TO LOCH LOMOND**
   Lochnagar
   Balmoral
   Braemar
   Linn of Dee
   Glen Tilt
   Blair Atholl
   Killiecrankie
   Pitlochry
   Loch Tummel
   Schiehallion
   Keltneyburn
   Fortingall
   Glen Lyon
   Bridge of Balgie
   Ben Lawers
   Loch Tay
   Glen Lochay
   Killin
   Glen Ogle
   Balquhidder
   Kirkton Glen
   Glen Dochart
   Ben More
   Inverlochlarig
   Loch Katrine
   Loch Arklet
   Inversnaid

2. **THE WEST HIGHLAND WAY**
   Crianlarich
   Tyndrum
   Bridge of Orchy
   Rannoch Moor
   Glencoe
   Kinlochleven
   Fort William

3. **BEN NEVIS, THE GREAT GLEN AND GLEN SHIEL**
   Ben Nevis
   Spean Bridge
   Glen Roy
   Laggan
   Invergarry
   Tomdoun
   Loch Loyne
   Loch Cluanie
   Glen Shiel
   Shiel Bridge

4. **WESTER ROSS AND SUTHERLAND**
   Loch Duich
   Loch Carron
   Strathcarron
   Achnashellach
   Coulin Forest
   Kinlochewe
   Lochan Fada
   Loch an Nid
   Little Loch Broom
   Dundonnell
   Loch Broom
   Ullapool
   Strath Kanaird
   Elphin
   Inchnadamph
   Kylesku
   Scourie
   Laxford Bridge
   Richonich
   Durness

5. **THE NORTH COAST**
   Loch Eriboll
   Tongue
   Bettyhill
   Melvich
   Thurso
   John O'Groats

Contents

Introduction

My love of Scotland, a country blessed with resplendent lochs and rugged mountains, encouraged me to write this book, which I regard as a pleasure. Such a statement from an Englishman is quite an admission, but I am convinced that this captivating country draws many admirers from England, some to repeatedly return, as Alfred Wainwright did.

Be assured that I am not sponsored by the Scottish Tourist Board, nor am I held in a stranglehold by a red-bearded giant named Jock as I write. By walking the length and breadth of the varied country, I realise that it's fiercely patriotic people revere their distinctive culture and are steadfastly proud of their roots. The sometimes wild and austere nature of it's terrain belies the kindness and hospitality always shown to visitors. Tradition and loyalty hold sway, manifested by remembrance of such famous ancestors as Bonnie Prince Charlie, Robert the Bruce and Rob Roy McGregor.

Red-blooded Sassenachs may at this moment be gnashing their teeth whilst furiously writing to their MP to pour ridicule on this glowing tribute. May I remind them of Scotland's immense contribution to international harmony, culture and humour. These are symbolised by the 'wee dram', which provides the harmony, Billy Connolly, who injects the culture, and Jimmy Knapp, to whom we are indebted for the humour. This may not cut much ice with my fellow-countrymen who believe that the best thing to come out of Scotland is the A74, which is currently undergoing metamorphosis into the M74. To such people, men in skirts, with severe draught problems, do not inspire hero-worship. The evocative sound of bagpipes taxes their eardrums, and 'tatties and neeps' are considered no match for roast beef and Yorkshire pud.

In my defence I rely upon Alfred Wainwright, who so loved Scotland that he spent all his holidays there, never wishing to go elsewhere. If such a renowned lover of the countryside could not stay away, it must have something special in my view. Although I never had the honour of meeting him I feel that I knew him well through following his inspirational guides across many parts of England.

I wrote an account of the following journeys, as a tribute to him, entitled *Plowright Follows Wainwright*. My initial long-distance foray was a walk around the Three Peaks of Yorkshire which stemmed from reading his *Walks in Limestone Country*. I then graduated to tackling the Pennine Way, a memorable experience, taking with me his *Pennine Way Companion*. This was followed by an exploration of the Lake District, accompanied by his Pictorial Guides to the Lakeland Fells, when I suffered some of the wettest weather known to man. Undeterred, I embarked on his Coast to Coast Walk from St Bees in Cumbria to Robin Hood's Bay.

I was introduced to the enchantment of Scotland by the television series in the late 1980's that featured Wainwright's travels through the country. Its majestic mountain scenery, secluded glens and rugged coastline nurtured my desire for exploration. One memorable shot during the series showed him and Eric Robson gazing over Loch Cairnbawn that lies in the remote north-west Highlands. The dramatic beauty of that view made a great impact upon me and I vowed to see it for myself. His very popular large format book, *Wainwright in Scotland*, was published around that time and its superb illustrations complemented the views that I had seen in the television series. This served to increase my appetite, in addition to offering a perpetual memory of Scotland's charms. When I can no longer walk the fells those pictures will provide a welcome substitute, transporting me to places of enduring beauty. I was thus encouraged to explore the country so loved by him and I embarked on a series of walks that would cover a large proportion of it.

This book could have started life in a different vein, if I had not been beaten to the punch, as it were. Shortly after completing the first of my Scottish walks, vanity decreed that I had to commit to paper my pioneering achievement of linking the Pennine Way and West Highland Way footpaths by walking from Kirk Yetholm, near the Scottish border, to Milngarvie near Glasgow. The route of that particular journey was of my own making and, being forever the optimist, I visualised myself as the first walker to officially link these well-established long-distance footpaths, thus bringing closer the prospect of a recognised cross-country route from Lands End to John O'Groats.

Pride comes before a fall, as the saying goes, and it was not long before I received my just desserts. I had barely commenced my epic account, when, passing a local bookshop, a new publication displayed in the window caught my eye. Unbelievably the book was entitled *Pennine Way to West Highland Way*. Desperately fighting the urge to heave a missile through the window, I pressed my face against the glass, much to the consternation of the assistant arranging a display behind it. I had to discover the perpetrator of the dastardly publication. It turned out to be Hamish Brown, author of *Hamish's Groats End Walk* and *Hamish's Mountain Walk*, the latter being an account of his continuous traverse of all the Scottish Munros. Cursing him for getting his latest book in first, I dashed into the shop, grabbed a copy and enviously scanned its pages. His route, I observed, varied significantly from mine, but this was of no consequence because he had already committed his account to print. From his viewpoint it would be merely an addition to his previous books, but to me it was a veritable knife in the back.

Dejectedly I trudged homewards, my expectancy dashed. Eventually my annoyance turned to acceptance and I began to think more positively about the issue. At least I had not spent a great deal of time on my account and I would be sure to check for competing publications in future. Realising that I could not break new ground, the splendid alternative of recording a journey in the footsteps of Wainwright, who had already provided the inspiration for many of my walks through England, came to mind. Thus were sown the seeds of the following story.

I travelled in the opposite direction to the route he describes in *Wainwright in Scotland* with the object of finishing at the north-east tip of Britain. Commencing my walk with an ascent of evocative Lochnagar, which overlooks Royal Deeside, I headed south-west to join the West Highland Way at Inversnaid on the banks of Loch Lomond. This most popular of Scottish long-distance footpaths was followed to its termination at Fort William, where a celebratory ascent of Ben Nevis was made. A descent into the Great Glen launched the next stage of my journey, to Glen Shiel. Remote Wester Ross and Sutherland followed, where habitation is sparse and much of the terrain inhospitable. When Durness, near Cape Wrath, was reached, the final lap of my journey, along the north coast to John O'Groats, began.

Lace your boots tightly and gather your strength if you wish to involve yourself in this testing adventure. You will experience some of the finest scenery that Britain has to offer, meet many interesting characters and share experiences unique to such a journey. Good Luck!

Alan Plowright. 1997.

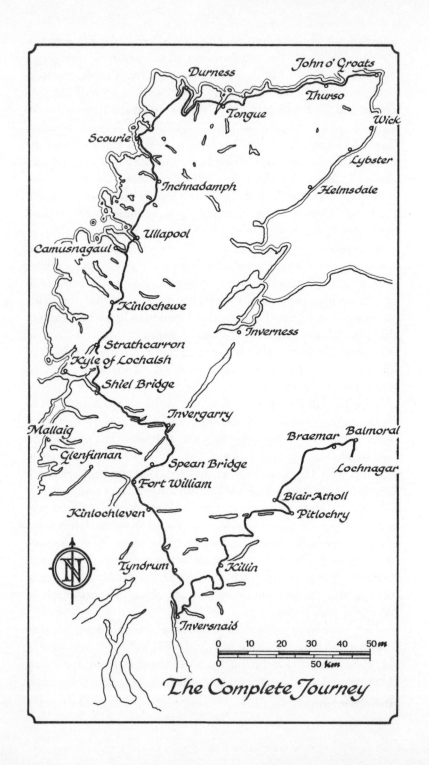

The Complete Journey

CHAPTER ONE

Deeside to Loch Lomond

DAY ONE: BALMORAL - BRAEMAR

The view from my imposing vantage point on the summit of Lochnagar was panoramic. Under a May sky of vivid blue the irregular outline of distant mountains soared above a tapestry of lush meadows sprinkled with diverse woodland. The cloud which had accompanied my approach to the dramatic ridge on which I now stood had miraculously rolled away. Six miles to the north lay Royal Deeside, the starting point of my journey to the north-east tip of Scotland. How easy it was to see why the Royal Family have cherished this area since Queen Victoria and Prince Albert fell in love with it in 1848.

The river Dee traced its eager course through the rich valley, intermittently secreting itself amongst protective clusters of trees. A path issuing from the rock-strewn lower slopes of Lochnagar snaked into the distant confines of the Balmoral estate that flanked the mercurial river. Straining for a glimpse of Balmoral Castle was useless for it remained stubbornly hidden amongst wooded grounds

1

that were barred to visitors that day. I had thus been denied the privilege of starting and ending my journey at distinctive Scottish buildings. The castle would have provided an auspicious launching site and also a powerful contrast to the simple crofter's cottage for which I was bound - now known as the Last House at John O'Groats.

Only an idiot could have failed to check that Balmoral grounds and gardens were accessible each day of the week. Never assume as I had, that ensuring their availability from early May until the end of July was sufficient. I was blissfully unaware that they were closed on Sundays and subsequently paid dearly for my stupidity. The polite refusal of entry which I received to the royal precincts also enforced a circuitous route to the foothills of Lochnagar. How inconsiderate of her majesty not to welcome me or provide a member of the Royal Family to launch me on my travels. On the other hand, how could I explain to a royal personage, with their protected lifestyle, the attractions of covering a substantial part of Scotland on foot?

Such tribulations were cast aside as I enjoyed the exhilarating view from my towering perch. In retrospect my visit to Balmoral was not entirely fruitless, for I had toured the Royal Lochnagar Distillery where fine malt whisky lay maturing in oaken casks following its age-old processing. The crystal-clear streams flowing from Lochnagar and the barley from surrounding fields have provided the raw materials for this most delicious of spirits since the distillery was established in 1845. Queen Victoria came to test its qualities and was suitably impressed. The modern Visitor Centre houses an exhibition recalling her memorable visit.

On my way to the Distillery I had seen the attractive Crathie church and one of the prominent memorials in Balmoral grounds, albeit from a distance. I caught sight of the spire and distinctive red roof of the church through an infinite variety of foliage that clothes the banks of the River Dee. The Royal Family worship there whilst in residence at Balmoral, its foundation stone being laid by Queen Victoria in 1893. Numerous memorials to past monarchs, members of their families and even their dogs inhabit the castle grounds. Some take the form of cairns strategically sited on wooded hilltops and one of these provided a fitting backdrop to the local golf course, its triangular outline silhouetted against an unfriendly sky.

Passing outlying estate buildings and some rich pastureland, I had begun my approach to Dark Lochnagar, immortalised in the famous

Map One

ROADS --------
RAILWAYS ++++++

song. It had glowered over the River Dee on my arrival at Balmoral, its stark outline impossible to ignore. Standing on its lofty pinnacle gave a tremendous feeling of achievement. I tentatively peered over the edge of the jagged, near-vertical wall of rock that hurtled precariously from beneath my feet. In the sunlight I could clearly see the extent of its grey, fissured face, seemingly scoured by a giant rake.

An unexpected voice startled me and I quickly retreated from the edge, not wishing to make an impromptu entry into the dark waters of Loch Nagar nestling in the corrie hundreds of feet below. I turned to face a sprightly and athletic-looking young walker. He must have made a quick ascent for he had been nowhere in sight a little earlier. Despite his exertions his breathing was relaxed. In fact, everything about him looked pristine, right down to his immaculate boots. His attire was spotless, each item displaying the poser's motif and oozing quality. This fellow has superb taste in walking gear, I thought, as I studied the natty, woollen hat sitting perfectly symmetrically over his head.

I felt pangs of jealousy welling inside me. Why couldn't he be human and sweat like the rest of us? The fellow had just climbed 3780 feet dammit! He should have looked like the crumpled sack that I resembled, my hair furiously tugged in all directions by the fierce wind. As we made our introductions I discovered that his name was David who hailed from Aberdeen. It transpired that he knew the surrounding territory very well from his numerous visits, which explained his fitness and rapid ascent. He then outlined his ascents of many Scottish mountains in all weathers and I became grudgingly impressed by this seemingly accomplished walker.

A wry smile came to David's lips on hearing that I was from Yorkshire. Apparently he viewed English walkers and climbers with some scepticism, considering the majority to be naïve as far as Scottish mountains were concerned. Many, he felt, were ill-prepared, foolhardy and thoughtless; quite oblivious to danger and showed no regard for any rescuers who may have to risk their necks to save them. He quoted the example of a tragic climber who had died in a blizzard the previous winter after falling 800 feet whilst attempting to climb one of the gullies in the wall of rock beneath us. The mountain rescue team were unable to reach him in time; beaten back for many hours by atrocious weather conditions. I silently hoped that he did not group me with the foolhardy.

We moved to a nearby viewing indicator, mounted on a stone pillar, which identified the names and locations of the host of mountains encircling Lochnagar. I was particularly interested in the Cairngorm group that lay to the north-west. David pointed out some of its outstanding peaks, recounting the delights and hazards of their inhospitable higher reaches.

I listened with fascination to his account of the challenging mountain range that was as yet unknown to me. In fact I felt quite sorry when he made his apologies and departed, saying that he still had many miles to cover. As he rapidly descended from the summit I inwardly smiled at his immaculate appearance, which suggested that today's outing was a casual stroll. Not a bead of sweat or speck of dirt had I seen on this remarkable man who seemed far removed from your average sweaty, mud-splattered walker.

It was comforting to see that my descent to the south-west started with a gentle slope, a pleasant contrast to the rock-strewn approach to the Lochnagar ridge. The narrow path threaded an easy course through stubbly vegetation inlaid with a patchwork of smooth stones, towards the dome-shaped summit of The Stuic standing a little to the south of its own dramatic ridge. This barrier of rock appeared determined not to be upstaged by its more familiar neighbour. Beneath its craggy slopes lay the small Loch nan Eun from which an energetic stream flowed down to the minute Sandy Loch, glistening cheerfully in the midday sunlight.

My easy downward passage from Lochnagar's summit eventually deteriorated into a steep descent to the head-stream of the Alt an Dubh Loch which tumbles jauntily into Dubh Loch. I could see David far below me heading for the secluded loch maintaining a punishing pace. Despite his speed I could visualise him completing his walk without a hair out of place.

Curlews circled over this serenely attractive scene, their liquid calls providing a pleasant accompaniment. Time dictated that I kept moving as I still had to reach Loch Callater which lies five miles from my destination at Braemar. I intended to cover over twenty miles on my day's journey. The path traced a circuitous route around Carn an Sagairt Mor and Creag an Loch that led me down to Callater Lodge on the shore of Loch Callater. Although I had enjoyed many captivating views that day, the loch and its setting proved a revelation. Blue, expansive waters glistened as they gently rippled in the teasing breeze that scurried through the glen. Boulder-strewn shores glinted invitingly beneath a backdrop of protective mountains flanking the approach to Auchallater that lies on the main road to Braemar. Those stately guardians of the glen alternately shimmered and glowered as scudding clouds hurried over their summits.

As I surveyed this tranquil splendour I was approached by a middle-aged couple, who, although clad in walking attire, looked clearly out of condition. They enquired if it was far to the summit of Lochnagar and I told them that it was more than five miles away over rough terrain. As it was already well into the afternoon I advised against attempting such a trip. They had apparently set out on foot from Braemar around lunchtime, which was much too late for such a venture in my opinion, and had so far only covered a relatively easy five miles along road and track. To attempt to reach Lochnagar and return to Braemar that day would be foolhardy, considering their age and fitness. I suggested that they took a more comfortable walk along the lochside path towards a nature trail I had seen identified on the map at the far edge of the loch. They readily agreed to this sensible alternative, realising that more than half a day would be required for the testing walk to Lochnagar. Pleased that they had taken my advice, I silently hoped that they would take a little more care with their planning in the future.

Bidding them farewell I passed a flock of meadow pippits eyeing me suspiciously, the 'peep peep' of their alarm cry hanging on the breeze. As I walked I mused over a missed opportunity on Lochnagar. According to the couple I had just left, the mountain was once a source of precious stones, particularly in the nineteenth century. Quartz and the very popular cairngorm were hewn from its granite cavities to supply the Highland jewellery industry. Had I known these facts earlier I would have taken a closer look at its rocky slopes, whilst carefully avoiding those alarming fissures in its soaring cliffs. That would be a task for heroes.

Retracing my steps past Callater Lodge, for I had deviated a short distance along the shore of the loch to enjoy the splendid views, I wondered if I should have told the two over-ambitious walkers that Queen Victoria and Prince Albert climbed Lochnagar from there, albeit on ponies. It was difficult to know whether the knowledge would have inspired their confidence or induced a feeling of inferiority. Threading my way through the steep-sided glen I crossed the accompanying Callater Burn which squeezes between the slopes of Creag na Dearcaige and Sron Dubh. Escaping these confines it joins the Clunie Water at Auchallater, from whence it accompanies the A93 road, through a broad valley, to Braemar.

I was greeted on the outskirts of Braemar by a sign indicating that I was re-entering Royal Deeside and my anticipation heightened. The village lay below me, within the ancient Forest of Mar from which its name was derived. Its full name is Castletown of Braemar which relates to Kindrochit Castle, whose ruins still stand in the village. This ancient fortification was used as a hunting lodge in the fourteenth century by Robert I. A modern hotel in the village now marks the site where the thirty-ninth Earl of Mar raised his standard on the Braes of Mar in support of the Old Pretender and the Jacobite cause in 1715.

Oblivious to its history I hurried into the welcoming village to find it alive with visitors bustling around tempting shops. Mingling with the throng I came to a bridge in the main street that spanned an impressive gorge along which sliced the Clunie Water as it rushed to join the Dee. The view was splendid, a veritable magnet for the eager photographers busily taking shots from all angles. Their next objective would probably be the historic Braemar Castle on the outskirts of the village, which I aimed to visit the following morning.

The prospect of a relaxing bath followed by an eagerly awaited supper drew me to my night's accommodation. I had engendered a ravenous appetite and further exploration could wait. My greeting by the lady who ran the B and B was civil if slightly wary. Did she find it strange that I was walking alone? Leading me up a narrow flight of stairs, which emitted loud creaks at every step, she opened the door of my bedroom, which seemed cosy enough. I fully expected a floor that groaned in sympathy with those protesting stairs. I recalled spending several sleepless nights in an otherwise comfortable hotel that boasted three hundred year-old oak floorboards that were so noisily springy that I literally bounced around my bedroom, broadcasting to the other guests my every movement. Consequently I was awakened continually by other guests retiring late at night and by certain bedtime activities. Thankfully this bedroom floor remained blissfully silent, for which I was eternally grateful.

My host proved highly efficient, despite her taciturn manner, performing every task at great speed, particularly the preparation of supper. I was still luxuriating in a steaming-hot bath when the call for supper came. Feeling that it was unwise to cross this formidable lady, I dressed hurriedly and gingerly descended the lethal staircase, accompanied by creaks and groans. I had hardly seated myself at the dining table before a dish of soup was thrust in front of me, accompanied by a look that implied I was to get a move on. As I tried not to slurp my soup, yet maintain a lively pace, I was joined at the table by an elderly couple who, I discovered, were German tourists. They were greeted with a withering look for daring to keep her waiting and hastily apologised. The wicked thought ran through my mind that I was taking part in a sketch from Faulty Towers with the lady playing the female equivalent of Basil Faulty. My fellow guests, Hans and Eva, were very pleasant and friendly, but like me could not prize much conversation from the human dynamo hovering around us. Her answers to our questions were delivered in staccato tones as she steered us quickly through the meal. As each course was finished, crockery was plucked away for immediate washing in the nearby sink; the dining room and kitchen being conveniently combined. A gastronomic record and a bout of indigestion seemed imminent as I devoured the remains of my sweet course. My two companions were striving to keep pace when I was whisked away to the lounge to take coffee in more comfortable surroundings. This, I assumed, was my reward for uncomplaining co-operation during the meal. What a wimp I was.

My new-found German friends were quickly ushered into the room and in an instant a tray of coffee and 'after-dinner' mints appeared. The mints were an extra bonus, I thought, suppressing a smile. When the whirlwind had retreated to her quarters I ventured that it had been the quickest meal on record, prompting a laugh from Hans and Eva. They had apparently been staying for several days and were accustomed to these daily endurance tests. It was their first experience of such accommodation over here, for they usually stayed in hotels. They assumed that guests eating rapidly in such establishments was a peculiar quirk of the British.

We often criticise our German neighbours for ignoring queues and laying out their territory-claiming towels, but I wonder how many Brit's make the effort to discover the true flavour of the countries they visit? Hans and Eva earned top marks for knowing so much about Scotland and especially the activities at the heart of the local economy. They could roll out the yearly itinerary in and around Braemar, to sustain and encourage tourism, at the drop of a hat. Having discovered that skiing is the mainstay in winter, with nearby Glenshee as its centre, they had made a point of visiting its facilities for a first-hand view. How its chair-lifts, ski-tows and parking space for over 1200 vehicles compares to the amenities in the German Alps, they courteously avoided to mention. They did, however, stress that at peak times there could be 9000 people on the slopes at Glenshee and many of them stay in Braemar. On the mornings following a snowfall, they smilingly said, snow-ploughs are out at 6am to clear the nine miles of road between Braemar and Glenshee, thus providing access for vehicle-loads of skiers who queue on the outskirts of the village from 7.30 am in order to get a parking spot at Glenshee. Apparently a frantic race to the ski-slopes begins around 8.30 am when the snow-ploughs return. Despite the depths of snow that must be experienced in the Alps, Hans declared the local snow clearance to be no mean feat, adding that often the only means of detecting the line of the road to Glenshee is by the long poles that protrude from its flanks.

Now in full flow, Hans told me that angling is the magnet for visitors in the spring and summer months. The season evidently starts in March when sections of the lovely Dee are allocated by the Laird's estate staff; permits being available at the Invercauld Estates Office. Some anglers apparently return to fish the same stretch of river each year, which is not surprising with trout in plentiful supply and salmon leaping the falls.

As the angling season draws to a close, he informed me, stalking comes to the fore at the end of September. This activity lasts for one month and forms part of the deer-culling system. Did I know that currently there are probably more deer in Scotland than in the time of Robert the Bruce? Eva asked. In response to my silence she elaborated thus. If field sports, run by estates such as this, ceased, most of rural Scotland would no longer exist as it is today. When the welcome stalkers have returned home the indigenous gamekeepers complete the culling to supply venison for markets around the country. They also cull foxes and other vermin to combat damage to trees and domestic animals.

When I tentatively asked about grouse-shooting Hans had a ready answer. This apparently had been sparse for two years due to insects devouring the heather shoots that form the mainstay of the grouses' diet. Capercaille, the largest and most handsome of the grouse family, could, he told me, be found in neighbouring Ballochbuie Forest, a remnant of the ancient Calledonian Forest that formerly blanketed much of Scotland. The succulent buds of the Scots pines are evidently one of its favourite foods, but despite this source of nourishment the birds' numbers have seriously declined. So, now you know.

In return for my companions' amiable and informative company I felt obliged to explain what I was doing in the area. It is often a dubious pleasure to divulge that you are undertaking a lone walk of several hundred miles. Common reactions are incredulity or pity, but this friendly couple were very interested in my aspirations. When I mentioned my aim of following Wainwright's route through Scotland, I received an immediate murmur of recognition at the sound of his name. I learned that they had visited the Lake District during their holiday and were aware of his writings, having seen many of his books on display in the shops.

Engrossed in conversation, I completely forgot the time and my intended reconnoitre of the village. The remainder of the evening was spent discussing such diverse topics as walking in the Bernese Oberland, an unfulfilled ambition of mine, to touring the snickleways of York. Bedtime furtively crept upon us, demanding another climb of that protesting staircase, to a chorus of creaks and sighs from its vociferous steps. Those tortured noises did at least assure me that an intruder would stand no chance of a furtive raid of our bedrooms.

DAY TWO: BRAEMAR - LINN OF DEE

The sun shone pleasurably through the bedroom curtains as I awoke to the sounds of birdsong, doors slamming and crockery being manhandled. Wogan's lilting brogue issued from a radio, competing with the cacophony; his Irish wit probably lost on my indomitable host. As I washed and dressed I savoured the thought of a leisurely day of exploration, for I only had a six-mile journey to the Linn of Dee to cover. After a walk of over twenty miles on my first day, I convinced myself that I deserved a rest, especially as I intended covering twenty-four miles the following day through wild, uninhabited country.

The stairs proclaimed to all within earshot that I was heading for the breakfast table, where I half-expected to see a dish-full of cereal awaiting me, to save precious time. Remarkably I was given a choice, but the lady hovered as I put the last spoonful of porridge to my lips, ready to rapidly exchange my dish for the groaning plate of fried food that she was wielding.

As I was rounding off my enormous breakfast with a portion of toast, I was subjected to a rapid interrogation regarding my plans for that day. The questions flew at me like bullets, with hardly a moment to reply between salvos. As I left the table she suddenly blurted out her good wishes for an enjoyable journey. Feeling guilty, I was reminded never to judge a book by its cover.

Ascending the stairs to collect my belongings from my room, I came face to face with Hans and Eva. Amidst much manoeuvring to avoid a collision, the creaking rose to a crescendo, an invisible orchestra signifying the culmination of our time together. They were reluctantly returning home that afternoon and after exchanging farewells we promised to keep in touch.

Another fine day was in prospect as I made for a row of cottages set back from the main road running through the village. The sun glinted on brightly-painted walls and lichen-speckled roof tiles as I approached Castleton terrace, searching for one significant cottage. Robert Louis Stevenson stayed there in 1881, unfortunately suffering continual lashing rain and high winds for the duration of his vacation. The foul weather had its compensations, however, for he amazingly wrote a chapter per day of *Treasure Island* during the nineteen that he spent there. Such a prolific output probably produced callouses on his fingers and set his pen aglow. What a fantastic output on such an enduring novel. Who knows what he could have accomplished with the aid of a word processor? I found the cottage in question, still unsure why I had sought it out. Was I unrealistically hoping that some of his immense talent would rub off on me?

Taking the road out of the village I was accompanied by the splendidly-blue waters of the winding Dee. In the distance loomed the impressive wooded slopes of Creag Choinnich and in the midst of a sun-drenched scene stood Braemar Castle on a strategic mound by the riverside. A blue and white flag fluttered hospitably above its distinctive roof turrets, beckoning me to its portals. I joined a party of eager visitors for a guided tour of the fortress which was originally built in 1628 by John Erskine the incumbent Earl of Mar. Braemar's strategic position on the ancient road from the south had long been recognised by the building of the mediaeval Kindrochit castle. The Erskine family, however, were keen to re-establish themselves as a force in Aberdeenshire following the return of the estranged estates of the Earldom of Mar by Mary Queen of Scots in 1565. Thus Braemar Castle, a fine Tower House, was erected with the dual purpose of providing a hunting lodge for the Earl's use and of controlling his turbulent neighbours, the Farquharsons. It was reduced to a ruinous shell in 1689 by John Farquharson of Inverey who set fire to it and restoration was not forthcoming until 1748, when it was re-inhabited. The reconstruction of the upper floors is an example of early 'Adam' work, not by the famous Robert, but by his elder brother John, who held the post of Master Mason to the Board of Ordnance in Scotland. He was entrusted with the task of adapting the ruinous castle for use as an army garrison.

Our guide gave an absorbing account of the castle and its

associated history, which set me wondering how many hundreds of times he had to perform this ritual and how he kept his commentary fresh and alive. Did he make subtle alterations or throw in deliberate mistakes to see if his charges would notice? He told us that the building was currently owned by the Farquharsons of Invercauld whose seat was the nearby massive Invercauld House. The present Laird and his family occasionally resided in the castle, probably to keep warm in its more compact surroundings. Thus many of the rooms portrayed a lived-in appearance which added greatly to their authenticity and appeal. The Farquharsons purchased the property in the late eighteenth century and immediately leased it back to the army, its previous incumbents. Evidence of military occupation was highlighted by a Hanoverian sergeant's name gouged in a Drawing Room window shutter. This proved that vandalism is not a modern phenomenon; the inscription was the historic equivalent of 'Kilroy', who gets everywhere these days.

In addition to the lavish decor and furnishings I was impressed by the wealth of history contained in maps and artifacts, particularly a map of the world drawn by A.Arrowsmith in 1797 identifying recent discoveries by Captain Cook. This was complemented by another wall map showing the entire Scottish clans and their territories. Memories are often cemented by compelling detail and the castle provided a rich store of these. Two rusted and pitted cannon balls fuelled my imagination and the gruesome Laird's Pit grabbed my attention. The latter was a tiny dungeon set beneath a stone-flagged passage, its only access being through a metal grill in the floor. It epitomised earlier barbaric times and closer inspection revealed a pile of bones and some coins littering the base of the pit. The sight of those bones made me gulp, a salient reminder that justice was summary in those troubled times and human life was cheap. In the Morning Room I was mentally hoisted onto the cliffs of Lochnagar by the sight of what must be the world's largest cairngorm, weighing all of fifty-two pounds.

Before leaving I spoke to the helpful guide about the excellent management of the local estates. He turned out to be a keen walker and we discussed the extensive provision of access to open land in Scotland, and my recent ascent of Lochnagar. Well aware of the unfortunate climber who lost his life on its unremitting cliff-face he told me that accidents had claimed no less than thirty-seven lives in the area during the previous severe winter. A sobering statistic for those pitting themselves against ensnaring mountains. Enough of such morbid talk!

The sun smiled on me as I left the castle and returned to the village, heading for a park on its western fringe. Passing through ornate gates I was greeted by a sun-drenched amphitheatre set amongst heather-clad hills; home of the famous Braemar Gathering. This annual spectacle is a magnet for thousands of people who can enjoy a memorable day in the company of members of the Royal Family, which by tradition has patronised the event since Queen Victoria's reign. It would be a bleak and stony soul that was not stirred by the sights and sounds of the Gathering which encompasses much more than the Highland Games themselves. The evocative sound of massed pipe bands reverberates around the surrounding hills and greetings are delivered by representatives from Scottish Societies all over the world, proudly proclaiming allegiance to their roots in the homeland. Traditional features of the Gathering include mounted march-pasts by brigades of Guards and the Beating of the Retreat by drum and pipe bands. The Games provide competition and spectacle as befit the most famous of their kind in the world. Tests of strength and endurance, such as tossing the 132 pound caber and the race to the summit of Morone, a nearby mountain, are probably the most gruelling, but inspiring of all the events.

I was moved by the atmosphere of the arena, its emerald heart surrounded by tiers of brightly-painted seats starkly outlined against a canvas of pines and gnarled hills. The Royal Pavilion stood passively, as though awaiting the Royal party who would watch the proceedings in a refreshingly informal manner, whilst enjoying a day out like any other family. I could almost hear the lilting sounds of the pipes and the excited chatter of the watching crowds, as I vowed one day to return and experience them for myself.

The time to leave Braemar had arrived, for the morning had sped by and I began my journey to the Linn of Dee with a short climb towards the Morone Viewpoint, which according to my map was set in a nature reserve above the outskirts of the village. My approach was by lane and winding track which took me past a delightful and expansive duck-pond lying amidst one of the finest examples of upland birchwood in Britain. The bewitching setting was enhanced by an encompassing blue sky of extraordinary richness and the sunlight dancing on the pond's placid surface. The ducks appeared oblivious to their striking surroundings as they lazed on the banks of the pond, warmed by the sun's generous rays. A little further along the track stood an hexagonal stone pillar topped with an etched indicator plate, reminiscent of the one on the summit of Lochnagar, that showed all the peaks on view. The display to the north-west over the valley of the Dee was stunning, the heather clad slopes in the foreground overshadowed by the dark, dramatic indentations of the mountains beyond. I was reintroduced to the majesty of the Cairngorms, albeit still from afar, and could appreciate all the more why Wainwright chose to end his Scottish journey in this area. Braemar bade a final goodbye as it lay beneath me, its buildings protruding from the cocoon of trees that clothed the valley-bottom.

This enthralling landscape provided fitting lunchtime entertainment as I sat by the indicator, enjoying my sandwiches in the invigorating Deeside air. It was a wrench to leave such an idyllic spot and begin a gradual, mile-long descent to the quiet road that winds through the valley to the Linn of Dee, but from a vantage point by the roadside I was treated to another unforgettable sight across the meandering waters of the Dee. Quoich Water oozed from the beautiful tree-lined Linn of Quoich to join the Dee beneath a vista of intriguing mountains that looked even better at closer quarters. Carn na Criche and Carn na Drochaide stood sentinel over a scene that etched itself in my mind like a fond childhood memory. I decided to visit that lovely glen for a closer inspection, for I saw from my map that it was accessible via a thin ribbon of road that ran along the opposite side of the river. This road is actually a continuation of the one by which I was standing, that crosses the river at Linn of Dee only to return along the opposite bank and expire at Linn of Quoich. Exhilarated, I struck out along the Linn of Dee road heading for Victoria Bridge that spanned the river a mile and a half away. My feelings were further stimulated as I paused to study another striking cleft in the hills; the Linn of Corriemulzie. Deeside certainly had much to offer on that gloriously sunny day and the more I saw of it, the greater I could appreciate Queen Victoria's love for the area. She and Prince Albert acquired their treasured castle at Balmoral without previous sight of it or the land in which it lies. Encouraged by her physician, Sir James Clark, to partake of the exceptionally healthy Deeside air, the purchase was made on his recommendation and proved extremely fortuitous, for they soon realised in what beautiful countryside it resides.

Crossing the bridge which bears her name, its iron construction functional rather than aesthetic, I noted that an archway over its entrance bears the inscription 'Victoria 1848'. On the opposite bank I ventured along a driveway that leads to Mar Lodge, a focal point within the surrounding Forest of Mar. An impressive building, with the black and white latticework of its multi-gabled roof contrasting with the pristine cleanliness of its stone frontage, the Lodge gave an appearance of recent large-scale restoration. It was built as a royal hunting lodge by Queen Victoria in the late nineteenth-century for her grand-daughter Princess Louise and her husband the Duke of Fife. The National Trust for Scotland has recently purchased it and has plans to revert its lands to their former state; Caledonian Forest. This is a far-reaching investment, for such a project would take hundreds of years to mature.

Returning to Victoria Bridge I took the narrow road along the opposite side of the Dee that ends abruptly at an insubstantial bridge over Quoich Water. This spot overlooks the entrance to Linn of Quoich and a car park lies beyond the bridge; a convenient starting point for walks around its lower reaches or more substantial treks into the Caingorms and Beinn a' Bhuird mountains. My detour proved worthwhile for the glen itself was even more impressive at close quarters. The secluded Quoich Water danced over stony beds and through narrow rocky channels, shafts of sunlight vividly highlighting the innumerable tints of the enveloping woodland. A little way up the valley lay the Punch Bowl, a large natural hollow which the Earl of Mar reputedly filled with punch for his supporters when they assembled there before raising the standard in 1715. What an auspicious start to a rebellion - reducing the participants to a drunken rabble!

Returning to the Dee, I perched on a rock for a quick coffee-break before back-tracking to Victoria Bridge where I re-crossed the river and headed for Linn of Dee. The day had proved extremely satisfying thus far and seemingly, to augment my enjoyment, a red squirrel scuttled across my path and disappeared into the protective woodland and an occasional woodpigeon fluttered warily amongst surrounding trees, nervous of my presence. I was not so lucky with the wild cats that reputedly lurk in the pine forests of Deeside, for they remained unseen.

The uninspiring appearance of the nearby hamlet of Inverey pricked my bubble of satisfaction. A dreary series of cottages flanking one side of the road displayed no signs of life as I passed.

The lonely War Memorial squatted forlornly on the opposite side as though shunned by the remainder of the small settlement. With malicious timing, the sun, which had been my faithful companion up to that point, disappeared, intensifying the dullness of my surroundings. Not wishing to do Inverey a profound injustice, I tried to visualise its earlier importance during the Jacobite period when it was the home of John Farquharson who set fire to Braemar Castle in 1689. He was popularly known as the 'Black Colonel'. One of the most romantic figures in the history of Deeside, he supported the Jacobite cause against the Dutch King William. His motive for burning the castle was to prevent it falling into the King's hands. Frequently escaping from the pursuing English Dragoons, his most audacious flight led him on horseback up the precipitous north side of the Pass of Ballater. From these escapades evolved a legend, which also featured his reputed habit of summoning his servant to the table by firing his pistol.

Inverey nestles at the foot of Glen Ey, which had also assumed a sombre appearance devoid of enhancing sunshine. Standing on the bridge over the Ey Burn I could observe its rapid, tumbling progress through a narrow rock-strewn and leafy channel, before it surged beneath my vantage point to mingle with the more placid waters of the Dee. Several rowan trees, resplendent bright red berries dangling from their branches, stood guard over the banks of the lively stream. In brighter conditions Glen Ey would assume a mantle of significant beauty.

A short walk from the bridge brought me to the Youth Hostel at Muir Cottage. A compact building with no pretensions of grandeur, it comprises one of the Scottish YHA's smaller premises, but is none the worse for that. It is in such places that the true spirit of hostelling is usually found. Situated in peaceful countryside, away from the tourist centres, the hostel was to be the launching site for my forthcoming trek to Blair Atholl.

Linn of Dee lay a further mile along the road and as there was time to spare before checking into the hostel it was pertinent to explore the Linn and save valuable time on the following morning. The sun remained elusively behind threatening clouds as I reached this popular beauty spot. A shapely stone bridge with impressive castellated parapets carries the road across the surging river, enabling it to head in the reverse direction for the Linn of Quoich. Hurrying to the bridge I peered into the dark chasm below. White foam, produced by hurtling, tortured water stood out starkly in the semi-darkness. The gently-rippling river that flowed peaceably from White Bridge was transformed into a raging torrent as it squirmed through a rocky defile rimmed with glowering pines. Eager to see it at close quarters I began to descend the fragmented rocks lining the narrow gorge, being very careful where I placed my feet. Several lives were lost here, probably through a mixture of bravado and stupidity. Wet rock and rushing water are a lethal combination for unwary feet, so I only ventured as far as was prudent. The view towards the bridge was awesome despite the surrounding gloom and it was hard to imagine that salmon inhabit such a writhing stretch of water. Unseen, they rest below concealed ledges in the forbidding channel, immune from human predators.

A rumbling stomach ensured a prompt return to the hostel for supper, where I was enthusiastically received by the friendly warden. The amenities were basic but quite adequate after spending an intriguing day in the exhilarating Deeside air. Two young walkers joined me at supper who had travelled twenty-eight testing miles from Aviemore, which made my leisurely stroll from Braemar seem puny by comparison. They had walked along the Lairig Ghru Pass through the Caingorms, but despite the distance and their aching limbs had thoroughly enjoyed themselves. They were clearly elated by their achievement, chattering enthusiastically about their day. The journey had taken ten hours, which, they pointed out was nothing to the times achieved by the supermen who take part in the annual Lairig Ghru race. The current record of three hours and twenty minutes, a time beyond my comprehension, has apparently stood since 1976 and could only be eclipsed by a superbly fit athlete.

Nerves tensed in my stomach as I told them of my impending twenty-four mile challenge to Blair Atholl. Their eyes lit up, for they also planned to take such a journey through the Forest of Atholl. Their trip would unfortunately have to wait for they were destined for Ballater; to complete their current circuit of the Grampian area. Good weather had accompanied them so far and they had found good stopping points at Tomintoul and Grantown on Spey.

We chatted avidly throughout the meal and well into the evening until terminal yawning forced us to our beds. My companions had earned a good night's rest and I needed to be on my metal the next day. Sleep came quickly, courtesy of Deeside's therapeutic air.

DAY THREE: LINN OF DEE - BLAIR ATHOLL

I awoke with a start, as often happens when a tricky day is in prospect. My mind rapidly ticked over like a Formula One engine on the starting grid, projecting images of me wandering helplessly in hostile countryside. Switching off these alarming pictures I peered through the curtains to see what the weather had in store. The sky looked quite friendly as wisps of white cloud moved swiftly across a pale blue backdrop. Could be worse, I thought, further sleep banished by my excitement. A refreshing shower massaged my senses and encouraging sounds emanated from the kitchen; breakfast was imminent.

I ate a substantial breakfast to fortify myself, whilst listening to the hum of conversation around me. My mind was on my forthcoming walk and I was not the best of company. My table companions seemed unabashed, encouraging me with their good wishes, and jokingly threatening to ask the warden to muster a search-party.

A speedy departure was followed by a return along the road to Linn of Dee, to which I gave a passing glance of recognition. The river continued to thrash itself merrily amongst the rocks in the brighter setting of a clear morning. A sign caught my eye as I crossed the bridge, which alerts walkers to the two long-distance routes that commence there. These are the Lairig Ghru and the path that I was to take to Glen Tilt and Blair Atholl.

Passing through a gate near the sign I struck out along an inviting ribbon of track that would lead me to White Bridge. It was a pleasant three-mile walk to the bridge with the Dee a close companion. The wide, green strath was illuminated by occasional shafts of sunlight which danced on the grassland and surrounding heather-clad slopes. Jagged rocky outcrops soared upwards from the valley floor at intervals and from one of these stone had been hewn, the resultant quarry now deserted and partially overgrown. The occasional stubble of spruce and pine complemented the lighter hues of the valley, creating a scene of memorable richness. By contrast the distant prospect of the mountains of Glenfeshie Forest glowering beneath menacing clouds was sobering, for they lay close to my intended path. I did not dwell on that unsettling view, for I had no shortage of companions at this stage. A cyclist hurried past followed by a frisky dog which, glad of the opportunity for a rest, sniffed inquisitively around me. Finding nothing of interest it romped after its master who was disappearing into the distance. Several parties of walkers were in view, all striding purposefully with the energy born of a new day.

Wild beauty encompassed me as I approached White Bridge, its sturdy stone pillars thrusting from the river which tinkled an accompaniment to my footsteps. No habitation was discernible, merely the sight of two tracks fanning out from the far side of the bridge and heading for gaps in the surrounding mountains. The Chest of Dee lies beyond the bridge which forms a veritable parting of the ways. One path swings north into the confines of Glen Dee to join the Lairig Ghru path, as it heads north-west from Derry Lodge, and accompany it through a channel in the Caingorms to Aviemore. Such a journey was enticing for the source of the enchanting Dee lies along the path, tucked between mighty Ben Macdui and Cairn Toul, amidst some of the country's wildest and most exciting mountains. However, I had been discouraged from taking this route by the accomplished Scottish journalist, author and broadcaster, Bruce Sandison. A chapter in his book *The Hillwalker's Guide to Scotland* is entitled 'Avoiding Aviemore' and it opens with the following observation: 'Set amidst some of God's most glorious scenery, this once attractive village has been devastated by mass tourism'. This indictment is followed by: 'In my opinion Aviemore is a fearful monument to man's insensitivity to his environment'. Turning to *Wainwright in Scotland* for a second opinion I noted his comment: 'The place has become brash, garish, noisy'. This was enough to make me avoid the throng of sightseers in that commercialised Speyside village, which is a mandatory halt on the high- speed tourist's itinerary. The 'Been there, done that' brigade pause for breath in Aviemore during their whirlwind tour of Scotland.

To be honest, it is extremely pompous of me to pontificate on the imperfections of transient tourists. What would happen if they suddenly decided to leave the comfort of their vehicles and explore the countryside? We would be walking on each other's heads, that's what. A heaving mass of humanity blotting out the sky and eroding everything in its path. Traffic lights would be needed at junctions of the most popular paths, together with other human traffic-calming measures, to prevent mass trampling underfoot. I am indebted to the transient tourist and gratefully acknowledge that he is not likely to follow me from the car park and dog my footsteps over the fells.

My chosen route lay along the track heading south to pass the tiny and remote Loch Tilt and the Falls of Tarf, before cutting through deep Glen Tilt to civilisation. Somewhere in the midst of that mountain wilderness lay the point of no return, where the only option would be to press on to Blair Atholl - a sobering thought. Habitation was non-existent, the isolated buildings identified on the map were ruinous.

Striking out from the bridge I looked around for accompanying walkers, but the ones seen earlier had disappeared and I was completely alone. Nature usually piles on the agony at such uncomfortable moments and exactly on cue the first drops of rain spattered on my dampened ego. The clouds gathering overhead goaded me into action as I strode between an extensive pine forest and a tributary of the Dee.

My progress was halted a mile ahead when I was confronted by the wide Geldie Burn which rushed across my path. The rain was now enjoying itself, hurtling into its grey waters, churning them into submission. Optimistically searching for a bridge over this obstruction I noticed the forlorn supports of one that had long since capitulated. Three pillars stood apologetically amidst the invading waters, a fourth having inconsiderately tilted over and died. Things were not looking good as I retreated hastily to a convenient semi-ruin, the remains of Geldie Lodge, huddling nearby, having no wish to ford the offending burn in a deluge. Fortunately the roof of the derelict building was reasonably intact, its bulky wooden beams still solidly embedded in thick stone walls. The windows and doors had disappeared, but I was thankful for the shelter it afforded as I crouched in one corner surveying my surroundings. The remains of a massive stone fireplace hugged the wall at one end, its great lintel shoring up a less than airtight wall above it, through which a patchwork of light filtered. Debris littered the floor, signifying that kindred souls had taken refuge there, some overnight, judging by the remains of a discarded tent and the variety of food and drink containers on display. A makeshift fireplace had been made on the floor using loose stones, its interior bulging with ashes. The original wooden floor, I learned later, had been ripped up to provide warmth.

The faint, unsettling smell of rotting flesh hung in the air prompting me to search for the culprit, half expecting to see the corpse of a stranded walker. Finding no evidence around me, I was in no mood for a drenching search outside. I frequently feel uneasy in derelict buildings, when imagination clicks into overdrive and intruders are sensed lurking around every corner. Pouring coffee from my flask - whisky would have been more appropriate - I tried to convince myself that only walkers would venture there. Sipping the hot, comforting liquid, I listened to the rain beating a monotonous tune on the roof. Trying to ignore the smell and the angry weather I studied the graffiti decorating the walls, but slogans such as 'Free Scotland Now' and 'Bugger Off English' did nothing for my peace of mind. In fact, they provided the final impetus to grasp the nettle and escape that creepy place. Draining the remains of my coffee I braced myself for the battle ahead.

The rain lashed me with a vengeance as I ventured outside and it was accompanied by a distinctly unfriendly mist rolling down from the hills. When troubles come, why do they always arrive in bunches? Retracing my steps to the burn, I placed a tentative boot in its hostile waters, grimacing as it immediately filled with numbing ice-cold water. I had noted its rock-strewn bed earlier and decided that it was better to soak my boots and socks than risk cutting my feet to ribbons. Lurching drunkenly across the watery divide, I all but pitched over, with surging currents tugging at my calves. Eventually staggering onto the opposite bank, my relief was tempered by the enveloping mist that meant my travelling blind on the most testing part of the journey so far. The route to Blair Atholl seemed straightforward on the map; but routes usually do on paper. It couldn't be simpler, I told myself, just follow the gap between the mountains and don't be lured into any side valleys. To buck up my spirits I loudly hummed a favourite Scottish ditty as I squelched through the mist. This stopped abruptly, for out of the gloom filtered an eerie, but colourful, glow. To my great relief two walkers appeared clad in day-glo waterproofs, their matching orange jackets and overtrousers shining like ethereal beacons. They paused to enquire where I was headed, grimacing when I told them. With pity in their eyes they remarked that only an idiot would attempt to reach Blair Atholl in such weather. Apparently they had only ventured as far as Loch Tilt, which lay shrouded in mist three miles ahead, and were returning to the safety of Linn of Dee. With their warning ringing in my ears a feeling of isolation engulfed me as they disappeared into the mist. Life can be tough.

I struggled onwards until my path was again barred by an

annoying burn, fortunately narrower than the previous one. I scrambled across the few available boulders, but I was forced to immerse my boots once more in chilling and numbing water. Fortunately my antics went unseen and my curses unheard.

The ruin of Bynack Lodge materialised from the murk but I ignored it, my feet heartily protesting at a second soaking. I was in no mood to linger as my desire to escape from that bleak and featureless wilderness intensified. Hugging the indistinct path like a limpet I plodded through soggy moorland, the cloying mist draped around me. Having only my map and compass for company I concentrated on steering the correct course, hoping against hope for a glimmer of light.

At times of such anxiety my yellow streak expands into a broad band. Frightening, irrational thoughts tumble into my brain and my imagination runs riot. Wainwright's warning that this journey should not be attempted in misty conditions insidiously lurked in the corner of my mind whilst other imponderables fought for the remaining space. Why had I foolishly ventured here alone? What would happen to me if I lost my way? Could Blair Atholl be reached by nightfall? As an antidote I strained to recall some outstanding feats from my past, in order to boost my sagging confidence. None would materialise. Instead, the embarrassing memory of two hours spent on a frame of snooker with a friend without potting a single ball reared its ugly head. A fine time to be reminded of such ignominy when what I badly needed was reassurance. My thoughts turned to David, whom I had encountered on Lochnagar and I imagined him in my present predicament. I could visualise him striding purposefully through the mist, his navigation unerring and his appearance immaculate. Why couldn't I be like him? I felt an uncontrollable urge to shout for my mum.

Water began seeping insidiously into my unprotected crevices as I ploughed through a no-man's land, which could have been the surface of the moon for all I cared. How debilitating is the incessant beat of rain on wilting waterproofs. Forcing myself to study the only other thing that moved in my eerie amphitheatre, I gazed at the nearby burn, its surface tormented by the persistent deluge. If my bearings were correct it was just starting life, eventually reaching the safety of the Dee.

Somewhere above me in the surrounding haze lurked the tiny and reclusive Loch Tilt, secreted behind an invisible ridge. It was

Lochnagar.

ear Linn of Dee.

View from summit of Be[n] Lawers.

Falls of Dochart, Killin.

Balquhidder churches and graveyard.

versnaid Hotel, Loch
omond.

View from Ben More to Crianlarich and Strathfillan.

Maurice near Auc

annoch Moor from
challader.

Ben Nevis and Mamore
Forest from Devil's
Staircase.

Maurice at Loch Loyne

Beinn Eighe and Lo
Coulin.

apool.

Strathnaver.

Castlehill Qua
Castletown.

Last House, John
o'Groats.

pointless to forsake the life-saving path, sketchy though it was, to search for this secluded source of the River Tilt. My map indicated that I should have reached a watershed that marked my entry into Glen Tilt. Such a landmark was undiscernible in the atrocious conditions. Dark and foreboding masses appeared out of the gloom on either side of me like gaping jaws. I was certainly entering a valley, but was it the right one? My fears were calmed when a little farther along the path I pinpointed a junction of several streams that rushed from the enveloping mountainsides to form the Allt Garbh Bhuide, the forerunner of the River Tilt. This comfortingly confirmed that I was in the welcoming channel that leads into the depths of Glen Tilt. Hallelujah !

My feeling of total isolation rapidly receded with the realisation that the worst was over. Provided that I stuck to this valley, I was home and dry. In hindsight this was an ambitious thought, for I still had four and a half hours of gruelling walking ahead of me. Progress became harder as the narrow path became stony and writhed in and out of clefts in the precipitous fellsides. Rocks protruded from its surface, eager to catch the unwary foot and these were interspersed with stretches of crumbling peat; a lethal combination. I was jerked to a sudden halt by the ghostly sound of a horse neighing. Was my mind playing tricks? Would the spectre of a headless horseman materialise, doomed for eternity to roam the desolate glen? These chilling thoughts were rebuffed when I turned round to find a horse and rider, thankfully complete with head, approaching along the path. As the horse halted I could see what a magnificent animal it was. Its sleek and shiny coat signified excellent grooming. An air of calm obedience radiated from it as it surveyed me with bright eyes. The rider uttered a surprised greeting, as he had plainly considered himself the only person to venture through the glen in such weather. When I mentioned my fright, he laughed and said that my appearance was quite a shock to him. It transpired that horse and rider were training for a forthcoming thirty-mile Endurance Time Trial, roughly the distance of their current journey from Braemar to Blair Atholl. The opportunities for practice were limited, which explained their presence in such poor conditions. When I suggested that the horse must be very sure-footed to negotiate a path fraught with pitfalls, the rider said that he dismounted on the most severe sections as a safeguard. The gentle animal stood motionless during our conversation, even allowing me to stroke it in a friendly fashion.

As we wished each other a safe journey I stood aside and watched them disappear into the mist and rain, marvelling at the carefulness with which the horse placed its feet on the treacherous ground.

A mile further on I stood straining to catch the sound of rushing water that signified the approach of the Falls of Tarf, the first significant landmark in Glen Tilt. Frustrating minutes passed before I heard what began as a low murmur and gradually grew into roar. Rounding the corner of a wide, rocky defile I was greeted by a double cascade of milky-white foam that appeared incandescent amidst its surrounding pall of mist. What a splendid spectacle this would present in fine weather. I watched in admiration as the torrent hurtled down the ravine and squirmed under a fragile-looking bridge that spanned it. Tentatively climbing the steps that took me onto the narrow wooden platform of the bridge, I clung to the metal cables that were its only means of support. The unnerving structure bounced merrily as I lurched drunkenly to its centre, where I stopped to allow its contortions and the clanking of its cables to subside. I had the wild notion of jumping up and down to work up enough momentum to scale the falls with one almighty leap. Instead I marvelled at the tenacity of the trees and clumps of heather that clung to the bare ramparts of surrounding rock. If weather and circumstance had been different this would have been a convenient spot to rest and admire the boiling cataracts, but I wanted to keep going; relaxation could come later. Bouncing my way off the bridge I rejoined the path which soon broadened into a track. Thereupon the going became easier and I struck up a good pace as I joined the infant River Tilt, which, not to be outdone, pitched animatedly through its own series of mini-cascades.

With a lighter heart I made good progress over the next four miles. As the steep sides of the glen began to relent I reached a forest beyond which I hoped to find the first sign of habitation since leaving Linn of Dee. Anticipation spurred me on as I fairly galloped down the gently-sloping track. So intent was I on my objective that I barely noticed an easing of the rain and a glimmer of brightness in the sky. As it intensified the rain stopped and I caught sight of the anticipated building ahead of me. Its austere appearance was immaterial. Forest Lodge was a joyous sight and comforting smoke curled from the chimney of an adjoining cottage. With perfect timing, the first rays of a watery sun pierced the rapidly-dispersing clouds. A stunning rainbow straddled the sky, forming a triumphal archway over the glen. I had to capture it on film, so I hurried to the lodge, threw off my rucksack and took out my camera. Imagine my chagrin when I discovered that it was the last shot on the film and therefore not guaranteed to come out. Shrugging my shoulders, I decided to take a chance as I did not relish unpacking my rucksack to get at my unused films. I sank to the ground and took a refuelling stop now that the pressure had eased. Sifting through the wreckage of my packed-lunch, I scrabbled amongst the empty bags, wrappers and sachets for signs of remaining nourishment. What little I found was devoured quickly as I leaned against the convenient backrest provided by a large block of local stone set into the lawn adjacent to the lodge. I savoured my upsurge of fortune as I gazed around me. A veil had seemingly been lifted to reveal a scene of unrivalled beauty. The glen, quite wide now, was awash with colour and at its heart the bubbling Tilt danced between rocky, tree-lined banks. The spectacle, probably born of relief, ranked with the finest that I have ever experienced. I was amidst vivid green meadows, overlooked by amiable mountains, their harshness softened by the sun. Things were definitely on the up.

Fighting complacency, I roused myself for I had a further two hours of walking to combat. The sun was well beyond its prime and the shadows were beginning to lengthen. My pace became less frenetic as I tried to conserve my remaining energy. I did not want to run out of steam near the end of a tough day's walk.

The lower reaches of the glen were delightful. Scattered dwellings became more numerous and at one point a former sheiling, now a tidy and attractive bothy, beckoned from across the river. There was no sign of a path on the far bank and the only visible access to the tiny stone cabin was by a steel cable that hung languidly over the water. Of a pulley or winch there was no evidence. A van was parked by the track on my side of the river, evidently used by the man who stood in the doorway of the bothy. He waved in a friendly manner as I passed. Puzzled as to how he had crossed the river, I could only deduce that the folding step-ladder that lay on the opposite bank was used to support and hence tighten the cable when in use. The remaining necessary equipment was probably stored in the bothy for safe keeping.

As the glen expanded further the vegetation became more varied. Verdant copses clothed the banks of the widening river that continued to gurgle happily over its rocky bed. A party of young canoeists was fighting the swift and turbulent currents under the watchful eye of an instructor. Their dazzling water-proof outfits introduced a splash of vibrant colour to the surrounding greenery.

A testament to the vagaries of the local weather caught my eye as I passed the neat and diminutive cottage bearing the impressive name of Marble Lodge. The occupants had hung a collection of colourful cagouls in the entrance porch. Marble was formerly quarried in the area and dispatched to Edinburgh for the princely sum of one guinea per cubic foot, hence the lodge's name.

Within a further mile the glen's character changed once more. The impressive mountains receded to be replaced by rounded hills thickly coated with woodland. A sign indicated that I left the track and took to a broad green path that climbed into the woods. Having enjoyed a gradual descent for many miles, it seemed an imposition to toil uphill. The day's exertions were beginning to take their toll and it was an effort to attain the cool confines of the variegated plantation. Due to my fatigue I did not pay my surroundings the attention they deserved. Birch, alder and larch mingled with beech, spruce and pine to provide a rich diversity of cover. I stopped to examine the substantial part of a sheep's fleece that clung to a nearby fence, regretting that I had not picked up a similar one that I had seen further up the glen. The two combined would have been sufficient to take home and make into a woolly jumper.

Emerging from the cover of the trees into the softness of rolling meadows I was treated to the glorious spectacle of journey's end. The wide strath of Glen Garry lay below me flanked by undulating hills, their upper reaches decked with dark forests and expansive moorland. At the hub of this gratifying scene, amidst lush pastures and rich woodland, lay the inescapable towers and turrets of Blair Castle, their dazzling whiteness riveting to the eye. A warm glow of achievement filtered through me with the realisation that I had survived the rigours of my marathon journey from Linn of Dee.

It was a short walk along a farm track to the quiet road that would lead me into Blair Atholl. As I strolled leisurely into the valley I studied a challenge yet to come, for the distant hump of Schiehallion beckoned, its summit embedded in shapely cloud, beyond the Tummel valley. The sun was slipping behind the hills as I approached my night's lodgings and I was convinced that sleep would come easily that night.

DAY FOUR: BLAIR ATHOLL - PITLOCHRY

After the long haul of the previous day I was looking forward to strolling a mere eight miles to Pitlochry. It proved to be one of those short walks that take all day. My anticipated mileage was as the crow flies and believe me Scottish crows are canny. They find much shorter routes than I do. To be fair, they don't stop to admire Blair Castle or the Pass of Killiecrankie as I did.

I took my time over breakfast, knowing that I did not have to rush away. It was, however, dangerous to relax too much for lethargy waits to pounce. As time was plentiful I began with a stroll. Blair Atholl is a quiet village, thankfully by-passed by the busy A9 road. Its railway station, although tiny, is handily situated on the main Glasgow to Inverness line. I smiled when I saw the remnants of a now defunct line end in the garden of a nearby cottage. Old Blair, the original hamlet, lay less than a mile away amidst quiet lanes on the banks of the tinkling Banvie Burn. Peaceful parkland and gentle woodland were the hallmark of this seemingly timeless and secluded gem.

Inevitably I was drawn, like the proverbial moth to a flame, to Atholl's centre-piece, Blair Castle, home to the Dukes of Atholl. I added a further mile to my day's journey as I walked up the long and impressive driveway, frequently overtaken by vehicles, a testimony to the castle's popularity. They halted at a kiosk, obliged to pay for entry to the car park and grounds. The friendly lady inside waved me through, saying that access was free to those on foot, but I would have to pay for admission to the castle. As I approached the imposing stronghold, visitors were tumbling from coaches and cars, eager to stretch their legs on the rolling lawns. Others reclined on seats flecked around the spacious grounds which were illuminated by arrays of rhododendrons and colourful flowerbeds.

I searched eagerly for the resident Piper who supposedly performed in front of the castle on most days of the season, but he was nowhere to be seen. Why was a Sassenach longing to hear the pressure released from a cloth bag squeezed under someone's left armpit? Hadn't I been a confirmed bagpipe-hater since an unfortunate seaside holiday with my family as a young boy. We spent most of that week trying to shake off the Dagenham Girl Pipers, who regularly appeared from nowhere to dog our footsteps. This awesome pipe-band had an even greater effect on my younger sister who fled in tears at their approach. Time is a great healer and after undergoing therapy with Bagpipes Anonymous I changed my tune. I now thoroughly enjoy the sound that resembles a haggis being tortured.

Feeling aggrieved by the absence of the Piper, I grudgingly paid my admission fee and entered the distinguished portals of Scotland's most visited Historic House. In hindsight, it was churlish of me, having gained free access to the castle grounds, to expect a Piper to be at my beck and call. It was akin to envisaging the Duke's private army, the Atholl Highlanders, parading for my inspection.

My tour of the magnificent building was all too brief, and I did scant justice to the thirty-two fully furnished rooms, but saw enough of them to appreciate their grandeur. I was transported into a world of beauty and elegance. History was plentiful for those prepared to study the vast array of artifacts, weaponry and costumes. The Tullibardine Room particularly caught my eye. It is dedicated to the Jacobites who had associations with the castle. Lord George Murray, son of the first Duke, was an accomplished Lieutenant-General to Bonnie Prince Charlie in the 1745 uprising. Another impressive feature was the Larch Passage, its panelling made from a tree brought from the Tyrol and planted at Dunkeld in 1737. Whole forests of larch were developed on the surrounding estate by the fourth Duke.

A helpful guide told me that Queen Victoria had visited the castle in 1844 and during her lengthy stay she had driven up Glen Tilt and found it stunningly beautiful. She declared that words could hardly do it justice. Amen to that, I thought. It transpired that the newly-appointed guide was born in the same county as me and had studied at a farming college not far from the grammar school that I attended. It is a small world.

I left the castle and returned to Blair Atholl to begin a journey which encompassed quiet roads, appealing woodland and engaging river scenery. Crossing the River Garry by a footbridge I joined a little-used road that follows the river to Killiecrankie. Initially I was walking within sight of the busy A9 road, its embankment towering above me. Traffic was scurrying along this main artery that links Perth with Inverness. In contrast to those rushing travellers, I took my time, savouring the otherwise peaceful setting with the river rippling alongside me. On the opposite bank I could see the Tilt tumbling into the more sedate Garry. This short but engaging river, that I had followed from its spawning grounds, ended its life amidst a cloud of spray, as though shedding tears at the loss of its unique identity.

A quarry slashed the hillside above the tiny settlement of Shierglas, the probable source of the attractive stone from which many of Blair Atholl's buildings were constructed. The hillside had been gouged into a series of huge steps that ravaged an otherwise commendable view. I passed through an archway under the A9 road, traffic noise echoing around me and hurriedly returned to the peace of the river and surrounding meadows. Herds of cattle and sheep shared the grazing land, paying me little heed as I passed. Circling gulls called raucously from above, evidently regarding me as a possible food supply. They were not going to get their beaks into my sandwiches. A couple of chaffinches, more timid than the scavenging gulls hid in a roadside tree that reverberated with their rollicking cadence.

My contentment was abruptly shattered by four cyclists who bore down on me from behind, startling me as they screeched to a halt. Bells seem uncool to the modern cyclist who now chooses to shout at an obstruction or fly past walkers with inches to spare. The luckless victim, if not bowled over by the back-draught may escape with a minor coronary. This particular quartet, resembling fugitives from a psychedelic trance in their multicoloured lycra outfits, enquired if I had seen their two companions who had inconsiderately gone missing with all their food and the only camera. Their frowns deepened when I told them that I had seen no-one else in that quiet backwater. With muttered curses they remounted and hurried away, their skin-tight gear glinting in the charitable sunshine. I recalled the cycling days of my youth when khaki shorts and short-sleeved sweaters were all the rage. How different to the splendid attire into which today's cyclists have to be poured. I grimaced at the sight of the disappearing quartet as they rode, four abreast, ready to mow down unsuspecting pedestrians.

The sun felt good on my back as I passed a chain of farms that lay placidly amongst the lush meadows. On the outskirts of Killiecrankie I crossed the bridges spanning the river and railway that forged side by side through the valley. As I entered the village, its name immortalised by the bitter conflict of 1689, I found it a tranquil place of tidy cottages and well-tended gardens. Things would have been much more frenetic when William III's English troops under the command of General Mackay were routed by the Jacobite forces led by Viscount 'Bonnie' Dundee. At the moment of triumph Dundee was slain and a stone in the grounds of Urrard

House marks the spot where he fell.

Just beyond the village a prominent sign led me to the Killiecrankie Visitor Centre that perches on the rim of the famous pass. I discovered that it housed an exhibition recreating the battle which includes displays of weaponry, maps and paintings. My curiosity sated I wandered to the nearby picnic area where tables squat amongst congenial gardens, offering a birds-eye view of the gentle woodland that clothes the sides of the steep gorge. Here was the perfect spot to attack my lunch pack and I made short work of its contents. To passers-by and other picnickers I must have resembled an ill-fed wretch who hadn't eaten for days. I was oblivious to all but the exhilarating ambience of this popular beauty spot; it was a lovely place, permeated by the fragrant smell of delicate flowers and new-mown lawns.

A steep path led me from the Visitor Centre to a rocky promontory that juts into the chasmic gorge. A shallow stone wall surrounds this superb viewpoint which is identified as the Soldiers Leap, another reference to the eminent battle. A trooper is reputed to have leapt over the gorge from there in an attempt to escape the Royalist Highlanders. It looked one hell of a leap to me, but I suppose anything is possible if you are being chased by ferocious clansmen brandishing claymores and discharging deadly haggis fumes from their hairy nostrils.

I peered along the dramatic cleft to the point where the A9 road cuts a spectacular swathe along its side, high above the river. The highway is supported on gigantic concrete pillars, in marked contrast to the majestic stone arches of the railway viaduct that sweeps along the gorge at a lower level.

Sunlight filtered through the encompassing trees as I descended a stony track that slanted into the narrow floor of the gorge. The graceful railway viaduct towered above me, its massive supports displaying a solidarity that is the hallmark of Victorian workmanship. As it wriggled around constricting boulders, the river had become much more animated than during its sedate journey from Blair Atholl. It was enjoying itself as it tumbled and cavorted its way through idyllic surroundings towards Garry Bridge. A large stone, smoothed by the friction of countless feet, lay embedded in the track, only its long curved top visible. Known as the Balfour Stone, it marks the grave of Brigadier Barthold Balfour, of the Dutch Brigade, who commanded the left wing of General Mackay's army in the battle. He was killed in the subsequent rout by one of Atholl's men. A little farther on I gazed at the lofty metal and concrete finger of Garry Bridge that straddles the gorge at a tremendous height. It resembled a mammoth girder that had wedged itself between the crests of the valley-sides.

The remainder of that warm and carefree afternoon was spent meandering along forest trails. It was a time for unhurried enjoyment of nature and scenery at its finest. I reflected on Wainwright's belief that 'The true walker is never in a hurry'. How right he was and how often had I foolishly sacrificed the simple pleasures of observation in my quests for long distances. I savoured my first view of the Tummel, a river ravaged by man in his thirst for hydro-electric power. Where it once flowed free and unfettered it is restricted by mighty dams and expanded into artificial lochs. At the point where the Garry flows into the Tummel I was introduced to Loch Faskally, created by the construction of Pitlochry dam and the flooding of a large section of the valley. In this particular case, I am happy to say, man has produced a water source in harmony with its surroundings. This stretch of water possesses a tranquil beauty which belies its function as a generator of hydro-electric power. My walk through its garland of alluring woodland was memorable.

As a result of loitering, my short walk had lasted well into the afternoon, but Pitlochry proved to be worth waiting for. I was impressed by the town that lies virtually in the centre of Scotland. The place is popular and therefore busy, which it fully deserves to be. An excellent base for touring, it welcomes visitors with an air of friendly hospitality and unhurried charm. Amenities are good for the traveller and tourist, who can replenish supplies or browse amongst its diversity of shops. Its reputation was built on tweed and whisky, a worthwhile combination, and it has the appearance of a capable frontier town. For those interested in history, the town's origins go back to prehistoric times and the remains of a 2000 year old Pictish fort can be found on its modern golf course. No, I am not sponsored by the local Tourist Board, if that is what you are thinking, I just like the place.

I wandered along its cosy main street, content to mingle with the crowd, a friendly mixture of local townspeople and eager holidaymakers. Some people gave a cheery greeting as I passed, which was gratifying. I find that an acknowledgement is often received from passers-by in the countryside, but rarely in towns and cities. Perhaps these kind people felt sorry for me, a tired-looking walker, weighed down by his ample rucksack.

Time was slipping surreptitiously by and I realised that five o'clock was rapidly approaching. It was pertinent that I found my accommodation and removed the day's grime. A short search took me to the 'upside-down house' as it was described when I was welcomed inside. I was given a tour of the tastefully furnished living quarters that formed the upper level of the building before being taken downstairs to my room. The house occupies a prominent position, high above the town and the view over the valley from the expansive lounge window was superb. A panorama of rural splendour on the outskirts of Pitlochry spread itself as far as the eye could see. Beyond a nearby belt of delicate trees, the Tummel wound through a green and captivating landscape. Traffic heading through the wide strath could be plainly seen. The ramrod-straight A9 road carried hurtling vehicles past the town, leaving local traffic to the more sedate and winding former main road. If Rob Roy had been active in these parts my vantage point would have provided an ideal look-out post. Government troops would have been quite unable to approach him unobserved unless they came stealthily by night. Present day traffic can, however, be easily observed in the darkness, the golden pools of their headlights clearly visible as they flit through the black void that encompasses the house.

Mealtimes were enlivened by the opportunity to sit by the dining room window at the 'viewing table', as it was dubbed and admire the view whilst eating. If conversation during the meal was preferred the alternative 'chatting table' could be used and it was here that I encountered a likable Australian couple who were coming to the end of an extensive European tour. They had visited many countries during their trip but declared Scotland to be the finest. In fact they intended to return the following year for a more thorough exploration. We agreed that Pitlochry will always be synonymous with that lovely house and its unforgettable view, which made our short stay so memorable.

DAY FIVE: PITLOCHRY - TUMMEL BRIDGE

Into every life a little rain must fall. Things were to go sadly awry during the latter part of this day's journey, for a cruel turn of events prevented me from reaching my original destination at Dunalastair.

The day began well enough for there was plenty to interest me as I left Pitlochry. A short distance from the town centre, overlooking the energetic Tummel, I came across the Festival Theatre, a resplendent modern building that offers a commanding view over the valley. Theatregoers can enjoy a relaxing meal in the restaurant and a superb view through its spacious bay windows over the resplendent lawns that roll down to the river. Across the water unfolds a pleasing panorama dominated by the shapely outline of Ben Vrackie that entices red-blooded fell-walkers to climb it. Despite its modest height of 2760 feet it offers an extremely satisfying ascent that only becomes laborious for the final few hundred. Your reward, as you enjoy a well-deserved rest on its rugged apex, is a bird's-eye view of the Tummel valley that spreads itself expansively beneath you. If mountain scenery is your delight look north-westwards for a glittering array of peaks which include the Forest of Atholl and the distant Caingorms. This friendly mountain affords an ideal excursion from Pitlochry on a fine evening when softening sunlight adds lustre to a landscape of bold mountains, heather-clad moorland and delightful woodland.

The narrow band of tarmac that wound along the riverside brought me within sight of the daunting Pitlochry Dam, a concrete monster that holds innumerable gallons of water in its grasp. Its mighty ramparts rose intimidatingly above me as I stood transfixed by its awesome presence. I could see tiny figures on its parapet that resembled ants on a giant concrete mound. In order to tame this brute I made for its base to begin the long haul to its top. A series of water-filled chambers, in the form of steps, lay at the approach to the dam. They form the beginnings of the famous salmon ladder that represents one of Pitlochry's main tourist attractions. These watery stairs provide access in season to the energetic fish as they leap from chamber to chamber to reach the tempting depths of Loch Faskally. The salmon were evidently having a rest day, for there were no signs of activity in the chambers as I passed.

Some minutes later I became one of the minuscule figures that paraded on the roof of the dam. I gazed in awe over the river below and traced its progress through the spread-eagled town. Behind me lapped the captive waters of Loch Faskally that I had admired the previous afternoon. My morning's course would run initially through the picturesque woodland that fringed its banks. This time

I would see the area from a different viewpoint as my route lay along a Nature Trail on the opposite side of the loch and in the reverse direction to my previous day's walk. From my aerial balcony I admired the coloured mantle of vegetation through which I would soon be burrowing.

The leafy avenue of the trail, sprinkled with vivid rhododendrons, enclosed me as I headed north and away from the dam. It was mildly frustrating to be walking in the wrong direction but my course would turn west after a few miles and lead me to Loch Tummel. Occasionally emerging from cover I enjoyed invigorating views along the tranquil expanse of Loch Faskally, the sunlight glinting on its mirror-like surface. Eventually the path led me from the woods to join a quiet road that climbed high above the loch, twisting and bucking in the manner of a roller-coaster. Traffic was sparse and I was able to enjoy my surroundings without fear of being mowed down by passing cars. A small oasis of green fields was visible at the northern end of the loch and within them stood a sturdy and eminently pleasing country house. How long it had occupied that idyllic spot I had no idea, but it must have witnessed a radical alteration of its surroundings for where once a sprightly river cavorted lay the broad reaches of the man-made loch.

On a brow of the writhing road my attention was caught by an imposing stone archway that, I discovered, formed the entrance to a nearby power station that lay hidden beneath the folds of the hillside. It was flanked by well-tended flower beds and a bench seat was conveniently provided for passer's by to enjoy the distinctive view over the valley in comfort. Etched in the stonework, in bold lettering, was 'Clunie Memorial Arch' and a plaque informed me that it was erected by the North of Scotland Hydro-Electric Board. The Arch is an exact representation of the cross-section of the Clunie Tunnel which forms part of the Clunie section of the Tummel-Garry project. Built between 1946 and 1950 the tunnel itself is 9158 feet long and carries water from Loch Tummel, two miles distant, to Clunie Power Station that reclined furtively in the valley below.

My camera was busy now, and when I reached the brow of the next hill I captured a long distance view of the Pass of Killiecrankie lying beneath the nostalgic backdrop of Atholl Forest. So engrossed was I that I failed to notice an elderly walker approach at a tidy pace. He surprised me by enquiring if I was tired and in need of a rest. Indicating my camera I assured him that I was merely pausing to take a photograph. In a broad Scots accent he complained that he was no longer able to walk at speed as his knees had gone. They seemed alright to me for he had caught me up in sprightly fashion and when I told him so he seemed genuinely pleased. Visibly brightening he suggested that I descend to the River Tummel a little farther on where I would be rewarded by the sight of salmon leaping over exciting waterfalls. Turning on his heel he hurried away whilst I watched for signs of his knees buckling.

At the point that he had indicated I dropped rather precariously down a wickedly steep and stony path towards the river. At the bottom I had to clamber over jagged boulders in order to reach the water. My struggle proved worthwhile for it was an enchanting spot, deep in the heart of the Linn of Tummel. The frenetic river rushed between a pair of miniature cataracts that lay a hundred yards apart. The brown peaty water was churned into a froth that could grace pints of ale as it rushed through the cascades. Selecting a conveniently flat boulder beside the lower falls I enjoyed a leisurely drink from my flask as I searched the churning water for signs of energetic fish. Once again my quest for leaping salmon proved futile, but despite my disappointment I sat entranced by the beauty of the place. My secluded haven possessed a heavenly quality with the sound of rushing water providing a fitting symphony. As I basked contentedly in the sunshine I noticed an inquisitive red squirrel approach stealthily and study me from a safe distance. Perhaps he hoped that this heavy-booted intruder would provide a tasty morsel.

The fish were still keeping a low profile as I left the river and rejoined the road that traverses the rim of the Linn of Tummel. It led me to Coronation Bridge, a footbridge that carries one of the numerous Nature Trails across the Tummel. Nearby an eye-catching notice-board displayed a large-scale map of the locality and identified the labyrinth of trails that permeate the surrounding woods. These are obviously popular judging by the parties of visitors and walkers that could be seen in the vicinity. A crowd of people studying the comprehensive map were joined by a large group of cyclists. Coronation Bridge is a focal point that fairly buzzes with activity.

Swinging west the road undulated and cavorted towards Loch Tummel amidst rowan, ash and alder, with the scent of moss floating on the air. Now an extremely narrow highway it had passing places that were fortunately little used, so light was the traffic. It afforded sanctuary from the busy tourist route that runs along the north side of Loch Tummel. I was safely immune from that bustle of activity which lies a mere half-mile away.

A mile of exhilarating progress brought me to the Clunie Dam that seals the east end of Loch Tummel. Now a reservoir, like its smaller neighbour, Dunalastair Water, it forms another link in the chain of the Tummel-Garry project. The bulwark of the dam controls the flow of water into the adjacent section of the Tummel that lies many feet below it. It also marks the beginning of the two-mile-long tunnel that runs to Clunie Power Station.

I threaded through larch and birch as the road began to jink along the south shore of Loch Tummel. Tinkling streams tumbled from the forests that straddled the hillsides and squeezed through gnarled mossy clefts before rushing into the sparkling waters of the loch. Through the trees I caught occasional glimpses of the placid expanse of water that stretched for seven miles to Tummel Bridge. Not so pleasing were the carrier-bags containing rubbish that periodically littered the shoreline and some of the road's passing places. There was even a crude fireplace, clumsily built with readily- available stones. It appeared that other travellers had selfishly abused this quiet route.

To take my mind off the wanton despoilation of this beautiful area I hummed a refrain of *The Road To The Isles*, recalling its appropriate lyrics 'By Tummel and Loch Rannoch and Lochaber I will go'. I teased myself with the question of where this ancient route to the Isles had run. Was I actually following it, or did it trace a path along the line of the modern tourist route? In my opinion, the only virtue of this busy corridor is its proximity to the superb viewpoint of Queen's View, set high on a promontory above Loch Tummel. Made famous by Mary Queen of Scots, who deeply admired the prospect over the loch, it has endured as a popular beauty spot. Allegedly, the present viewpoint is not the original one, which was reputedly at a lower elevation. The reason for its move to a more prominent position is that as the vegetation surrounding the loch grew it obscured any long-distance views.

The sun deserted me as I approached some isolated homesteads near the west end of the loch. Under heavy skies, with rain beginning to fall, I reached the hamlets of Donlellan and Foss, the road having forsaken the lochside and veered south-west. The scattering of buildings had a sombre appearance in the worsening conditions and my excitement began to wane. Walking had felt effortless at the outset as there was much to see, but it now became mechanical, a means to an end. I cursed myself for allowing a blip in the good weather to dampen my spirits. There was the forthcoming attraction of Tummel Bridge to look forward to, I told myself.

The neat and trim Parish Church in Foss was given scant recognition as I trudged past, barely stopping to read the sign that indicated it lay in the Parish of Foss and Rannoch. Both hamlets were dealt an injustice, for I was preoccupied with the deteriorating weather. My belated apologies to Donlellan and Foss, which deserved more of my time and attention.

A mile of stepping in time to the beat of the rain on my waterproofs brought me literally to the end of the road. I was forced to abandon my peaceful companion and join the busier and wider B846 road that links Tummel Bridge with Keltneyburn. Gone were the uplifting lochside views, obscured by a dense pine forest as I made for Kynachan on the outskirts of Tummel Bridge. The anticipated views of Schiehallion to the south-west did not materialise, for it was annoyingly obscured by low cloud. What I could see, however, were the long snow poles that lined the road, reminiscent of those around Glenshee. Descending to the point where the River Tummel flows into the west end of Loch Tummel I could see that the area had no pretentions of prettiness. Gaunt industrial complexes signified Kynachan's sacrifice to power generation. A substantial electrical sub-station and a power station bordered the road that was now hugging the river as it headed, straight as an arrow, for Tummel Bridge. When I reached the eagerly awaited crossing point of the Tummel I found its impact disappointing. Nowhere looks at its best when viewed through a drizzly haze, but this renowned beauty spot had, in my opinion, been ruined by the trappings of modernity. Alongside the original high-arched stone bridge stood a steel monstrosity that looked completely out of character with its surroundings. Unable to cope with the demands of ever-increasing traffic the old discarded bridge could only watch forlornly as cars hurried across its garish counterpart.

Determined to give Tummel Bridge and its vicinity a fair viewing I crossed the river and within a short distance I was greeted by the Tummel Valley Holiday Park. This straddles the main road through the valley and its wooden chalets and caravans intrude into the embracing woodland. I was unimpressed by this tourist corridor that displayed the all too familiar litter of cans, ice-cream wrappers and plastic bags. Without hesitation I turned on my heel and hurried back to the bridge, eager to put this unappetising place behind me. Tummel Bridge is one of the few places that I was glad to leave.

My plan for the afternoon was to follow the valley westwards to Dunalastair Water and seek accommodation at the nearby hamlet of Dunalastair. The road was to be discarded in favour of tracks through the forest that lies on the south side of the Tummel. It was no wrench to join a back- road that led from the village, its tarmac surface soon disappearing as it entered the forest. I did not anticipate any hardships that afternoon as Dunalastair lay barely five miles away. The sky began to clear as I struck a good pace through extensive clearings where trees had been recently felled. I felt that fortune was on my side once more and Dunalastair Water would be reached in no time at all. However, my confidence turned out to be sadly misplaced for fate had other ideas. The first two miles were dispatched with ease and things were looking good. A benevolent sun shone with renewed vigour as I surprisingly joined a metalled lane that could have been laid for my benefit. Unfortunately it wasn't, for it accompanies an aqueduct that feeds the power station at Tummel Bridge. The area was deserted and there were no warning notices signifying that I had no right to be there. According to my map the lane and the aqueduct were heading in the right direction along the fringe of the forest, so I blessed my good fortune and followed them. The surface of the aqueduct had turned a vibrant blue under the benevolent rays of the sun and striking reflections of the surrounding foliage danced on its waters. A mundane man-made channel was thus transformed into a thing of beauty. Several footbridges spanned the aqueduct but they were sealed off by barbed wire. I assumed that these barricades prevented people from trespassing onto the far side, but later events proved me wrong.

All went well for a further mile as I enjoyed the warm sun on my back, obligingly tempered by a slight breeze. I had not met a soul since leaving Tummel Bridge and wondered why no one else was enjoying such fine environs on a pleasant afternoon. People did not realise what they were missing, I thought, but I was too busy enjoying myself to worry about their misfortune. The view over the Tummel was startling. A sward of rich forest bordered the distant horizon. Between this dark- green mass and the tree-fringed river lay a band of delicately purple moorland, so attractive that you felt the urge to reach out and touch it. Into this inviting landscape protruded the arrowheads of riverside pines that rose gracefully from a russet cloak of riverside bracken. Through a gallery of stately silver birch I could see a small but impressive Tower House nestling on the opposite riverbank. It had an adjoining castellated archway that presented a most imposing facade. When I discovered, a few minutes later, who owned such a delightful property, it came as a great disappointment.

My route began to veer towards the river and after a short distance I arrived at another huge concrete barrier that spans it. Beyond this structure the Tummel has been widened to form an artificial lake, supplied by Dunalastair Water. Was the river to have no peace? It has been subjected to a series of floodings and strangulations that have destroyed its original character. Access to this gigantic concrete funnelling device was barred by a high fence and a notice proclaiming strictly no admittance. I could see a narrow road leading from the other end of the dam to my coveted Tower House and archway. The mystery was solved. This whole complex, including the house, was in the hands of the hydro-electric company. How sad it was to see such an imposing entrance permitting access to this commercial undertaking.

Here I had to say goodbye to the lane and the aqueduct. The former disappeared beneath well-secured gates and headed for the barrier whilst the latter ran into the lake to take in water for the thirsty power station at Tummel Bridge. I was obliged to join a sketchy path in order to continue my journey to Dunalastair Water, but not for long. My progress was soon halted by another high fence that stretched across my path and down to the river. It was extremely frustrating to see the footpath continuing on the far side of the wire fence and there was even the remains of a small stile a short distance along it. My route had evidently been a right of way at one time, but was now of no use to me whatsoever. In desperation I decided to leave the river and follow the fence to see if there was a way around it. After stumbling through tangled vegetation for several hundred yards I found myself completely hemmed in by another fence that joined it at right angles. I was now completely cut off from the remainder of my walk and the realisation dawned that the encircling fences signified that I had no right to be in the area at all. All became crystal clear. The lack of people, the barbed wire on the footbridges over the aqueduct that was obviously put there to prevent people from entering the property that I had been walking through. Who could fail to pick up such tell-tale signs? Anger and frustration welled inside me. Why had there been no notices as I entered the forest? What should I do now? I struggled to gather my thoughts. To try and scale the intimidating fence would be foolhardy. I would have to forego Dunalastair unless I was prepared to back-track to Tummel Bridge and follow the road on the opposite side of the river, which involved a further nine miles of walking. This was not an attractive proposition. I decided to cut my losses and merely return to Tummel Bridge and seek accommodation there. This would not severely disrupt my following day's journey, but it would involve an approach to Schiehallion by road instead of my planned cross-country route.

My enjoyable afternoon had now degenerated into a retreat. To compound my misery, Schiehallion was beckoning provokingly from above, its triangular summit clearly visible in the intensely blue sky. So near, yet so far, I thought. Bowing to the inevitable I struggled back along the fence to rejoin the path. I narrowly escaped further disaster by just avoiding a giant ant's nest secluded in the undergrowth, a heaving mass of frantic activity waiting to erupt onto a careless foot. Subsequently I very carefully watched where I was treading, which brought to my notice some of the largest fir cones that I had ever seen.

Retracing my steps along the path I began a frustrating return journey to Tummel Bridge which I had earlier been eager to leave. Seemingly, I couldn't escape from the place. My eyes were peeled for warning notices but I never saw any. I found this puzzling as I rejoined the road into the village. Here I at last met someone, a friendly couple from Yorkshire who were accompanied by an identical pair of black labradors. As we stopped to chat the dogs fussed around me and, amusingly, when I bent down and stroked one of them, the other wagged its tail. Jack, I discovered, was a keen fisherman and he and his wife Beryl had rented a nearby holiday cottage so that he could fish the river and Dunalastair Water. When I poured out my tale of woe they invited me to their cottage for some refreshment. Whilst I was enjoying a welcome drink Beryl suggested that I spent the night there, as there was a spare room and it was getting late for finding other accommodation. This was manna from heaven and I quickly accepted their generous offer. I was treated to a huge meal that rendered me immobile and afterwards, in the comfort of armchairs, we talked well into the night. My day had not turned out too badly after all.

DAY SIX: TUMMEL BRIDGE - KELTNEYBURN

I awoke with a start, as though a switch had been activated in my mind. It may have been the subconscious thought of climbing Schiehallion that jerked me from my deep sleep. For a few perplexing moments I had no idea where I was. Sunlight streamed through the bedroom curtains and I recognised the compact quarters that I had generously been accorded. The recollection that I was still in Tummel Bridge and of my enforced change of plan, came flooding back. Scrabbling for my watch, I found that it was almost eight o'clock and I needed to get a move on. A hurried wash and shave brought me back to life and I tried not to dwell on the previous day's debacle as I dressed.

Trotting downstairs I was hopeful that today would go according to plan. Jack had already left, armed with fishing tackle, for Dunalastair Water. Whilst I enjoyed a breakfast of cereal, pancakes and toast, Beryl busied herself with household chores, cheerily humming to the radio as she swept and dusted. She paused to ask where I was headed and when she learned that the main item on my agenda was Schiehallion, she quipped that I at least had good weather for it. This was true, for the sky was bright and clear, a perfect day for tackling mountains.

As I departed I thanked Beryl and offered to pay for her hospitality. She would have none of it, saying firmly, but politely, that I had been a welcome guest and money was not necessary. She teased that she and Jack might appear unannounced on my doorstep sometime, for our homes were not many miles apart. I told her that they would always be welcome, for it would give me a chance to repay their kindness.

I left Tummel Bridge for the second and, hopefully, the last time, by the same road on which I had entered it. The day would be tough and I had no wish to blunder across pathless countryside. The B846 road would have to suffice. It would form a major part of my day's route to Keltneyburn. I would have to leave it for a while, however, whilst I dealt with Schiehallion.

A climb of the hill that I had descended the previous day now presented itself. The Tummel and its power station were left behind and I began a meandering four-mile ascent to Loch Kinardochy which lies near the crest of a ridge that Wainwright considers to be a fine viewpoint. Conditions were a vast improvement on those of the previous day, when rain and murk had blotted out any views. Thick forests flanked the road as I laboured doggedly up the long incline and eventually met the Allt Kinardochy that tumbles from tiny Loch Kinardochy, now only a couple of miles above me. The lively burn hid shyly amongst the trees but the sound of its gurgling accompanied me almost to the top of the ridge. When the road finally levelled out I was able to relax and take stock of my surroundings.

The loch lay smooth and serene above the long strath of the Tummel Valley and beyond it a vast canvas of rippling mountain tops filled the horizon. An adjacent car park bore testament to the popularity of this vantage point and I could see why Wainwright was so taken with it. The nearby stub of a disused lime-kiln chimney intrigued me and clambering over the spoil heaps left from limestone quarrying I peered into it, only to find its interior filled with shale. Now a sad relic, the kiln had formerly served a very useful purpose. Much surrounding land had been reclaimed from bog and desolate moorland by drainage and the addition of lime formerly supplied by the kiln. The distinctive acid soil was thus neutralised and the nutrients from the lime had encouraged plant growth. Looking westwards from the kiln I was treated to a new perspective of Schiehallion, the great hump of its summit ridge now exposed.

This sight goaded me into action once more and I began a hurried search for the narrow, winding road that would lead me to its foot. I soon found its junction with the B846 road, where a convenient sign displaying 'Schiehallion Road' pointed the way. A pleasant two-mile walk ensued along the quiet road that threaded through attractive birchwoods. I was chaperoned by invigorating sunshine which filtered through outstretched branches to dance at my feet.

The car park near Schiehallion was bulging - obviously a popular spot. My meandering six-mile walk from Tummel Bridge had put me behind the majority of the day's human traffic that liberally spattered the slopes of my objective. As I hurried towards the start of the footpath at the far end of the car park I was stopped by a dubious-looking character who enquired if I was about to climb

Schiehallion, and if so, could he accompany me, adding that I should call him Ted. He had an unsettling, unkempt appearance, accentuated by a rapacious beard that a flock of swallows could happily nest in. I recalled my misjudgment of Philip, whom I had met at his lovely B and B in Patterdale. He had displayed a similar wild appearance, which was totally alien to his character. This chap may not be as bad as he looks, I thought, though still curious about someone who hung around for a walking nursemaid. As though reading my thoughts he explained that he was very inexperienced, a fact well advertised by the grubby trouser legs tucked into flimsy socks, themselves embedded in massive hobnailed boots. He hardly looked like a walker and those boots would take some hauling up a mountain. I reluctantly said that he could join me, more out of pity than logic.

Hoping that I would not regret my decision we left the car park and passed a footpath sign displaying the picture of a large boot sole, which made me smile. Our ascent had barely begun before I was subjected to a condensed version of Ted's life story, which began in the Glasgow slums and went downhill from there. This verbal barrage continued non-stop until he began to gasp for air, whereupon I felt tempted to echo the adage 'Save your breath to cool your porridge'. Obviously superbly unfit he whinged about his aching legs, the chafing straps of his rucksack and his painful lungs. Nothing but complaints and we hadn't reached the serious climbing yet. Already rueing my sympathetic gesture I was sorely tempted to place a strategic boot on his backside to help him on his way. I could callously imagine him struggling up the steepening path displaying the imprint of a boot sole, identical to the one on the footpath sign. Fate kindly intervened, for a little further on he collapsed onto a simple memorial cairn, groaning that he had to rest. Enough was enough. Seizing the opportunity I told Ted that I had many miles ahead of me and could not keep stopping. Giving him no chance to argue I strode up the path ignoring the permeating feeling of guilt. Luckily there were no walkers in the vicinity - heaven knows what they would have thought of my performance. Without a backward glance I romped the next stretch of path, half-expecting plaintive cries from my abandoned acquaintance, but none came. As the going became harder I was forced to slow my headstrong pace. Halting briefly I snatched a view over the Tummel valley, much of its wooded depths exposed amidst ribbons of water glistening like priceless gems.

Clambering over fragmented rocks and scree is frustrating and curse-ridden. The upper slopes of Schiehallion has them in abundance, seemingly scattered by a malicious giant seed-sower. My progress was slowed by the combination of steep gradient and offending quartzite fragments that severely tested legs and ankles. The path, barely discernible at times, was helpfully marked by cairns; invaluable in poor weather conditions. The summit rocks finally hailed an end to my tribulations which paled into insignificance beside the magnificent spectacle below me. How true is the saying: 'No pain, no gain'. Amidst the fierce wind that threatened to tear me from Schiehallion's grasp I cautiously pirouetted on a convenient flat rock, squinting at the friendly sun, which, although extremely welcome, needed its dimmer switch tweaking.

To the north-west I could discern tiny Kinloch Rannoch teetering on the edge of the promontory that separates Loch Rannoch and Dunalastair Water. Its minuscule buildings were seemingly about to be swamped by the larger Loch Rannoch which dominates the valley, carpeted on its north side by the extensive Rannoch Forest. This collection of alder, rowan, silver birch and the ubiquitous pine is a surviving remnant of the ancient Caledonian Forest. Distant jagged, hostile peaks frowned upon a vast landscape which embraces the wild and untamed Rannoch Moor, an area that I planned to encounter on my way to Fort William.

Mountains were arrayed all round me as I struggled to identify some of them. I was concentrating on the main group to the south-west when I was joined on my platform by a young lady and her companion, a friendly terrier. Unsurprisingly docile after manipulating its stubby legs over the rocky assault course the dog lay on the rock panting. Noticing the 'Three Peaks of Yorkshire' emblem on the lady's rucksack took me back to my early walking days and my first attempt at the twenty-four-mile Yorkshire Dales marathon. We chatted about those lovely dales, home territory for both of us, for she lived in the pleasant market town of Skipton. Eventually seeking shelter amongst the myriad rocks we attacked our respective lunch packs, appetites honed by exertion and fresh, mountain air.

Descent can be harder than climbing over rough terrain, the knees taking the strain of tussling with gravity and unstable footing. Thus my downward journey was a mixture of tedium and elation, relief from the ensnaring rocky screes being provided at intervals by patches of well-trodden snow. Landmarks that had appeared minute from the summit were dramatically enlarged before disappearing behind the indentations of the lower slopes. Approaching the memorial cairn with trepidation I kept a wary eye out for my deserted companion. Thankfully he was nowhere in sight, presumably realising his limitations and calling it a day. I often wonder what happened to him.

Being so eager to escape my dubious limpet I had barely given the cairn a second glance, but now I gave it a closer look. 'In loving memory of Alexander Frazer, resting in the place of his choice on Bonnie Schiehallion' read the inscription on the plaque cemented to it. This tangible tribute from his wife signified a rather unusual preference for that particular spot rather than the mountain's more dramatic summit. Could permission have been denied for such an edifice on the summit, as it had been for a Wainwright memorial on several Lakeland fells?

With the mountain conquered I joyfully retraced my steps along Schiehallion road. A shorter, cross-country route to Keltneyburn had appealed to me, but it involved an unorthodox descent of Schiehallion and a traverse of rough country before a track could be reached at the isolated Glenmore Bothy. That area of land is owned by the Glenlyons, who may not like people wandering at will across it. I decided to play safe and continue my journey by road.

The air was still clear and fresh, tantalising to the nostrils and untainted by traffic fumes. It felt good to have the hardest of the day's walking behind me and I soon returned to the B846 road that I saw was identified on my map as General Wade's Road. This gives reference to the very efficient network of roads laid at the General's instigation to enhance the movement of English troops around Scotland between the Jacobite risings of 1715 and 1745. Although the General has received the credit for all such roads, he was only responsible for their construction between 1726 and 1737. He was ably assisted by Major Caulfield, who did all the work and got none of the recognition, until he succeeded the General and filled out the basic framework already constructed.

The modern B846 road links Tummel Bridge with Aberfeldy and as far back as those troubled times formed a strategic route between the valleys of the Tummel and the Tay. As I surveyed this dead-straight ribbon of road, no longer the dusty track of the Jacobite period, it stretched temptingly before me bounded by a series of flimsy-looking plastic posts topped with reflecting strips. In the dark these strips give the impression of wild-eyed animals when caught in the harsh glare of car headlights. Pine-woods flanked one side of the road, the trees huddling together to blot out any light beneath them. The Keltney Burn fought its way through the unyielding trees on its journey to the hamlet that bears its name. An attractive white-walled farmhouse stood impassively nearby, its accompanying barn containing an imposing collection of gleaming farm machinery. The area surrounding the barn was less impressive, portraying a veritable graveyard of rusting and long disused implements. Such a sight convinces me that farmers are reluctant to throw anything away. This however, is a hyper-critical observation by a person whose bulging and over-loaded garage bears testimony to my maxim that every piece of junk hoarded on its groaning rafters and around its walls might come in handy one day.

I strode along General Wade's road, light-heartedly humming a tune to myself and feeling that all was right with the world. Although many miles had been covered since leaving Lochnagar I was bearing up well despite some long daily mileages. I was suddenly jerked from my reverie by a screeching of brakes, as a large and very impressive car skidded to a halt alongside me. I visibly jumped and stared with a startled expression at this monster which had seemingly appeared from nowhere. Its driver, obviously used to giving orders, barked through the open window, demanding the location of the Ben Lawers Visitor Centre. His wife looked pleadingly at me from the back seat. Had she been banished from the front passenger seat, I wondered? Evidently she had been given the task of route-finding, for a map lay open on her lap. Her attempts had obviously failed and the anxious look in her eyes indicated that she would be very glad of some assistance. She lowered her window to await my response and I put my arm through the opening in order to point out the desired route on her map. As I had already concluded, she was not adept at map-reading and had difficulty interpreting my instructions. After a few minutes of drumming his fingers impatiently on the steering wheel her husband could apparently wait no longer and snapped petulantly that he would ask at the next village. Ignoring the fact that I was still leaning through the open window he slammed his foot on the accelerator and his wife shouted in dismay. Luckily I shot my arm from inside the car and was left staring incredulously at the rapidly disappearing vehicle.

All my pleasant thoughts had disappeared as I stood transfixed, silently cursing the uncivilised driver who was obviously far too important to wait around whilst a simple walker tried to give route instructions to his wife. When my heart had stopped pounding I began to feel a great compassion for that poor woman who had to live with his ignorance every day.

Dismissing thoughts about the unfairness of life, I headed for Keltneyburn accompanied by disconcerting power lines, their attendant pylons marching across the surrounding countryside like spectral beings. My imagination in overdrive, I pictured a severed cable lashing down and reducing me to a cinder. What a relief it eventually became to banish those menacing coils and reach my destination.

The hamlet comprises a pleasant collection of neat and well kept stone buildings. Many of their walls displayed contrasting coloured stonework and evidence of recent re-pointing. Its main attraction, apart from the hotel, is the Old Smithy which houses a showroom for visitors. The blacksmith, however, has moved with the times. He was working in the yard, not with hammer and anvil but with a brazing torch, which he was using to repair a broken component from an excavator.

The peaceful hideaway basked in late-afternoon sunshine as I ambled towards the nearby bridge for a glimpse of the Falls of Keltney. I did so under the watchful gaze of a statue; that of Major General David Stewart of Drumcharry and Garth. This gentleman, attired in full Highland regalia, was a renowned historian of the Highlands and its regiments. Hoisted onto his plinth in 1925 by the Stewart Society and other admirers, he was able to scrutinise passing locals and visitors from his commanding position. What did he think of the red-haired, sorry, I'll correct that, sandy, greying- haired lone walker ambling beneath him. In all probability I was pigeon-holed as one of the English hoards.

Attaining the bridge, I was rewarded with the sight of the sparkling Keltney Burn, turning to boiling foam as it dashed over the rocks below. The sight of so much froth reminded me that a reviving drink was called for. I callously dismissed the engaging falls and sought the local hostelry where I planned to spend the night.

As the froth of the local brew slithered deliciously past my parched tonsils I was beckoned to one of the tables in the hotel bar by a chap who cheerfully introduced himself as Jimmy. He had watched my arrival a little earlier and seemed eager to discover who this lone traveller was. Roughly my own age, he displayed an inquisitive, but friendly, interest in my journey. The reason for his scrutiny became apparent when I learned that he was a life-long resident of the village who now lived alone. He told me much about the locality before enquiring if I had seen the local castle. I told him that I had noticed what resembled a fortified tower hiding in woodland as I had approached the village. His eyes brightened as he asked if I would like to see Garth Castle, as it is known, at close quarters. He seemed keen to take me, so, ensuring that he had no other commitments, I readily agreed.

He led me through the village to a track that follows the Keltney Burn as it heads towards the castle that lies about a mile away. As we walked he recounted the building's chequered history. Built in the fourteenth century for the wayward son of Robert the Bruce it fell into ruins until it was restored by the Curry family five centuries later.

Eventually we forsook the burn and followed the steepening track which wound towards the castle. Jimmy explained, as we laboured up the steep approach, that modernisation in the nineteen-sixties had bankrupted the owner of the fortress. Since that time it has housed several occupants, some using it as a holiday home. Recently, he told me, it had been vacated by its Dutch owners who were awaiting a purchaser.

When the tower loomed above us, gaunt and foreboding, I could see that it occupied a commanding position on a promontory, set high above the valley. We spent a while circling the eerie, deserted fortification, unfortunately denied a view from its turrets towards imminent Tayside.

Eventually my stomach reminded me that my delayed supper would be welcome, so Jimmy and I returned at a brisk pace to the village. Here we parted company, but not before I had thanked him and wished him well. He gave a cheery wave as I headed for the hotel to quell my rumbling innards.

DAY SEVEN: KELTNEYBURN - BRIDGE OF BALGIE

My initial task was to set a course for Fortingall. The lack of defined footpaths necessitated following a quiet road for roughly three miles.

This section was not arduous as it followed the low-lying valley of the River Lyon that emerges from Glen Lyon beyond Fortingall and flows past Keltneyburn to its confluence with the River Tay. Craggy hillsides rose sharply from the valley floor on its north side, whilst the view to the south was dominated by the tree-lined slopes of Drummond Hill, an area with an abundance of forest walks. I discovered Garth House and the adjacent dwellings at Drumcharry sheltering beneath those steep northern slopes. The inscription on the plinth of David Stewart's statue in Keltneyburn therefore made more sense as I now knew the location of Garth and Drumcharry.

Maintaining a lively pace ensured that in slightly less than an hour I entered the village of Fortingall, which was a delight to behold. I stood entranced by the sight of white-walled cottages topped with impressive thatched roofs, nestling alongside the main thoroughfare. Not to be outdone, the church stood doggedly nearby, its brightly-coloured west wall displaying an ornate, steeply-arched window. The building appeared to be defiantly resisting the ravages of time and weather, for it looked as clean as a new pin, right up to the small bell-tower perched on its roof. Part of the west wall was obscured by the spreading branches of an enormous yew tree. I entered the churchyard for a closer look. An adjacent notice advised that although the tree was much photographed I was not to forget the lovely church alongside. Obeying these instructions I took camera shots of them both. The massive yew, I learned, is a specimen of primeval forest. It is 3,000 years old and believed to be the most ancient surviving piece of vegetation in Europe. A long history is also attached to the church, its site having been used as a place of worship since the seventh century.

I paused for a drink from my flask outside the neighbouring hotel. Looking around me I discovered a thatcher repairing the roof of one of the nearby picturesque cottages. He eventually descended his ladder and lit up a cigarette. I took the opportunity to wander over to him for a chat. He was very happy to explain the intricacies of thatching, which, he was at pains to point out, is a craft and not an art. I was surprised to learn that it is still widely in use, there being currently over 1000 exponents and their numbers are on the increase. The angle of the roof, he told me, is an important criteria; it needs to be steep in order to facilitate the speedy shedding of water. I had never realised that alternative kinds of material can be used; straw or reed. Straw thatching can apparently last up to forty years depending on weather conditions; a dry climate being desirable, as rain and dampness cause it to deteriorate. Good quality reed thatching, he said, would last for over seventy years in good conditions.

In answer to his query regarding my day's journey I told him that I still had twelve miles to cover to my destination near Bridge of Balgie. When he asked if I had seen the Standing Stones on my approach to the village, it appeared to me that everyone I met in the area wished me to visit a site of historical interest. I replied that I had seen very little of anything in my haste to reach there. What a fool I had been, for they were clearly marked on the map and I had marched within a hundred yards of them, paying them no heed. Feeling that I must make amends, I told him that I would take a look at his thatching and then retrace my steps along the road to see the stones. Fortingall had much to offer and it would be a shame to rush away, but I began mentally preparing myself for a concerted assault on those remaining miles when the time came.

I stood for a while watching the thatcher, whose name I learned was Mark, at work. Doubtless his friends called him Mark Thatcher and ribbed him about the Iron Lady. He skillfully secured the new sheaves of thatch to the roof with strips of hazel and showed me how the pointed ends of the strips were pushed into the old thatch to create a stapling effect. His nimbleness was impressive as he effortlessly climbed the ladder carrying bundles of thatch, apparently oblivious to the height at which he was working. Thanking him, I took my leave, smiling at his parting remark, which implied that he would much rather be on his roof than walking the countryside with me.

It was only a short walk to the Standing Stones that squatted undramatically in one of the roadside fields. They comprised nine irregular-shaped stones arranged in three groups of three; each group being some distance apart. I was intrigued by this unusual configuration and made a mental note to do some research on my return home. This later revealed that they were the remains of three stone circles, or rectangles to be precise, that marked one of the megalithic sites set on the terrace overlooking the River Lyon. Originally there were eight stones in each rectangular setting, with the largest stones at the corners. They remained intact until the late eighteenth or early nineteenth century when the extension of agriculture into marginal lands gave an incentive to farmers to blast or haul away stones of such obstructive circles. In this particular case, five stones from each rectangle were deliberately overthrown and buried, but thankfully, superstition dictated that the remaining three stones were left erect. Part of the site was excavated in 1970 and two of the buried sets of stones were unearthed.

Walking back through the village I waved to Mark who was still hard at work. My progress was soon halted once more when I stopped to admire Glenlyon House, its iron gates firmly closed. This seat of the Campbell family stands in splendid isolation from the village as though wishing to remain aloof from it. Situated a good distance from the road at the head of a tree-lined drive, it appears reluctant to reveal its charms for those trees obscure an ample view of it. I could, however, discern some of its fine features, the most prominent being a circular turret that is typical of the Scottish tower-houses on which its construction was based.

My next task was to find the entrance to Glen Lyon that lies a short distance away. Wainwright called this glen 'a half-day's detour of sustained delight', but intimated that you had to keep a sharp lookout for its entrance. I soon came to a signpost that pointed the way into the glen and indicated that Bridge of Balgie lay eleven miles along it. Another sign warned that it was unsuitable for caravans, coaches and heavy lorries. Glen Lyon is ranked as one of the finest glens in Scotland and this accolade was certainly supported by the enticing view on display. Here was Highland scenery at its best as I surveyed the outlying spurs of Ben Lawers and Carn Mairg that guard the narrow entrance. Their snow-tinged summits contrasted sharply with the wooded lower slopes, forming a scene of rugged grandeur. I was full of anticipation as I set out to explore the glen's innermost secrets.

The road hugged the River Lyon and I thankfully noted from my map that I would be able to leave it shortly and join a riverside path, albeit for only a mile. Before doing so I passed magnificent woodland on either side of the narrow gorge, particularly admiring the impressive beech trees. Five great larches stand at the point where Gregor MacGregor is said to have leapt across the river to escape from the pursuing Campbells in the sixteenth century. The place is identified as MacGregor's Leap, in recognition of his amazing feat. The hills forming the Pass of Lyon towered above me, barely allowing room for the narrow road and its companion, the lively river. Beyond the Pass the glen opens out and for about nine miles the river flows contentedly between farms, emerald-green fields and woodland. At higher level, snow-capped peaks towered over heather-clad hills and the air was heavy with birdsong. Moss-covered boulders lined the roadsides and some stark skeletons of trees, stripped of their foliage, contrasted dramatically with their lush surroundings. I passed a parked car containing a couple who, despite the glorious sunshine and superb setting, were reading a book and a newspaper respectively.

My progress was carefree, yet determined, as I took the river-side path, glad to be free of passing vehicles for a while. Luckily, I did not have much more walking to do along the modern road because I was able to climb the lower flank of Carn Mairg by a steep path that eventually joins a track above the tiny settlement of Invervar. Here I had only to cross the river to join a minor road, conveniently unsuitable for cars, that probably formed the original route through the glen. This provided peaceful surroundings, untroubled by traffic, through which I strode purposefully towards my night's destination, a farmhouse that lay six miles farther along the valley on the outskirts of Bridge of Balgie.

I was beginning to tire as I approached the farm along a steep, winding track. I was made very welcome by the farmer's wife who instantly told me to call her Marjorie. She solicitously enquired how far I had travelled that day and if I had found my journey enjoyable. She beamed when I ventured the opinion that she lived amongst some of the finest scenery that I had yet encountered.

After a relaxing soak in a piping-hot bath I was introduced to her husband Alistair, who sat in one corner of the large dining-cum-living room. He asked me to join him whilst his wife went off to the kitchen to prepare supper. I took a nearby chair which was reluctantly vacated by a friendly-looking sheep dog with only one eye. She had lost it in a fight, the farmer told me, which was not of her own making, as she was a truly good-natured animal. As I scanned the room it displayed an air of homely clutter. Belongings were scattered on every convenient surface, including the sturdy oak-legged table that dominated the centre of the room. Farming magazines and books filled shelves that had long since reached saturation point. The overflow littered chairs, window sills and the already groaning table. A cat lay oblivious to our presence in front of the stone fireplace on a pegged rug that was commonly found during the austere days of the second world war. Another one regarded me haughtily as if to question my intrusion. Alistair proved to be a friendly and talkative character with the amusing trait of mispronouncing words. He was quick to tell me of his proud position as secretary of the Black-faced Sheep Breeders' Association. He gave me a lengthy description of its aims and how it operated but he omitted to mention who had the black faces; the sheep or the breeders. My study of the room had not gone unnoticed for he was quick to point out that at his wife's urging he had begun to improve its ambience. His first task, he told me, had been to fix pelvises above the windows from which now hung neat and colourful curtains. Next would come the renovation of the fireplace, followed by the varnishing of the furniture; assuming that it ever became accessible.

A fragrant smell of cooking wafted through the open door and I sniffed expectantly, which made him smile. 'Och she's a grand cook and a good worker, but her one vice is adding yon spices to the food' he said. 'She's never been the same since she saw those cooking experts doing it on the television. I can't say that I hanker after the taste of origami and funnel, you can't beat pepper and salt'. Struggling to keep a straight face I told him that I was also a lover of plain food, whereupon he leapt from his chair, remarking that he had better warn Marjorie not to be heavy-handed with the compliments.

His worries were unfounded, for I enjoyed a sumptuous meal which engendered a lovely feeling of contentment. I was then treated to a couple of glasses of his finest whisky that induced an even greater soporific effect. It took an extreme effort at the end of my strenuous but satisfying day to keep my eyes open as Alistair launched into a series of anecdotes that I felt were intended as after-supper entertainment. I hung on with my eyelids drooping for as long as possible, but finally had to excuse myself and retire to bed, where I enjoyed the sleep of the innocent.

DAY EIGHT: BRIDGE OF BALGIE - KILLIN

The following morning I awoke to find the sun streaming through the bedroom window, indicating that the spell of good weather which I had been enjoying seemed likely to continue. What a contrast to my first Lakeland outings, I thought, when I had to battle through persistent rain and mist. It is remarkable what a little fine weather can do for the spirits.

Eager to be on my way, I was soon seated at the only clear corner of the expansive dining table; some of the belongings having been moved aside the previous evening to allow me to eat my supper, Alistair and Marjorie had obviously resorted to eating in the kitchen, as space was at a premium. Bess, the sheep dog, came fussing round me, then placed a friendly paw on my lap and sat motionless, fixing me with a gaze from her single eye. As I stroked the dog's head Marjorie bustled in carrying a dish of steaming porridge and signalled to Bess to return to her favourite chair. 'This will set you up for your walk; I trust that you like porridge', she said, placing the quivering mass in front of me. I accepted it politely, hoping that she had not flavoured it with salt in her customary zealous manner. Possessing a sweet tooth where porridge is concerned, I normally shrink from this Scottish tradition. Thankfully it was unseasoned and proved quite enjoyable despite its unyielding texture.

Marjorie reappeared with what I can only describe as a breakfast bursting with cholesterol. The enormous plate contained several slices of bacon, barely visible under a mound of fried eggs, tomatoes, mushrooms and baked beans. As I stared in awe at this gigantic offering she said with some concern, 'You must not go hungry if you are walking all the way to Killin today'. Not wishing to worry her further with the revelation that I intended a round trip through Glen Lochay on my way, I said nothing. Thinking that if I ate a meal of those proportions I would not be able to go anywhere, I manfully began to make in-roads into the daunting heap on my plate. I did my best, but was finally defeated by that edible mountain and looked guiltily at Marjorie when she returned to check on my progress. 'I hope you aren't sickening for something', she said. A worried frown appeared on her face as she studied me intently. Whilst trying to convince her that I felt fine, I had nagging expectations of the chest pains that had afflicted me when leaving Earby on the Pennine Way after a similarly hearty breakfast. On that particular occasion I was convinced that I was about to expire with a massive heart attack. Thankfully the pains were caused by mere indigestion, but I was not to know that at the time. I was grateful that Alistair was working around the farm, for if I had disclosed my fears to him he would have doubtlessly told me that they were purely a pigment of my imagination.

As I waved goodbye to the good-hearted couple a short time later,

I was patently aware of the friendliness and hospitality that was so often extended to me. I headed for the Bridge of Balgie, thinking how evocative its name sounded and found it straddling the River Lyon at the point where a narrow, winding road enters the glen from the south. There is a small settlement scattered around the bridge, the neighbouring Innerwick providing a more compact set of dwellings, adjacent to the only place of worship. Although houses are sparse there is a school, a post office and an unusual War Memorial. The latter comprises a conical pile of stones topped with two large, weathered stones. From a distance it resembles a tall cairn, but closer inspection reveals a neat inter-locking of stones of varying shapes and sizes. An arched recess is set into its front, which housed a wreath of poppies, their vivid redness contrasting with the grey background. A series of neat stone steps climb the grassy bank on which the monument proudly stands, poignantly demonstrating that lives have not been forfeited in vain.

I said goodbye to Glen Lyon and took the narrow road that leads from the valley towards the Killin - Aberfeldy road. My immediate destination was Lochan na Lairige that lies in the watershed between Glen Lyon and Loch Tay. From there it would be a short walk to the Ben Lawers Visitor Centre. I had enjoyed my journey through Glen Lyon, despite missing out the wild and remote upper reaches of what is reputedly Scotland's longest glen.

Footpaths along my route from the valley were conspicuous by their absence and I was obliged to follow the road which gradually became steeper and more winding. I forced myself doggedly around a series of sharp bends where I kept well into the grass verge to avoid the occasional oncoming cars making their wary and quite tortuous descent. I was careful not to stray too far from the road however, because the ground fell away sharply, with drops of several hundred feet in places. A chattering stream, whose name I found impossible to pronounce, rushed past me on its journey to the River Lyon, tumbling over series of jagged stones in its haste.

The imposing peaks of Ben Lawers (3984 feet) and its neighbour Beinn Ghlas (3657 feet) appeared above a backdrop of wild hills carpeted with tussocky grass. Snow clinging to the folds and crevasses of their summits glistened in the morning sunlight as though warning me to be wary of hidden dangers. Beinn Ghlas would have to be scaled on the way to the apex of Ben Lawers and the climb would be no pushover.

Reaching the brow of the hill, with the gradient easing, I was able to absorb the atmosphere of my lonely setting. Lochan na Lairige lay in a cradle of surrounding craggy and unremitting hills. Their grassy lower slopes gave way to harsh, rocky pinnacles, purple in the vivid sunlight. I could see the concrete dam that holds back the dark waters of the Lochan, which, a sign informed me, is now called Lawers Dam. A portion of its grey and silty banks was still exposed, despite the heavy rain and snow of the winter and early spring. As I strode past the dam I was straining for my first glimpse of the Ben Lawers Visitor Centre that I knew lay just below me.

It soon appeared; an oddly shaped modern building that could have been one of the wilder creations of Henry Moore. Many vehicles clustered within the car park, demonstrating the Centre's popularity, and a path snaked from it to the lower slopes of Beinn Ghlas. There were several walkers on the path that signifies the beginning of the well-trodden route to the summit of Ben Lawers. My anticipation was in full flow as I approached this oasis of activity set in an otherwise remote and austere landscape. I knew that Wainwright, who normally avoided such crowded places, extolled the Centre's merits; therefore I was keen to see it. I was not disappointed, for it is efficiently run by the National Trust for Scotland who also own and preserve the summits and southern slopes of the Ben Lawers range. A nature trail around the Edramucky Burn had been restored in 1990 by the construction of a perimeter fence that allowed the vegetation within to recover and flourish. The one and a half-mile-long nature trail consequently passes through an area rich in plants that had previously been destroyed by intensive grazing. The displays in the Visitor Centre outline the types of alpine flora found in the locality and also exhibit examples of birds, butterflies and the influence of man and sheep on the landscape. I chuckled to myself when I saw that the local black-faced sheep were the culprits who had stripped the land of many rare plants, because I immediately thought of Alistair.

As I left the Centre I braced myself for the ascent of Ben Lawers. I had learned that the National Trust are not actively encouraging the climb because of erosion of the well-trodden footpath. Their efforts to combat this are evident from the boards that cover some of the initial sections. Motor -cycles and mountain bikes are thankfully banned from the Nature Reserve. I passed two ruined buildings, as I crossed the Edramucky Burn, that were formerly small dwellings, or sheilings, used during the summer months by graziers who drove their cattle onto higher ground to feed. This practice disappeared when the Highland clearances brought sheep onto the hills.

From this point the track began to climb steadily through the Nature Reserve to the former site of a further group of sheilings. Here the ascent began in earnest as the gradient rapidly increased. I was glad of the opportunity to chat to fellow-walkers whom I overtook periodically. A lady from Stirling, I discovered, was walking stages of the West Highland Way at intervals and had so far reached the head of Loch Lomond. She was apprehensive about the forthcoming stretch over Rannoch Moor, believing it to be remote and hostile. I told her that I would be taking the same route across that moor on my journey and promised to write and tell her how I fared. As I chatted to a young couple who were resting by the side of the path they explained that they were taking a day's rest from organising their forthcoming wedding. It was not very restful for them, as they were finding the going very hard, but they assured me that they were feeling the benefit. Their spirits were improved by the magnificent view below us, in which the blue waters of Loch Tay featured prominently. The village of Killin nestled in a picturesque wooded setting at the west end of the loch, beneath an array of snow-capped mountains that surround Glen Dochart. The most striking of these was Ben More that I had an appointment to climb in a couple of days time.

Wishing the couple well, I tackled the rock-strewn slope that leads to the series of minor peaks guarding the summit of Beinn Ghlas. Their rounded crests resemble a many-humped camel. Numerous fragments of quartzite lying on the path reflected the sun, their vivid whiteness contrasting sharply with the brown earth and myriad small stones. I doggedly traversed the humps until the summit was revealed, its small cairn beckoning a short distance away. Latent energy coursed through me as I hurried towards my initial goal. I could see two ladies by the cairn taking photographs of each other. Amidst much preening and posing they proudly recorded their achievement. We struck up a conversation whilst we all surveyed the dramatic col that links Beinn Ghlas to the massive dome of Ben Lawers. The twin towers of the latter's cairn and trig point were just visible on its jagged summit and the ladies were apprehensively looking at the sharp gradient leading to it. In order to take our minds off this daunting prospect we discussed Scottish

Munros and the books that have been written about them. At the mention of Hamish Brown, I told them why his account of linking the Pennine Way and West Highland Way had been of great annoyance to me. The ladies were themselves admirers of Tom Weir and his writings, considering him to be to Scotland what Wainwright is to England. I tactfully suggested that Wainwright is also very popular in Scotland.

Leaving them to further contemplation of their objective I dropped down into the col whose sides fell away at an alarming angle, particularly the one facing north-west. This sheltered slope still retained a great expanse of snow, but I was careful not to make too close a scrutiny of it as the path went perilously close to its top. It was a strenuous climb up the steep dome of Ben Lawers that was pitted with rocky, snow-lined channels, but a real thrill to conquer that final hurdle and stand on top of Perthshire's highest mountain. I noted that the trig point was badly cracked and balancing precariously on its badly eroded base and seemed likely to topple at any moment. Its companion, the small cairn, was all that remained of a twenty-foot high one that was built in 1878 at the instigation of Malcolm Ferguson of Glasgow who had hoped to raise Ben Lawers into the elevated company of Scottish 4000 foot mountains. His aspirations were unfortunately defeated for the cairn could not withstand the destructiveness of the elements.

Settling by the trig point, I celebrated with a drink and contemplated the sandwiches that Marjorie had kindly provided. The huge breakfast had kept me going until now and I suddenly realised that I had escaped the dreaded chest pains; my morning having been totally absorbing. I casually chewed on a sandwich as I surveyed a memorable view. Range upon range of snow-capped mountains stretched before me, having the appearance of brown waves flecked with white spume. The pyramid shape of Schiehallion could be clearly seen and beyond it, the Cairngorms. Closer to hand, Lochan nan Cat lay below the fearsome north-west flank of the mountain, its inky waters funnelling into the Lawers Burn that flows into Loch Tay. Above this enthralling panorama fluffy-white clouds floated in an expanse of blue that merged into a grey haze as it met the horizon. An unforgettable scene.

A young walker startled me by leaping on to my lofty perch. He was gone in an instant however, only finding the time for a quick greeting before hurriedly descending the path along the east ridge that leads down to the hamlet of Lawers on the shore of Loch Tay. Surely fell-walking should not be that frenetic.

My rendezvous with Glen Lochay in mind, I retraced my steps down to the col, passing the Scottish ladies once more. They asked if I had seen any Purple Saxifrage on Ben Lawers, which made me realise that I had not noticed one example of Alpine flora. I told them that if I did not set myself such demanding daily schedules I might see more of nature's offerings. Bidding them good luck with their search I carefully descended to the Visitor Centre, doing as Wainwright always instructed; watching where I put my feet.

I soon picked up a track which contours the slopes of Meall nan Tarmachan and Meall Liath as it heads for Glen Lochay. The long expanse of Loch Tay spread itself below me as I left the crowds, to be accompanied only by the warm, afternoon sun. As I descended to the west end of the loch I could distinguish the ruins of Finlarig Castle that lies near the entrance to Glen Lochay. This building once controlled access to the glen and was the home of one of the most ruthless of the Campbell chiefs. He was Duncan of Cowal and in the castle grounds can be seen the remains of his beheading pit and hanging tree.

Entering the glen I opted to follow the narrow road through it; the valley sides were steep and there were no discernible paths. Glen Lyon had been a delight, but here was a glen made in heaven. Wainwright insisted that it should not be missed and he was right to do so. It was a place of peace and infinite variety, through which the lively River Lochay and the quiet, dead-end road threaded their winding courses. Mature woodland lined much of the valley floor and the sun permeated through the gleaming foliage of alder, rowan and beech. I frequently encountered deer, sheep and pheasant contentedly wandering across the road, which was remarkably devoid of traffic. Set amongst these tranquil surroundings was a scattering of farms and cottages. I was brought to an abrupt halt by the unusual sight of a farmer taking sheep and lambs from a lorry and lustily throwing them over a fence into one of the fields. The sheep only looked a trifle disconcerted by this treatment, but the lambs tottered around in a bewildered fashion.

A little further along the valley I saw rows of Tesco carrier bags hanging from the roadside fences. They were intriguing and I longed to know their purpose. The even more disconcerting sight of a small Power Station soon confronted me. Convincing myself that it was a necessary evil and that hydro-electric power was vital to Scotland's economy I hurried past wishing that it could have been built in a less conspicuous spot. The great pipes plunging down the nearby fellsides, accompanied by ominous power cables, did nothing to ease my concern.

This distraction was soon flushed from my mind as I continued to enjoy the sights and sounds of the enchanting glen. Surrounding woodland melted away, permitting extensive views along the widening valley where the twin farmsteads of High and Low Botaurnie snuggle beneath the slopes of Creag Uird. The most impressive view of all revealed itself as I passed the farm of Kenknock and stood on a bridge over a fast-flowing burn that tumbles from the wild hillside. Where the glen comes to an abrupt halt about three miles further on, a wall of magnificent snow-ravaged mountains thrust themselves skywards. Their intimidating peaks form the Forest of Mamlorn that blocks access from the valley. Amongst the indentations of this great rock barrier I could just make out the steep north face of Ben Chaluim and the twin spurs of Creag Mhor. Longing to see those compelling mountains at closer quarters, I reminded myself that I had already ventured further into the glen than was prudent and that I must head for Killin.

I reluctantly retraced my steps through the glen, but my spirits were buoyed by the delightful surroundings and the distant views of Beinn Ghlas and Ben Lawers. The evening was well-advanced when I emerged from Glen Lochay at the end of a day's journey that would provide many happy memories, to which, someone applied the following astute description. 'They last, they can't get lost, they don't wear out and they can't be given away'. Feeling tired, but elated, I entered the welcoming village of Killin.

DAY NINE: KILLIN - BALQUHIDDER

Killin offers splendid hospitality to the walker and traveller, being a convenient stopping place on the scenic journey from Callander to Pitlochry. The place is adept at catering for hosts of visitors, but remains friendly and unspoiled. Good accommodation is offered and the outlying meadows are dotted with a variety of caravans and tents. It sits astride the area's jewel in the crown, the Falls of Dochart, which plunge beneath the attractive bridge at the head of the village.

It was pleasant to stroll along its main street after a satisfying breakfast, knowing that the day ahead would involve a relaxed walk of only twelve miles. Postcards were purchased; it was time to let friends and relatives know how things were going. The village appeared massive compared to recent stopping points and the area I discovered is steeped in history. It lies in the province of Breadalbane, the ancient lands of the Campbells and MacNabs. The latter have inhabited Glen Dochart for over 800 years and Kinnell House, on the outskirts of the village, has been the seat of the MacNab chiefs for 400 years following the destruction of Eilean Nan Castle which stood near the site of the present Killin Hotel. Inchbuie Island, set in the River Dochart, is the ancient burial ground of the clan. In the Breadalbane Folklore Centre by the Falls of Dochart are the healing stones associated with St.Fillan, the patron Saint of Breadalbane, whose Episcopal Church still stands near the present Parish Church. In former times this church was probably the centre of religious worship in that part of Scotland. I was to learn more of St. Fillan when I travelled through lovely Strath Fillan, which links Crianlarich with Tyndrum.

Killin is in the spotlight once more for an entirely different reason - it is the northern extremity of the new long-distance cycle route linking the centre of Glasgow with Loch Lomond, the Trossachs and Breadalbane. So, come on you walkers and cyclists, here is a golden opportunity to enjoy an attractive journey from Scotland's industrial heartland to the cradle of its beautiful Highlands. The attractive route follows forest trails, quiet rural side roads, disused railway trackbeds and canal towpaths.

Another local attraction is Loch Tay, which I had seen from my crows-nest viewpoint on top of Ben Lawers. It is one of the finest salmon and trout lochs in Scotland and is also the scene of a recent project to recreate a sunken culture that dates back 5000 years. A platform of trimmed alder trunks has been constructed in its waters to revive the habitat of a former race of loch dwellers. Artificial islands known as 'crannogs', basically massive huts perched on top of wooden piles, were built from 3000 BC up to the seventeenth century and this modern version has taken a year to construct using traditional methods. An exhibition area is planned for this ancient form of architecture, next door to the modern water sports centre at the east end of the loch.

My tour of the village reached its climax as I stood on Dochart Bridge overlooking the scenic falls. The waters do not plunge from a great height, but the effect is equally stunning. A series of mini-cascades transform the wide river into a writhing stretch of water that dances around wooded islands fringed with shattered boulders. A magnificent renovated water wheel compliments the nearby Visitor Centre, formerly the historic St.Fillan's mill, that now houses a Tourist Information Centre in addition to the Breadalbane Folklore Centre.

The view in the opposite direction is determined not to be outshone by the majesty of the falls. Through an archway of finely-sculptured trees the striking dome of Meall nan Tarmachan can be seen, keeping a benevolent watch over the village.

The main part of my day's route lay along Glen Ogle, a deep corridor linking Glen Dochart with Lochearnhead, along which conveniently runs the remains of a dismantled railway. This would hopefully provide pleasant walking and by further good fortune a former spur of the disused line would lead me out of Killin and into Glen Dochart to join the main line that swings out of Glen Ogle, about three miles away, heading for Crianlarich.

I soon picked up the abandoned railway, now a broad track scything through the forest that covers an extensive area to the south of Killin. It felt good to stride along the flat bed which provided an excellent footway, but it was hard to ignore the devastation wreaked upon an impressive and scenic railway. There is now no alternative to the long and demanding climb by road through Glen Ogle. In the days of steam a relaxing and rewarding passage was offered by train, allowing you to sit in comfort and take in the full splendour of your surroundings. I mourned the demise of this section of the old Glasgow to Oban line which was brought about by a landslide in the nineteen-sixties.

As I cleaved through enveloping mist I could see from my map that a short cut into Glen Ogle was possible by means of a series of forestry tracks. I decided to forego such notoriously fickle thoroughfares, which can either disappear altogether or be diverted due to the changing nature of the forest. A hard lesson had been learned when I got lost whilst trying to make my way out of Redesdale Forest above Byrness on the Pennine Way along a maze of forest tracks. My best companion would be the railway, despite its more circuitous route.

Several miles of forest walking can become monotonous and dulling to the senses. This proved to be the case as I progressed at a good rate farther into the forest, but there were compensations. I caught sight of numerous birds; the entire woodland seemed alive with their trilling. As I crossed a stream a timid dipper hurriedly whisked away, his short 'sip, sip' cries lingering sweetly on the morning air. The occasional blackbird swooped nearby, obviously sizing up this intruder. My tread was certainly purposeful as I burnt up the miles, keeping a watchful eye, but allowing my mind to wander over the eventful happenings of my walk so far. The cottage in Castleton Terrace, Braemar entered my mind's eye as I visualised Robert Louis Stevenson frantically scribbling his chapters of *Treasure Island*. Perhaps he was on a tight deadline with his publisher or was in great need of money. In my view he could have been the patron saint of long-distance walkers, for his famous quotation from *El Dorado* was prophetic - 'To tread hopefully is a better thing than to arrive, and the true success is to labour'. How right he is. When a long walk is finished a sense of anti-climax sets in, but during it one is facing daily challenges that, once overcome, produce a profound sense of achievement. I am sometimes asked why I walk long distances and the honest answer must be - to build a store of memories. A long walk is not only of the moment, it can be savoured for many years afterwards.

The loud, clattering cry of a pheasant jerked me from my thoughts as I approached the junction of the spur with the main line. It was time to change direction and leave Glen Dochart, but not for the last time. The following day I planned to return to a spot further along the glen and make my way to Ben More, a mountain I was determined to climb. The reason for my detour was to visit Balquhidder, the burial place of Rob Roy McGregor. This would entail a journey through Glen Ogle and a return to Glen Dochart along Kirkton Glen.

Two miles farther on I emerged from the forest and entered Glen Ogle. The sky was overcast with unfriendly clouds scudding overhead, borne by a fresh breeze. I could not complain about the weather for apart from that dreadful day in Glen Tilt it had behaved itself remarkably well. The rippling waters of a small lochan then accompanied me for a short distance, its slate-grey surface chilling and uninviting. I was now close to the busy A85 road that brings noise and fumes to an otherwise unspoiled Glen Ogle. A sizeable number of heavy lorries carrying cargos as diverse as 'Irn Bru' and ladies' tights were straining every sinew to reach their various destinations.

My grassy carpet, tiring of the valley-bottom, began a gradual but determined ascent, permitting more extensive views. It scours the valley wall as it passes over ravines and embankments, before starting the long descent to Lochearnhead. A fine retrospective view is offered of the four distinctive peaks of the Tarmachan Hills beyond Killin, their knobbly outlines resembling a giant crummack. These mountains are amongst the most popular in the Southern Highlands, the grandest of all being Meall nan Tarmachan that I had admired earlier from Dochart Bridge. Across the valley lay a region of undulating heather-clad hills and high moorland that stretches east to the Crieff, Aberfeldy road.

Although long-disused the bed of the railway is remarkably intact. The embankments, a little overgrown in places, are in good shape and the attractive stone viaducts provide a lasting tribute to the skill and tenacity of their builders. Conditions were harsh for the nineteenth-century railway constructors who dubbed this glen 'The Khyber Pass of Scotland'. With rail privatisation underway, here is a golden opportunity for an entrepreneur to resurrect the grandeur of this once popular line and to breath new life into it.

Those sentiments were shared by a couple of walkers whom I conveniently passed at that point. They could remember this particular section of line being in regular use, frequently travelling by steam train to Killin. Unfortunately none of us had the financial clout to realise our ambition and get it re-opened. We agreed that the line was a sad loss. We could always beg of course. Please send all donations to me, care of the Glen Ogle Railway Preservation Society!

The couple knew the area very well, intimating that a trip through Kirkton Glen would not be disappointing, but climbing Ben More would be tough. They were heading for Glen Dochart before returning to Balquhidder, where they had left their car. As they said farewell they advised me to keep a sharp lookout for the distinctive Ben Vorlich as I approached Lochearnhead.

My warped sense of humour makes me smile inwardly whenever I see the name 'Loch Earn'. It conjures up a picture of that great comedy duo Morecambe and Wise strutting their stuff, with 'Little Ern', the one with the short, fat, hairy legs, having his supposed wig adjusted by his partner Eric. So I smiled as I gazed over Lochearnhead, watching the extensive waters of the loch gradually merge into the distant dull haze. Ben Vorlich was visible, protruding over the closer Ben Our. I longed for a helicopter at that moment to carry me above its ramparts, for the plan view of that popular mountain is unusually X-shaped, due to a combination of ridges which branch from each other on its upper reaches. However, I could discern its impressive slopes gliding down to the shore of Loch Earn and the hamlet of Ardvorlich.

As it was a mere five miles to my destination at Balquhidder I ate a leisurely lunch at my commendable viewpoint, sharing my sandwiches with a pair of thrushes that hopped mischievously nearby. A study of my map revealed that Lochearnhead stands at a strategic junction of roads. The A85, heading west along the north side of Loch Earn, meets the A84 coming north from Callander. Three miles south of this junction lies the entrance to Balquhidder Glen where a narrow road leaves the A84 heading for Loch Voil.

My dependable track proceeded to snake round the base of Meall Reamhar and across the lively Kendrum Burn before aiming for the A84. This section of the disused line gambols in and out of woods and views were limited. A short distance beyond Kendrum Burn I exchanged my faithful companion, the rail bed, for a convenient footpath through pleasant pastureland, but paid for my desertion by wallowing in patches of glutinous mud. Eventually I came face to face with the busy A84 with no alternative but to follow it to the Kingshouse Hotel. Scurrying traffic roared past me and, buffeted by its slipstreams, I tottered along the roadside verge to an underpass near the hotel. Relieved of struggling alongside that frantic thoroughfare I walked under it engulfed by disconcerting swishing sounds, caused by the rushing vehicles overhead. As they subsided, I had a relatively quiet stroll along the minor road to Balquhidder to look forward to.

My approach to Loch Voil and Balquhidder unfortunately proved disappointing. I had to pass through the hamlet of Auchtubh which appeared to consist of untidy roadside farms and small-holdings each sporting a pack of dogs, their baying and growling becoming a tiresome cacophony. Casting frequent backward glances, I checked that none of these disconcerting animals had escaped their confines. I normally like dogs, but not aggressive ones that delight in attacking you from behind.

As I got out of earshot the view ahead was a marvellous consolation, steep slopes raking down to almost touch Loch Voil cradled before me in the fertile valley. The Braes of Balquhidder beckoned, richly festooned with forests of pine, larch and spruce. Such was my introduction to the great Scottish legend of Rob Roy, for he frequented those hills whilst on the run from the Hanoverian troops. I would be following a 'Rob Roy Trail', albeit in reverse, over the next few days. Balquhidder Glen was the area where he also spent the last years of his life, as he endeavoured to re-establish himself amongst his own folk. I hoped to see his grave in Balquhidder churchyard and to pass a series of dwellings with which he was associated, including his birthplace, on my journey to Loch Katrine and Inversnaid.

Rob Roy remains an enigma, for to some he is a scoundrel and to others a champion. Sir Walter Scott symbolises him in his novel as a man fighting for the lost cause of the Highland warrior against the modernising Lowland ethos; courage and honour pitted against commerce and industry. He was born in 1671 during the decline of the clan system which finally collapsed some years after his death and he portrayed a defiance of powerful, rich landowners and the Lowland forces of law and order. His father served under King Charles II, the incumbent Stuart King when Rob was born, and the boy with a flaming mop of red hair developed Jacobite sympathies from an early age. He had exceptionally long arms and became highly-skilled with the broadsword, which later added to his colourful reputation. Rob was in the cattle business; the mainstay of the area's economy. All rents were paid in beasts and they were also a measure of a clan chief's wealth. He became involved in cattle-droving, for many were sold in the Lowlands, and in addition to legitimate dealing and protection, he tried his hand at reiving. Rob has been dubbed a cattle rustler, but the Highland code of the time regarded cattle as communal property; they were regularly stolen and later recovered.

His troubles really began when his near neighbour, the Duke of Montrose, who dominated the lands around the south end of Loch Lomond and was involved in business dealings with Rob, gave him the princely sum of £1,000 to buy cattle for fattening in the Lowlands. Rob's chief drover, MacDonald, unfortunately disappeared with money. Rob had set his house as security and this was seized by Montrose. His family were evicted, all his stock and belongings were taken and he was declared an outlaw. Revenge was extracted on Montrose by stealing cattle and grain from the steadings of his family and tenants. MacDonald was never heard of again and Rob was ruined, but his eviction also had political overtones. Montrose had earlier asked Rob to swear that his rival, the Duke of Argyll, who had returned to politics after fighting abroad, was in collusion with the Jacobites. Refusing to lie, Rob had further infuriated Montrose who had already heard rumours that Rob had taken the £1,000 to support the arming of rebel Jacobites.

The rest, as they say, is history, for tales of Rob Roy and his exploits abound. All came right in the end, for he died peacefully at Balquhidder in 1734. Despite the efforts of Montrose, and later, government troops, he remained free and was eventually granted a King's pardon. During his outlaw days, legend was fuelled by his being captured three times and audaciously escaping on each occasion. Rob had supported the Earl of Mar in the raising of his standard in 1715, but it is not clear if he took part in the grand 'shindig' at the Punchbowl in Glen Quoich.

This potted version of Rob Roy's life is thrust before you because he holds a great fascination, not only for me but for other long distance walkers. My adversary, Hamish Brown, took an old copy of Scott's *Rob Roy* on his marathon journey from John O'Groats to Lands End, throwing away each page when read, presumably to lighten his load!

As I entered the enticing village of Balquhidder I took a probing look along Loch Voil, searching for the semi-circle of Crianlarich hills that, according to Wainwright, dominate the head of the glen. Although unsuccessful, an adequate compensation was the lure of my surroundings, which include the imposing Stronvar House, the local Laird's former mansion overlooking the loch. This now houses a Bygones Museum which displays a comprehensive collection of everyday items from yester-year.

I climbed the short gradient towards the focal point of the village where, in splendid array, stand the old and new churches with the rugged Creag Breac rising behind them like an avenging angel. The shell of the old church stands proudly beside its attractive and more modern counterpart amidst a cocoon of gravestones set in a bed of glorious green. This churchyard is pleasantly uncluttered, having ample space between a variety of graves which are dominated by the upright finger of a memorial cross. Tucked behind this and lying strategically outside the entrance to the old church is the all-important MacGregor family grave. A narrow path led me to the spot that I had been at pains to see. Expectantly I looked down on three stone slabs lying side by side, their carvings partly obliterated by weather and time. They are surrounded by a simple iron rail, its attached inscriptions denoting that Rob, his wife, Mary, and two sons are buried there. A simple headstone bears the motto 'MacGregor - Despite Them'. Surprised by the burial place's simplicity, I was nevertheless gratified to visit this historic place which I found fascinating. Queen Victoria, who keeps crossing my path, also visited the site a few years after the building of the newer church. She was doubtless interested in one of the English crown's former adversaries. I am sure that she found the visit pleasing and could appreciate why Rob wished to spend his latter years in the area. Balquhidder was a delight.

As I left the churchyard a signpost attracted my attention, indicating the track to Glen Dochart that runs through Kirkton Glen. I had conveniently found my route from the village, no search now being required on the following morning. The important, immediate task was to find my night's accommodation, for which I thankfully had plenty of time available. This was accomplished without difficulty and another satisfying day drew to a close as I enjoyed the customary hospitality of a neighbouring farm.

DAY TEN: BALQUHIDDER - PORTNELLAN.

The climb through Kirkton Glen, although steep in its final stages, proved a fitting follow-up to Balquhidder. To my pleasure and wonderment the weather that morning maintained its benevolence. Friends had solicitously warned about the vagaries of the Scottish climate, but so far it had earned high praise. Such good fortune supported my belief that it is better to be born lucky than rich.

A steady walk through Forestry Commission territory was the primary task, along a wide, and thankfully straightforward, track. The only hazard was posed by the predatory beak of a giant logging machine which man-handled the felled trunks with consummate ease, effortlessly transferring them from trackside stacks to a waiting lorry. This monster swung its load of embryonic matchsticks with such enthusiasm that I gave it a wide berth. The rasping symphony of eager chain saws provided accompaniment as assassinated trees fell to earth with remorseless rapidity. I was forced, however, to reverse a familiar proverb: 'That which ye reap also shall ye sow', for to the Commission's credit they were also engaged on a programme of replanting. Infantile, spindly stems sprouted amidst acres of decimated vegetation, bringing the promise of new life to those ravaged, barren tracts.

My steps shortened and my body temperature soared as the track, refusing to escape from the forest, forced me to transfer to a steep and rugged path that resolutely climbed through open country until the gnarled hulk of Leum an Eireannaich towered above me. The impressive crag dominates the head of the pass for which I was aiming, its dramatic overhanging nose a veritable magnet for aspiring climbers. Its challenging faces and crevices provide a fruitful playground for the Scottish Mountaineering Club. Each testing climb has its own evocative name, such as 'Garden Wall', 'Old Man's Groove' and 'Stella Major'. I was perfectly content to admire them from below, thank you. A massive boulder crouched in the shadow of the crag reminding me of the Cow and Calf rocks on the edge of Ilkley Moor near my home. According to legend the Giant Rombald, who inhabited that moor, dislodged the Calf boulder from the larger Cow rock, catching it with his heel whilst fleeing to escape his wife's wrath. How this particular boulder came to lie beneath Leum an Eireannaich is open to conjecture, but it did provide another illustration of the Rob Roy legend, for it is known as his 'Putting Stone'.

Several energetic minutes brought me to the delightful setting of Lochan an Eireannaich nestling in the watershed between Balquhidder Glen and Glen Dochart. Taking a breather, for I had made good time during my ascent, I sat by the gently-rippling water and enjoyed a leisurely cuppa. A large bird wheeled above me, obviously vetting this intrusive stranger who had invaded its privacy. Even I, with my limited knowledge, knew that it was too large for a kestrel or ptarmigan. Could it be a majestic golden eagle I wondered? From its very dark colouring I settled for the more mundane raven that is slightly smaller than the eagle. Probably nesting on the craggy buttress above me, it would be protecting its domain. The air smelt deliciously pure and the sun gently warmed my back, despite the freshness of the wind that tugged at my hair. My thoughts drifted to another walker who had passed that spot on his lone journey from Lands End to John O'Groats. He is the celebrated author, John Hillaby, a hero of mine since reading his evocative *Journey Through Britain*, an account of that epic walk, published in 1968. This acclaimed naturalist has explored much of the world alone and on foot. He is also the instigator of my earlier exploration of the Scottish Borders.

It was reassuring to read that a walker of his vast experience had trouble navigating through Kirkton Glen. He was foiled by a fickle forestry track that doubled back on itself and left him to blunder helplessly through thick mist. Searching vainly for a path he somehow ended up on Leum an Eireannaich. Wary of falling from the daunting crag he waited until the mist lifted, when he was able to gaze down on my current resting place. He described this tiny lochan as 'steaming like a cup of tea'.

Passing earlier through Strathyre, a little to the south of Balquhidder, John Hillaby had deduced that people in that area of Breadalbane took in great gulps of mountain air which had a tonic effect on their vocal chords. This he believed, induced them to burst into song at any opportunity. 'They were at it in the forester's lodge when I passed by; the house shook. There was also guitar-playing and singing in the pub where I ordered a meal. This was a spontaneous *ceilidh*'. I could vouch for the taste of the local air, but the only singing had been my own, sparingly dispensed and only whilst unobserved.

Leaving the lochan to its peace and solitude, I began a descent which would return me to Glen Dochart. At this stage I was truly walking in John Hillaby's footsteps, for he had made a wary descent from the crag to Lochan an Eireannaich and taken the path that I was now following. I had been amused to read his account of joining the dismantled Oban railway that subsequently led him to a tiny abandoned station at Luib on its way through Glen Dochart. He said of the station - 'you have the impression that the staff fled before the last train to Crianlarich pulled out. Clearly to be seen through the cracked windows of a Lilliputian left-luggage office are dusty trunks, labelled suitcases, a bundle of fishing rods and a bicycle with flat tyres. What on earth happened that night when Station Master Campbell went home, never to return?' I had made a mental note whilst reading this passage to seek out the station, if in fact it still existed, to check if those items still remained in the left luggage office. His tale intrigued me, reminding me of the discovery of the *Marie Celeste*.

I descended at a fairly rapid rate along the path that skirts the base of Meall an Fhiodhain and leads down the valley carved out by the Ledcharrie Burn which flows into the River Dochart. Conditions underfoot were quite arduous and the narrow path indistinct at times, but this was a minor annoyance, for I was treated to extensive views of Glen Dochart and the mountainous hub of Breadalbane. The glen itself straddles this ancient province which covers an area of approximately 1000 square miles and I was entering Campbell country, once controlled by the infamous Campbells of Glenorchy.

A group of shielings was clearly shown on my map around the half way point of the descent. Unfortunately there was no evidence of their remains but I fortuitously met a man in the vicinity, rather strangely carrying two metal divining rods. He was evidently on a similar mission because those rods, he told me, were the only means of discerning the whereabouts of the shielings that were no longer visible. Presuming that the rods would identify the water-sources of the former dwellings, I watched him for a while, but he had no success.

Leaving him to his unusual task I hurried into the heart of Glen Dochart for a reunion with the defunct railway. Progress was again speedier on this green highway and a short distance along the track I found what I was seeking, the eagerly awaited Luib. The diminutive station had undergone a transformation, for it now forms the centre-piece of a caravan park. Many of its original features are still discernible but there was no sign of the ghostly left-luggage office. The former stationmaster's house now contains the site shop and the adjacent railway workers' cottages are still occupied. The nearby platforms, the space between them filled in, are now merely grassy humps, but a water tank that replenished thirsty steam engines still squats nearby, aloof on its lofty metal perch. Despite being unable to solve the mystery of what happened when the last train pulled out, I was heartened to see that the station had not been completely abandoned. Public access was not permitted through the lines of shiny caravans, so I had to abandon the old railway at the site entrance and take the tarmac drive that leads to the A85 road.

Half a mile of road walking brought me to the point where the disused railway formerly crossed the A85. I picked up its line once more as it beavered through fields on the north side of the road. My love affair with this relic from the past began to wane, for the pleasant green track deteriorated into a quagmire. This was probably caused by the herd of Highland cattle that barred my way, eyeing me suspiciously. As I tentatively edged around them they thankfully proved to be docile beasts. To add insult to injury it was not long before I found my progress halted. After further wallowing I came to a bridge that was annoyingly fenced off. Beyond the fence the track had become so overgrown with trees that further progress was impossible anyway. I was forced to return to the road, where at last I had a stroke of luck, which slotted another piece of the Rob Roy jigsaw into place. I knew that thereabouts stands the remains of a cottage that Rob was given by the sympathetic Campbells after his family's eviction from their Inversnaid home by Montrose. The ruin apparently lies, not far from the road, on the slopes that border the foothills of Ben More. Re-crossing the road and climbing the steep, tussocky slope on its south side I hit the bullseye at my first attempt. On a ledge, out of sight of the road, I found the sad remnant of the building that had been burned by Government troops as they stepped up their hunt for Rob. Only one wall remains, upon which a chimney still perches. Spindly-branched bushes sprout from the top of the moss-covered wall, almost framing the remarkably preserved chimney. A gaping hole in the base of the wall signified where the fireplace formerly stood. Above the crumbling remains of the cottage dangle menacing power cables, clearly at odds with this historic setting.

I returned to the road to complete the last few miles of my journey to Portnellan, that shelters at the foot of Ben More, amidst scenery of the highest order. The glen was flecked with woods, their subtle tints complementing russet-coated fellsides punctuated with rocky outcrops. Brightly-painted farmhouses, oases of candescent white, shimmered in the sun's charitable glow. The meandering river eased along the valley floor, reluctant to stray from its ever-present companion, the A85 road. As a light-hearted distraction I carried out a census of the traffic busily threading its way through the glen, and nicknamed it 'Shearing's Corridor'. These popular touring coaches were ever-present. Glen Dochart was definitely a 'must' on their itinerary, its wide-eyed participants being whisked along on their pilgrimage to Crianlarich, Fort William and beyond. I could vividly picture the reclining coach drivers, feet resting on the steering wheel as they coasted on automatic pilot; the weekly ritual so familiar. My heart went out to the forlorn couriers struggling to introduce a new descriptive slant to scenery they knew like the back of their hand. Perhaps some gave up the unequal struggle and recited their commentary parrot fashion - 'Crianlarich .... Strath Fillan .... Tyndrum .... and so ad infinitum'.

I passed two lochs, each one a gem. Although very small by Scottish standards, their settings were unsurpassed, and they were no doubt brimming with wild brown trout and salmon that frequent the River Dochart which feeds them. Loch Iubhair and Loch Dochart, as they are known, were to miraculously diminish to the size of postage stamps when viewed from Ben More's summit.

The snow-capped dome of this mountain dominates the south side of the valley. At 3843 feet it is the highest of the group of Munros known as the Crianlarich Hills. As I approached, its awesome presence pervaded the whole area and I could see its north-west slope careering upwards at an alarming angle, seemingly only fit for nimble sheep. Wainwright describes it as 'a gradient of forty degrees without respite'. He continues 'I have a soft spot for Ben More, being another of the few Scottish mountains with a name I can pronounce with confidence, but affection does not extend to its ascent and descent. The climb directly from the road is an unremitting treadmill of 3,300 feet with toes pointing upwards every step of the way'. Given such a challenging write-up, I just had to have a tilt at it and eschew the easier and more popular western approach which scales the col between Ben More and Stob Binnein (3,827 feet). However, I would gain a night's respite before tackling the daunting slope that disappeared skywards.

A short walk brought me to the comfortable hotel at Portnellan. Here, in the shadow of my next morning's objective, I spent a relaxing evening in the company of a fellow-walker, Duncan, who hailed from Glasgow. He loved the Breadalbane area, visiting as often as his city job allowed. Ben More was an old friend to him and he confirmed that my ascent would be tough. He had climbed it from many angles and declared that he would never tire of doing so. When I mentioned my visit to Balquhidder and Rob Roy's grave he enquired if I had seen the nearby ruin of Rob's former dwelling. I told him that I had, also recounting my experiences thereabouts with the reluctant railway.

The evening sped away and sleep came easily in my comfortable surroundings, which was useful, for a hard day awaited me. In fact, so quickly did I lapse into slumber, there was no time for my usual recap of the day's events.

DAY ELEVEN: PORTNELLAN - INVERSNAID

How clean and fresh the Breadalbane air tasted as I left the hotel; as John Hillaby said, it made you want to burst into song. Conserving my strength, I declined, for there was a testing twenty-five mile walk ahead, including the small matter of conquering Ben More. My step was decidedly springy that morning for I was eagerly anticipating a companion joining me at Inversnaid. My walking-friend, Maurice, would hopefully be waiting at the Inversnaid Hotel with open arms and a supply of Kendal Mint Cake and sticking plasters - essential for our survival. Readers of *Plowright Follows Wainwright* will recall our meeting in thick mist above Patterdale on Wainwright's Coast to Coast Walk. He planned to accompany me to Shiel Bridge near the Isle of Skye - to keep me out of mischief, he said. Maurice is great company, being more gregarious than myself, and you should hear him sing! Arrangements had been confirmed the previous evening by telephone, including his assurance that bunting would be on display to celebrate my arrival at Inversnaid. Unfortunately, he said, his attempt at organising a pipe band had failed!

Steeling myself, I gazed at the impending slope of Ben More, its higher reaches appearing to touch the startlingly blue heavens. It was once again an ideal morning weatherwise, but the forecasters predicted a severe deterioration later in the day. Purposefully I attacked the severe gradient, keen to conquer the mountain tops early on, thereby allowing me to attain the more sheltered glens before poorer weather beset me. Despite its steepness the slope was comfortingly smooth and grassy. The Crianlarich Hills had weathered evenly, apart from small rocky outcrops, rendering them ideal for hill-walking. Pity about the gradient - puff ...pant ...puff ...pant; gravity inflicted an onerous toll, torturing limb and sinew as I clawed my way up. It was reminiscent of climbing Kirk Fell from Wasdale Head - 'the straightest and therefore the most direct ascent in Lakeland', according to Wainwright - except that I had an extra 1200 feet to contend with. Ben More is after all only exceeded in height by Ben Lawers in the Southern Highlands. Tussocky grass is very useful in such dire situations, providing something to hang on to and haul yourself up with. Occasional relief came through stopping to admire the view, which expanded with every step. A castle could be discerned squatting on the island in tiny Loch Dochart, one of many such strategically-sited Scottish fortresses, such as those in Loch Awe and Loch Alsh. The full extent of Glen Dochart was visible, its tarmac artery stretching to Crianlarich which lies a mere three miles away. Here it is joined by Strath Fillan, through which courses the thin web of the West Highland Railway as it heads for Bridge of Orchy and the awesome Rannoch Moor.

During one of my pauses for breath I noticed two young men below me who were striking a remarkable pace. No doubt we would meet soon as I could not match their furious rate of ascent. However, after a short time I observed that they had stopped, obviously not able to maintain their impetus. Perhaps I was not such a slouch after all; despite being a plodder I could maintain a fairly consistent pace. The pair below me probably belonged to the stop-and-start school of hill-climbing. Its devotees maintain a gruelling pace, interspersed with frequent stops, which unfortunately negates their intention of a fast overall climb. If they did catch up with me I hoped for a more cheerful greeting than that received from a couple I had met near Benmore Farm who barely spoke. Such an attitude was puzzling, a polite 'good morning' costs nothing.

As I steadily approached the mountain's higher reaches, I had to avoid the abundant rivulets streaming from the rocky summit, as the remaining late-spring snow melted. Thankfully I was unobserved, for I was lurching through the tussocky grass to avoid filling my boots with water. After my game of hop-scotch I found myself clambering through rocky gritstone pinnacles interlaced with veins of basalt. This final exertion sapped any remaining strength and my legs became lead weights. I was saved by a stony, but friendly, path that miraculously appeared. This led me to my goal, but when I finally stood on the summit my elation was blown away by a fierce and biting wind which made me hurriedly seek respite amongst the surrounding rocks. Here I treated myself to a well-earned coffee break, my woollen hat wedged firmly over my protesting ears. The sound of boots scuffling on the weathered rocks heralded the appearance of two male students who, I discovered, lived in Manchester. Their bronzed features suggested much open air activity and they seemed barely out of breath. One was tall and lanky, sporting a long mane of black hair which lashed around his head as though demented. His companion was the complete opposite, short and stocky with close-cropped auburn hair. They were both wearing shorts, but the penetrating cold made them dive into their rucksacks for additional clothing. Goose-pimpled legs were quickly encased in overtrousers; hats and gloves soon followed.

Chattering freely we sipped our reviving drinks whilst gazing over Breadalbane that sprawled beneath us, a splendid, giant tapestry. The Black Mount Hills of Rannoch Moor were now visible to the north-west, throwing down the gauntlet to all who dared to venture amongst them. Beyond them shimmered the mountains guarding Glencoe, the scene of the infamous massacre. Following my gaze, my young companions, Jim and Arnold, enquired if I was familiar with Rannoch Moor, to which I replied that I wasn't, but hoped to be very soon. They had apparently climbed in the Black Mount Hills on one of their Munro-bagging expeditions. This explained their fit and healthy appearance, for I learned that they had already climbed over 100 of the 277 Munros - Scottish peaks over 3000 feet, named after Sir Hugh Munro, the first man to compile an official list of them. They were out to capture a further six that day, the Crianlarich Hills providing rich pickings for them. Apparently there are eleven in the group, counting the east and west tops of Beinn à Chroin, within an area of twenty-five square miles.

When I told them I was heading south from that point, Arnold said that I could join them for a dramatic ridge walk that links that summit with those of Stob Binnein and Stob Coire an Lochain, both Munros. Before leaving I braved the wind and did a quick spin on one of the rocks, getting a superb all-round view of row upon row of snow-tinged peaks. The most prominent was Ben Lawers, now an old friend, dominating the prospect to the north-east. I was allowed no time to savour climbing that mountain a mere three days previously, for Jim and Arnold were already jigging a downward course through craggy rocks. Snatching my rucksack I leapt in pursuit, eager not to lose them.

As we descended into the col between Ben More and Stob Binnein we passed several walkers struggling upwards, who had evidently ascended by the main route from Benmore Glen. Our view of the ridge and the apex of Stob Binnein was dramatic. The ground fell away precariously on either side of our earthen tightrope suspended between the two mountain tops. Snow could be seen clinging to the north-eastern faces of the summits, contorted into astonishing patterns. The eastern face of the col was still plastered with a rippled snow coating that curled over at the top as though intending to slip away and then changing its mind.

From the depths of the col loomed a steep and intimidating climb to the top of Stob Binnein that looked far harder than it had appeared from Ben More's summit. Although tough, it proved mercifully short and we were soon standing on our second snow-kissed summit. A simple ridge walk took us to our next objective, Stob Coire an Lochain (3497 feet), and it was here I had to say goodbye to Jim and Arnold. They were eager to attack their fourth Munro, Meall na Dige, clearly visible a mile to the east. This did not appear too onerous a task for it stood 350 feet below us, linked by a convenient grassy ridge.

Hand-shakes and good wishes marked our parting. I had no doubt that they would bag their remaining three Munros that day as I started my descent into Inverlochlarig Glen, where I intended to join the track to Inverlochlarig that stands two miles to the west of Loch Doine.

I watched them rapidly descending the ridge towards their next objective, envious of their youthful energy, before carefully picking my way from the summit. It was no easy task as I studiously avoided the rocky crags of nearby Creagan Liatha that threatened to trap the unwary. My knees protested as I negotiated alarmingly steep fellsides, compelled to apply the brakes to prevent me from coming to grief. Eventually I staggered into the valley-bottom with my limbs thankfully intact and found the track which I was seeking.

The animated Inverlochlarig Burn accompanied me through the glen and ripples on its surface indicated the expected deterioration in the weather. A thick blanket of cloud suddenly blotted out the sun catching me unawares. The careful placement of my feet had so engrossed me during my precarious descent that I had been oblivious to all else. As the rain intensified I was thankful that I had escaped from the mountain-tops. Conditions would be most unpleasant up there, particularly as mist was now closing in and visibility was reduced to a mere few yards.

The presence of unseen mountains around you is paradoxically comforting yet disturbing. You know that they afford shelter, but the mist produces the effect of complete detachment from everything around you. It is akin to losing your sight and having to rely on other senses to guide you. Advancing through the clammy curtain my thoughts centred on a television programme which had featured an enthusiastic, but sightless walker. Blinded in the war, he described the sensations that walking had subsequently aroused in him. He maintained that he could manage without his sight, but not without his mountains and he continually ventured on to them with a companion. His senses were aroused exactly as they had been when he could see, creating a deep spiritual contentment. In the peace of the open countryside his acute hearing picked up a multitude of tiny sounds that he described as an active silence. Warming to this brave man's fortitude, I had felt humble to be able to enjoy the sights around me whilst he derived great pleasure from his darkened world. A little mist should not frustrate me, I thought, when he was thankful for so much less. Thus my step was lightened and I strode purposefully through the heavy pall until a gradual descent began to extricate me from it. Below me I could discern the remote collection of farms that comprise Inverlochlarig.

I had completed another 'U' turn, for the settlement lies near the west end of the Balquhidder Glen. It would have been simpler to walk west from Balquhidder along the shores of Loch Voil and Loch Doine to reach Inverlochlarig, but I was in no hurry and in so doing I would have missed Kirkton Glen, Luib and Ben More. My circuitous route had also uncovered another historic link with Rob Roy - the ruined dwelling in Glen Dochart. Rob also had connections with Inverlochlarig, where he lived for a period. Although nothing remains of his dwelling, I was keen to see the setting of the farmhouse that was once his refuge.

I surveyed this hideaway that lies at the end of the bucking-bronco of a road that runs from Balquhidder. The farmhouses and their numerous functional outbuildings sheltered beneath a semi-circle of imposing mountains. Beyond this cluster of habitation a rough track wriggled towards the desolate and boggy head of the glen, soon to give up the unequal struggle by petering out in a pathless wilderness.

The dull hump of Beinn Tulaichean, its summit lost in swirling spumes of mist, towered over me as I dropped down into the valley, clambered over a stile and reached the first of the white-painted farmsteads. During my descent I had closely observed the mountain's south-east slopes. They were strewn with menacing boulders which had formed deep fissures. It was alarming to think what might happen if one of those massive stones became dislodged.

A nearby immaculate shelter caught my eye and as the rain was persisting I thankfully took a rest inside it. Erected by the Countryside Ranger Service it houses rough seating made from logs that provide respite for tired limbs. As I left this sanctuary at the entrance to a deserted car park I read two notices attached to its outer wall. One welcomed me to Inverlochlarig with displays of the flora and fauna found in the locality. Red deer are apparently common and also the adaptable ptarmigan, whose remarkable camouflage protects it from predators. The other notice contains maps of the surrounding area and safety information for walkers, which includes a warning against venturing into the fells unannounced during the stalking season. Hopefully this prevents any careless intruders from being shot.

Making tracks through the farmyards in order to follow the River Larig towards the head of the glen, I was halted by the sight of a dead fox. This was probably intended as a deterrent to others of its kind from attacking the farmer's lambs. Propped against an adjacent wall lay one of the countless plastic bread trays that seem to litter back-yards everywhere. The thought of a bulky bread delivery van lurching its way through the long valley to the farm seemed incomprehensible.

A sign pointed towards three of the mountains that overlooked the desolation of the upper glen as I left the farms behind. The first of these was Stob à Choin for which I was headed. Thankfully I was not bound for the very head of the glen, intending instead to take a side-valley that runs between Stob à Choin and Stob an Duibhe. My plan was to follow the Allt à Choin burn that flows southwards through that defile to Loch Katrine.

Devoid of habitation once more I clung to the track that wound beneath craggy mountainsides which plunged from a dense blanket of cloud. For three miles I followed this umbilical cord through a sea of loneliness, with only bird-calls for company. I abandoned it before it disappeared in cowardly fashion beneath the wall of mountains that seals off the head of Balquhidder Glen.

Wild country lay ahead as I left the track to scramble across the River Larig, dousing my boots and socks in the process. Trying to ignore the discomfort of squelching boots I made for the yawning gap between Stob à Choin and Stob an Duibhe. At this point I was entering the Trossachs, often described as the Lake District of Scotland. Its more popular parts are usually thronged with rubber-necking tourists who follow its meandering network of roads. The mountain range that I was about to pass through displayed no such activity and is as much a part of the Crianlarich Hills as those of the Trossachs. Strictly speaking, the Trossachs originally covered an area of no more than one square mile - that is, the wooded Glen between Loch Katrine and Loch Achray. Over the years it has expanded to embrace the land between Loch Ard and Aberfoyle, to Lochs Katrine, Achray and Venachar. I was unlikely to meet any visitors during my lonely passage to Loch Katrine. The Allt à Choin burn would be my only companion.

My trek through the secluded valley had its compensations in the form of the indigenous wildlife that flourishes there, undisturbed by human intrusion. As I approached a tiny lochan at the source of the Allt à Choin I came face to face with a startled pine-marten which appeared most surprised to see me. It raised itself on its hind legs, sharp claws exposed, before scampering for cover. Rabbits darted for their burrows at my approach and I caught a brief glimpse of a deer that quickly disappeared into the mist.

Whilst I was crossing one of the numerous feeder-streams that lurched from the steep fellsides into the infant burn, a large bird swooped out of the gloom and, after giving me a quick inspection, soared away. My bird identification, as I have already indicated, is sketchy, but I am convinced that it was a golden eagle in search of prey. Sadly, these majestic birds are now confined to the Western Isles and the remoter parts of the Scottish Highlands, having never received the protection accorded to their neighbours, the peregrine falcon. Some years ago many young eaglets were mysteriously wiped out and the cause was eventually established as poisonous chemicals contained in fertilisers used on the surrounding lands. These poisons were consumed by sheep as they grazed, with no apparent harmful effects and were subsequently retained in the fat of their bodies. When the sheep were killed by eagles and fed to their young, which unfortunately had no resistance to the chemicals, they perished. Thankfully the harmful constituents were eventually banned from use in fertilisers, but untold damage had already been wreaked on the eagle population.

The pervading silence returned to be broken only by the drumming of the rain that merrily cascaded around me with renewed vigour. I had enjoyed plenty of good weather on my journey so far and I couldn't complain if nature decided to restore the balance, provided the pendulum didn't swing too far. The Allt à Choin began to dance vigorously under the deluge as though struggling to escape from the constricting corridor that guides it remorselessly toward Loch Katrine. The mountains on either side were concealed in a grey haze that I prayed would lift before I reached the loch.

My hopes were dashed as I approached it. Reluctantly the inky-black water eventually emerged, but nothing else was visible and the all-important first impression of a place of reputed beauty was destroyed. It was not all bad news however, for when I reached the loch I found a strip of tarmac encircling it. This forms a private road and permitted cycle-way that runs from the Trossachs Pier, situated at the east end of Loch Katrine, along its north shore and round to Stronachlachar, that lies part way along the south shore. It also provides a good surface on which to walk and I would hopefully make good time around the loch, apart from an intended stop to discover a little more about Rob Roy's haunts. A boat would have come in handy for Stronachlachar lay barely a mile away across the water, whereas, it would require a five-mile walk to reach it by land.

The first habitation that I encountered on the road was co-incidentally called Portnellan, as was my day's starting point. It is not often that you pass through two places bearing identical names on the same day. Progress was good despite the nagging rain as I headed for the west end of the loch and Glengyle House, the site of Rob's birthplace. Here he spent his early years, by the lochside. When I came upon it the house had an unkempt and disquieting aura in the murky conditions. It stands forlornly amidst overgrown lawns, its sombre, white walls disfigured with the stains of neglect. The once- attractive red of the castellated gable ends has also been dulled by the passage of time. I knocked with some trepidation on the back door and receiving no reply I circled the inhospitable house. Its abandonment was obvious when I looked through one of its curtainless windows into a lifeless room. Why was I made to feel so uneasy by this sad eighteenth-century house that stands in virtual isolation on the site of the earlier house in which Rob Roy was born? I do not believe in spirits, but this house exuded an unnerving atmosphere and I longed for a group of friendly cyclists or walkers to pass by. None came and I was completely alone, with only the haunting sound of the wind rustling the trees in nearby woodland. I was a good candidate for 'wimp of the year' as I retreated from the unwelcome ambience of this disturbing place. I half-expected to hear the clash of claymores and the fearsome sounds of skirmishes that were the hallmark of Rob's years as an outlaw. To compound my unease, a group of lively heifers, that had been grazing the lawns, aggressively approached. I felt a great temptation to bolt and head for Stronachlachar at great speed, but I forced myself to stay and search for another slice of MacGregor history that supposedly lay nearby.

Across the road from Glengyle House stood farm buildings that were also deserted. Where had everyone gone? I tentatively entered the adjacent wood and stumbled through its dark confines. I eventually found a path which led me to my objective that lay hidden deep in the wood. It was the burial ground of the MacGregor's and its appearance was no more reassuring than that of the house for it comprised an odd assortment of graves of varying ages that stood on a grassy mound enclosed by a high and forbidding stone wall. With my heart pounding I scrutinised the spooky final resting- place of several of the MacGregor Chiefs and some members of their families. An ornate stone cross dominates this compact array of memorials to the leaders of the turbulent clan. It bears an inscription dedicated to James MacGregor of Glengyle who died in 1870 and to his wife and son. Much in evidence throughout the graveyard were crests identical to those on the grave of Rob Roy and his family at Balquhidder. One of two stone tablets mounted on the boundary wall is in memory of Gregor MacGregor of Glengyle, nephew of Rob Roy, who died in 1777.

As I wandered amongst the gloomy edifices I realised the historical worth of this tiny graveyard sequested in a dark and remote wood. It recalled happier times when the locality was a busy place and Glen Gyle was a well-used trading route. This now deserted glen runs north-west from Loch Katrine and formerly lay on the drove road that ran from Dalmally to the Trossachs and Falkirk. There was once a thriving village at the head of the glen that has long since disappeared.

My curiosity satisfied, I hurriedly left the cheerless place and struck out for Stronochlachar with several miles still to cover. At the western extremity of the loch I crossed a garish metal bridge, totally out of keeping with its surroundings, that crosses Glengyle Water as it enters Loch Katrine. This modern bridge lies further west than its predecessor which was submerged when the loch was converted to a reservoir, along with neighbouring Loch Arklet, in order to supplement Glasgow's water supply.

Visibility improved slightly as my boots pounded around the loch. An occasional glance over the loch's reputably pure waters revealed a truer picture of the area's intrinsic beauty. Gnarled slopes, sprinkled with rocky outcrops clambered from the far shoreline. The emerald-green of their lower regions was slashed by narrow wooded valleys and I could appreciate why Sir Walter Scott had based his epic poem *Lady of the Lake* on such surroundings.

I had not met a single person since leaving Ben More and the first signs of life reappeared in the form of a couple sitting in their car that was parked on the pier at Stronachlachar. They were intently watching the progress of the steamship, *Sir Walter Scott* that was fast-disappearing across the dark and choppy waters of the loch. I cursed my bad luck at missing a close-up view of the renowned steamer that has plied between the Trossachs Pier and Stronachlachar since 1900.

In the prevailing conditions the pier was a bleak, windswept spot, which was a pity because it is surrounded by attractive parkland and provides a panoramic view of the loch. Colourful rhododendrons border the pier and the pleasant network of avenues that surround it. The only visible building was an old-fashioned amenity block that would have graced any railway station in the grand old days of steam. Its deserted café and opulent toilets were reminiscent of that bygone age. The gents toilet boasted some beautifully varnished internal doors and partitions, but I was most impressed by the gold-plated taps on the wash basins. Even the sink plugs were secured by gold chains, a rare contrast to modern public toilets where you are lucky to find a plug, let alone a chain.

The angry waters of the loch bombarded a tiny island that cowers a short distance from the pier. Despite its size it did prove secure enough for Rob Roy to imprison the Duke of Montrose's factor, or land agent, upon it. This act was in retaliation for the injustice perpetrated by the politically scheming Montrose. Rob knew that November was the month when the Montrose tenants paid their rent and calmly walked in on the factor as he sat counting his collections in the inn at Chapelarroch. The factor was made to write his own ransom note before being dumped on the Factor's Island, as it became known. Eventually he was released unharmed.

Four miles remained of my journey to Inversnaid as I left Stronachlachar and joined a narrow, unfenced road that winds along the north shore of Loch Arklet. The reservoir looked grim and hostile under the persistently leaden sky, but thankfully the rain had eased. A line of trees ran incongruously into the water, a reminder that meadows have been submerged. The road had begun to dry, which saved me from a dousing by the numerous coaches that bounced their way past me heading for the road's terminus at Inversnaid. Inquisitive faces peered at me from these travelling cocoons, which hailed from as far afield as Bath and Bury St Edmunds.

The view ahead was dominated by shapely peaks that thrust themselves skyward on the far side of Loch Lomond. These mountains, known as the Arrochar Alps, are amongst the most popular in Scotland. The weather-beaten features of Beinn Ime, Ben Vorlich and Ben Arthur displayed tracts of the treacherous Arrochar rock, predominantly a micha-shist with a coating of lichen, that is murderously slippery when wet. The finest of the six peaks in the group is Ben Arthur, also known as The Cobbler. Its three rocky summits have a unique outline that endears it to visitors and rock climbers alike.

An hour of purposeful walking brought me to the gaunt battlements of the dam at the end of Loch Arklet, where the restless swell of the reservoir spends itself in a flurry of spray on the wall of its prison. I was relieved to find that the road began to descend towards Inversnaid. My long day's walk was beginning to tell on me and I needed all the help that I could get.

On a prominent hillock above one of the numerous bends in the road stands Garrison Farm, which occupies the former site of the Inversnaid garrison that was built in 1718 to quell Rob Roy and his outlaw band. Rob's audacious capture and imprisonment of Montrose's factor had the unfortunate effect of so stinging the Duke that he used his influence to arouse attention to the outlaw in military circles. Consequently plans were laid to build a barracks, where Garrison Farm now stands, in order to crush Rob's troublesome band for good. Rob had the last laugh however, for he eventually attacked and ransacked it.

Inversnaid has earlier associations with Rob Roy, for after his marriage, the chief of the MacGregor clan, Archibald of Kilmanan provided land on the shore of Loch Lomond where Rob built a new house. In the next few years, before his subsequent eviction by Montrose, Rob's landholding expanded greatly and he came to own a great swathe of land around Inversnaid. Garrison Farm was the last of the buildings that I would pass with Rob Roy connections.

It was a great relief to see the road finally emerge from the forest, that drapes the east bank of Loch Lomond, and grind to a halt at the Inversnaid Hotel. This impressive building lies snugly near the water's edge, close to a jutting pier from which plies the popular ferry to Inveruglas on the west shore. I hurried towards it, hoping that Maurice would be there to greet me. It had been a strenuous day and it was already past seven o'clock in the evening. In the hotel forecourt one of the numerous coaches that had sped by me was disgorging its passengers, many of whom were stretching confined limbs, grateful like me that their day's journey was over.

I envied Maurice who, if on time, should now be refreshed and feasting in comfortable surroundings. Another night of luxury in a hotel was in prospect, but my anticipatory bubble was about to be cruelly burst. A glassy stare greeted my arrival at the reception desk. Did I detect a note of disdain in that searing look? This was far from the welcome I had anticipated, despite the fact that I had considerately removed my boots before entering. After confirmation of my reservation I enquired if Maurice had checked-in and after some delay I was informed that he had. There was no offer to enquire if he was in his room and at my prompting, the receptionist, who appeared to carry the cares of the world on her shoulders, picked up the phone to do so. At that moment Maurice emerged from the lounge with a broad grin. As he pumped my hand it reminded me of the congratulatory back-slapping episode that had marked our successful completion, at Robin Hood's Bay, of Wainwright's Coast to Coast Walk the previous year. Here we were, together once more, to continue where we had left off. It was touching to see that Maurice had patiently waited for me before starting his meal.

It came as no surprise to find that Maurice had also received a less than enthusiastic welcome. Despite this, the place was bulging with guests and was obviously a strategic halt on the tours of the Trossachs and beyond. Although he had worked up a healthy appetite Maurice insisted on waiting for me to shower and change before we ate and took the opportunity for a good natter about the forthcoming challenge of the West Highland Way.

I had been entrusted with booking accommodation for our nine-day journey to Shiel Bridge and was already having reservations about my first choice. Tentatively entering my room, I was relieved to find it reasonably comfortable . I did not want Maurice to feel that I had let him down.

Suitably cleaned and refreshed I rejoined him and we hurried to the dining room. It was virtually full and the prevailing hum of conversation enveloped us, resembling the buzz of an angry swarm of bees. The meal was an anticlimax; poor food complemented by slow and impersonal service. Our fellow-diners seemed impervious to such annoyances, chattering excitedly about their day. Maurice was eager to hear how my walk had gone thus far, and having no wish to bore him to death, I gave him the edited highlights.

Our meal over, we studied the comprehensive map of the West Highland Way issued by the Countryside Commission for Scotland. Tracing our next day's route, we noted any points of interest. Our plan was to follow the long-distance footpath to its termination at Fort William, which lay roughly sixty miles to the north. The complete path is ninety-five miles long, commencing at Milngarvie, a former mill town on the north-west fringe of Glasgow. At its inception in 1980 it was the first officially designated long-distance route in Scotland. My introduction to it was by courtesy of Jimmie MacGregor, the celebrated musician, walker and broadcaster, who had travelled along it during his television series. Its magnetism and scenic beauty combined with Jimmie's friendly commentary had deemed it an indispensable part of my itinerary. Unfortunately, Maurice and I would only cover two thirds of the path, missing out the lowland section that passes Drymen and joins Loch Lomond at Balmaha, that lies a day's walk from Inversnaid.

The map was eventually discarded, as our respective day's journeys began to take their toll. We were soon in our beds savouring thoughts of exciting days ahead. Sleep quickly overtook me and I dreamt of Rob Roy, whose legend had coloured my day. It would be nice to recall that I helped him in my dream with one of his daring escapes, but I simply fought alongside him against his arch-enemy, the Duke of Montrose. To my discredit, I cannot remember who won.

CHAPTER TWO

The West Highland Way

DAY TWELVE: INVERSNAID - CRIANLARICH

Prior to breakfast on a grey, unattractive morning Maurice and I had the temerity to request packed-lunches at the hotel reception desk. An embarrassing silence ensued. The receptionist was obviously disconcerted by such awkward guests. Eventually a grudging concession was made to investigate the possibility and we were asked to enquire again after breakfast.

During our meal we pronounced judgment on the hotel, whose ethos appeared to be; attract as many coach parties as possible, give them inferior food and get rid of them before they can cause trouble. Walkers were obviously an encumbrance, inconsiderately lumbering in with muddy boots and sweaty brows, which lowered the tone of the place. It was doubly unfortunate that one of the most popular long-distance footpaths in the country happened to pass the door. For those about to leap up and cancel their booking at the Inversnaid Hotel, have no fear, it is now under new management and its ambience has greatly improved.

As we checked out of the hotel we were each handed a couple of sandwiches filled with slices of cold pork. Reasoning that we were lucky to get anything at all, we made a quick exit before they could change their minds.

Departing hurriedly, we cast a hasty look across Loch Lomond. The view was unfortunately marred by an overflowing rubbish bin in the hotel forecourt. Maurice and I chuckled at the sight of this bulging bin which nicely summed up our opinion of the Inversnaid Hotel. Through the morning haze we could just discern Wallace's Isle on the opposite side of the loch. It is named after Sir William Wallace, the great patriot and chieftain who led the Scottish armies against Edward I. He was captured in 1304, condemned for treason in London and executed at Smithfield. His island lies at the mouth of Inveruglas Water that emerges from an array of Arrochar Hills, their summits on that morning enveloped by a blanket of unfriendly cloud. Slightly to the north lies Inveruglas Isle, the site of a castle once occupied by the MacFarlane clan. They ruled the west shore of Loch Lomond north of Tarbet and like the MacGregors gained a reputation as raiders and cattle thieves.

Our day's journey began with a tramp through the band of woodland that hugs the east shore of the loch as far as Doune Farm. The stony path threads a winding course that fluctuates from loch-shore to high on its flanks. As we blundered through a mass of vegetation, including oak, birch, rowan and hazel, we saw nothing of the wild goats, deer and grey squirrel that reputedly inhabit the area. Our untrained eyes probably missed many tell-tale signs. Through periodic gaps in the trees we peered over the loch for decent views of the Arrochar Hills, but they remained obstinately headless by courtesy of the annoying cloud.

Approximately twenty minutes of walking brought us to the site, indicated by the map, of Rob Roy's Cave. Much to our chagrin we spent half an hour scrambling over a jigsaw of massive boulders that littered the hillside and never found it. This was most frustrating because I now considered myself an expert on the outlaw, having found so many of his haunts. How are the mighty fallen. Worse was to come, however, for when we related this abortive tale in the guesthouse that evening, our embarrassment was complete. The object of our search, we were told, was not a cave at all, merely a deep crevice between two large rocks. It had, however, managed to shelter some of the MacGregors who met there before many of their raids

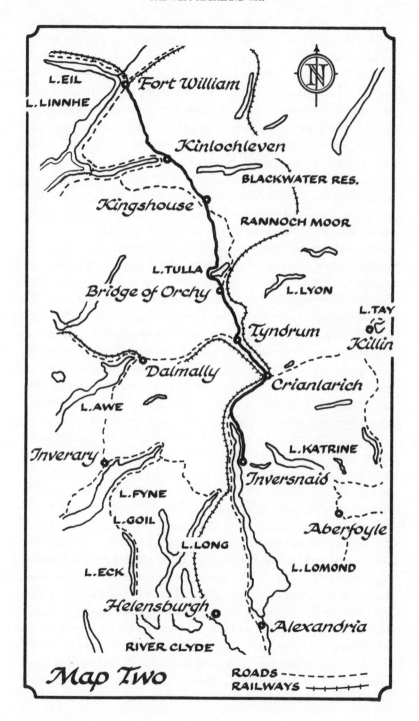

Map Two

ROADS - - - - -
RAILWAYS + + + +

and also Robert the Bruce, who reputedly spent a night there in 1306. Was this the scene of his famous rendezvous with the spider, I wondered?

Fed up with our abortive search, we relented and rejoined the path, muttering curses as we did so. We found the hillsides scoured by numerous streams which, during the heavy rains of previous years, created land-slips, some of these gouging channels across our path. A party of Royal Engineers was helpfully erecting a temporary bridge over a newly-created ravine. It was a scene of hard hats, squealing winches and barking orders. Maurice and I felt unspoken admiration for those soldiers, who were performing a very useful service, infinitely more helpful than polishing boot toe-caps until mirror-like, or painting the grass around their camp green.

At one point we stopped to look for a tiny island in the loch with the fascinating name of Island I Vow, which supposedly houses the remains of another castle. As we gazed over the loch, two ladies emerged from woodland a short distance away and strode along the path towards us. They stopped for a chat and we discovered that they were very accommodating - no, not towards Maurice and me, if that's what you are thinking. Their destination was Inversnaid where they would later rendezvous with their husbands who were following them, not on the path, but along the loch in a boat, whilst indulging in their favourite pastime of fishing. This apparently was a common occurrence, the ladies being sent ahead to a pre-arranged meeting point whilst their husbands enjoyed themselves. I can think of many wives, who, when handed such a proposition would gladly throw their husbands into the loch. These particular ladies were completely unabashed and evidently enjoyed their enforced marches. Earlier that morning they had been dispatched on the ferry from Ardlui and had alighted at Ardleish for the four-mile hike to Inversnaid. Showing a great interest in their husbands' antics, they explained that their boat would be hugging the lochside, as close to the overhanging vegetation as possible. The reason for this strategy being that from the trees and bushes dropped succulent caterpillars and grubs, straight into the waiting mouths of the fish congregating beneath. The shoreline obviously provided rich pickings for their husbands.

Bidding the ladies farewell we expressed the hope that their wait at Inversnaid would not be a long one, secretly feeling that their wretched husbands deserved to drown. We re-entered our arboreal tunnel to finally emerge near the head of the loch. Fine views were now available. The white-walled Doune Farm, recently restored, nestled on the gently sloping lochside amidst welcome turf and stunted bracken that stretched to the water's edge. Under a brightening sky the upper extremity of the loch was clearly visible, fringed by a circle of green hills. Ardlui lay snugly at its northern tip, alongside a cleft in the hills through which the River Falloch emerges to empty its waters into the loch. The entrance to Glen Falloch heralded the start of the final stage of our day's walk to Crianlarich. The Way follows this valley, which forms an integral part of the Loch Lomond basin, and passes into Perthshire at Inverarnan.

It was easier walking as we progressed to Ardleish and onwards to the head of the loch, where we stopped for some welcome refreshment. Maurice had worked up a fine lather in the humid conditions and stripped off his damp shirt, which he hung on a convenient tree branch to dry. He cautiously opened the sandwiches that had been provided at the hotel and gave them an exploratory sniff. Nothing if not cautious was our Maurice. His nose wrinkled, indicating his distaste, and they were returned to his rucksack. I was so hungry I recklessly ate mine and suffered later for my stupidity. By mid-afternoon I had a rampant stomach-ache which refused to subside until the late evening. More curses for the Inversnaid Hotel. Meanwhile, our pleasant lunchtime interlude was spent lazing on the lochside and watching enticing salmon leaping from the water, unfortunately out of our reach. Oh for a rod and line!

Time dictated that we turned our attention to Glen Falloch, its lower reaches a deep trench scoured by a retreating glacier. We enjoyed an exhilarating walk to Inverarnan, during which we were able to enjoy good retrospective views of the mountains sheltering the east side of Loch Lomond. Hidden behind their rugged outlines are Loch Katrine and Glengyle. Ahead of us, to the north-east, loomed the dark profiles of the Crianlarich Hills huddling under a cheerless sky. They displayed a totally new aspect to that presented in Glen Dochart. During the gentle approach to Inverarnan itself there was much to hold our attention. The remains of a canal was visible, which had been constructed in the mid-nineteenth century to link the Inverarnan Hotel with Loch Lomond. It was now a forlorn and overgrown channel, long-disused. The hotel itself is a former cattle-drover's inn, strategically sited on the old droving route from Glen Fyne in Argyll to Glen Gyle. Above us, the Ben Glas

Burn hurtled dramatically over a hillside cliff, but we were too close to the hill to obtain the best view of this lurching series of falls known as the Grey Mare's Tail.

Beyond Inverarnan the glen veers north-east, setting a course for Crianlarich, which would lead me virtually full circle to the west end of Glen Dochart. This beautiful valley was a revelation, particularly the Falls of Falloch. The sun began to shine benevolently on us, banishing the clouds away to the north. It was to remain a constant companion for nine consecutive days. The downside was that Maurice and I lost about two stones in sweat, each, during that period. In fact we were lathered by the time we reached the Falls. Some walkers are never satisfied, even by a remarkably long spell of sunshine! At this point an extremely lively section of the river twisted and swirled around myriad jutting rocks in a series of gentle, but extremely attractive cascades. Its waters seethed beneath the copious overhanging foliage of surrounding woodland. We basked in delightful surroundings sprinkled with pines and the stark carcasses of dead trees. The hoot of an owl surprised us. Evidently it was not on its usual night-shift. Maurice caught a fleeting glimpse of a capercaillie, far from its breeding grounds on the islets that sprinkle Loch Lomond. All might have been different if an earlier attempt to blast the lovely cataracts had succeeded. The intention of this reckless scheme had been to create access through Falloch Falls for fish heading for the river's upper reaches. Thankfully it failed.

A steady climb to the farms at Derrydaroch took us into open country, engendering a true moorland feel. Maurice's step became jaunty and he surged ahead as though relieved of an imaginary burden. He likes the moors. To our left we had a clear view of the A82 Glasgow to Fort William road threading through the heart of the glen, accompanied by the West Highland Railway. These twin lines of communication emphasise the importance of Glen Falloch as a strategic link between the lowlands and the Western Highlands. They are constant companions on this section of their journey to Fort William, having joined forces at Tarbet for a scenic journey along the upper west side of Loch Lomond before squeezing through Glen Falloch. Recently described by critics of British Rail as 'the busiest uneconomical line in the country', the West Highland Railway was declared unworthy of subsidy by the company, who tried to discontinue the invaluable sleeper service from London to Fort William. Thankfully, due to widespread public protest and a successful legal challenge to British Rail's plan, the service has been allowed to continue. I wonder how it will fare under privatisation?

We crossed the river near the compact collection of farms that form Derrydaroch - the 'oak grove'. One of the many fine Way signs directed us towards the road and railway line. We kept both of them company for roughly three-quarters of a mile, listening to the roar of the traffic before thankfully passing beneath the railway and crossing the busy road. Our path then struck across the moorland towards Keilator Farm and subsequently Crianlarich.

The upper reaches of Glen Falloch form a splendid display under a penetrating sun. We contoured the fellside beneath Craw Knowe along a grassy path that signified a reunion with General Wade's military road network. The broad tracks and clear pathways that form the modern remnants of his road system were to guide us for most of our route to Fort William. Maurice and I gave three cheers for the General. Across the widening strath Ben More's triangular peak appeared beyond the ridges of Cruach Ardrain. I couldn't resist a little boast to Maurice about standing on its summit the previous day and looking over much of the forthcoming section of the Way.

The one-mile journey to Keilator Farm seemed twice that distance. We first saw the farm from afar but it appeared reluctant to come closer. This may have been due to our feeling the effects of the heat and our eagerness to reach Crianlarich. Maurice and I jokingly likened that mile to those we found in Swaledale on Wainwright's Coast to Coast Walk. They had seemed so long we had deemed them to be on the unique 'Swaledale Scale'. After what seemed an age we passed above the farm and traversed the tiny Bogle Glen, which is supposedly haunted by bogles - Scottish ghosts or goblins. We did not see any apparitions, but we were startled by the angry cry of an indignant grouse that rose from the bracken a few feet from us. It obviously did not take kindly to uncouth walkers lumbering through its territory.

At the head of the glen we climbed a high stile over a deer fence that runs along the watershed that lies above Crianlarich. Here the drainage pattern changes from south-flowing into Loch Lomond to north-east flowing into Strath Fillan and eventually the Tay. Below us huddled the sporadic buildings of Crianlarich, an extremely popular village which extends a warm welcome to holidaymakers. Despite a resident population of less than 200, it's popularity as a tourist centre swells its summertime inhabitants to many times that number. A good proportion of visitors are walkers and climbers, reflecting its excellent position for outdoor pursuits.

The tantalising thoughts of a cooling drink and a chance to refresh ourselves carried us rapidly down the Old Military Road and into the village. Here we mingled with a variety of visitors ranging from casual sightseers to hardened walking types sporting thick beards and sweatbands. A party of youngsters bustled from the railway station full of excited chatter and expectant gazes. Crianlarich sported two stations when the old line from Callander was still in use, but is now reliant on the busy West Highland line. Finding a convenient pub, we enjoyed a deliciously cool drink and struck up a conversation with three walkers, Don, Derek and Peter who were also tackling the West Highland Way. They had taken up walking later in life, as we had done. Like most novices they experienced some hairy moments at the outset. Apparently their first walk of any distance was the Pennine Way, on which they embarked with no training or experience. Being as 'green as grass' they had problems with route-finding, particularly on their first day. They set out, without any food, armed only with a map, which they couldn't read, and attempted to cross the notoriously featureless and boggy plateau of Kinder Scout. Their map soon sank into one of the treacherous peat groughs, rendering them completely rudderless. After wandering aimlessly amidst the peat they eventually found their way off it, unfortunately several miles from where they intended. Blundering on to a nearby road they sought directions at a pub and miraculously found the path to their next objective, Bleaklow Head. Here they joined forces with a group of experienced walkers who guided them to their destination at Crowden Youth Hostel. They decided that things from then on could only get better and decided to persevere. Purchasing another map they completed the next day's walk successfully. Bolstered by this they progressed all the way to Byrness in Northumberland without serious mishap, when ill-fortune struck. Derek went down with a gastric infection and was unable to continue. His companions ensured that arrangements were made to get him home before pushing on without him to complete the final lap across the Cheviot Hills to Kirk Yetholm. Derek returned to Byrness at a later date, determined to complete the walk, and finally achieved his ambition. We discovered that the three friends were also staying over-night in the village and arranged to meet them that evening for a meal.

Our guesthouse lay in a fine setting on the outskirts of Crianlarich and I looked from the window of my room over a vista of the now-familiar Crianlarich Hills. Ted, the proprietor apologised for not providing supper and suggested we eat at the pub. We told him that this was already arranged and he appeared relieved, saying that he was running the place on his own for the time being. By way of atonement he showed us a couple of vintage cars standing in his large garage, explaining that he was an enthusiastic collector. The other hobby of this busy fellow, we discovered, was painting.

Later, we returned to the pub to find the lounge bar heaving with an assortment of walkers and climbers. Finding Don, Derek and Peter tucked in a corner we squeezed in alongside them. Sitting alongside us were another couple of West Highland Way walkers, Reg and Tony. Reg's feet were in a very poor way for he had collected a blister on each of his toes. He had covered them with plasters and Tony had considerably bound his feet with bandages to allow him to carry on walking. Despite suffering badly and having oversized feet Reg had discarded his boots in favour of trainers and persevered for the past couple of days. He was bolstered by the fact that Crianlarich lies halfway along the Way, which made him determined to reach Fort William. I sincerely hoped that, if he did manage to complete his uphill struggle, God would grant him a new pair of feet.

We concluded that the room should be re-named the 'Blister Bar' because we met another party of West Highland Way walkers suffering from their ravages. These abused feet belonged to six female nurses from Glasgow who were bravely, or foolishly, walking the Way to raise money for their hospital's charity. Unused to covering great distances in debilitating boots their feet had rebelled. One of the young ladies was hobbling nearly as badly as Reg and she would be very lucky to make it.

Throughout the evening we chatted to many other walkers, swapping accounts of past experiences and outlining ambitions for future walks. It was a pleasant change for me to be surrounded by kindred souls after many days of lone walking. I was also feeling pleased with myself for passing the 200 mile point on that day. Maurice toasted my achievement and added that I would soon reach halfway. What an inspiring thought.

Our evening had assured us that the West Highland Way was extremely popular and attracted a great variety of walkers. It was a good example of why walking is now recognised as Britain's foremost participation activity, over twenty million people are now reckoned to be regular walkers. The pastime has recently been classified as a sport by the government, who as I write, are issuing grants towards the repair of eroded footpaths. Maurice and I are convinced that friendliness is one of its greatest attractions.

DAY THIRTEEN: CRIANLARICH - ACHALLADER

The following morning Maurice and I enjoyed a hearty breakfast before bidding farewell to Crianlarich. The sun beamed cheerily upon us and another warm day was in prospect. We were delighted. Tyndrum was our initial destination, the next village in the 'Shearings Corridor', with which I had become re-acquainted. The valley of Strath Fillan, which we would follow for much of the day, joins Glen Dochart at Crianlarich. We would doubtless see more of those well-known touring coaches that morning.

Retracing our steps to the deer fence that we had crossed the previous afternoon, we took the broad track that snakes to and fro across the wide strath, as though uncertain which side of the River Fillan to follow. This track initially winds through an extensive forest to the north-west of Crianlarich. When the West Highland Way was being formulated, the Forestry Commission were heavily engaged in planting in the area. Consequently, gaps were conveniently left in parts of the forest to permit views along Strath Fillan and many species of trees were planted to add visual variety for walkers and visitors.

A long and gradual descent led us back into the valley and we emerged from the forest to re-cross the A82 road and the West Highland Railway. The river is spanned at this point by Kirkton Bridge, and the views along Strath Fillan are truly memorable, highlighted by a most pleasing aspect of Ben More and Stob Binnein. From this vantage point, the finest features of these mountains are revealed, making it a favourite spot for photographers. Maurice was so enthralled by the shimmering peaks that he was sorely tempted to abandon his day's walk and climb them, but I assured him that I wasn't going to wait around. With muttered curses he reluctantly left the bridge to accompany me along the opposite riverbank.

His good temper was restored as we approached an intriguing reminder of one of Breadalbane's early religious influences, in the shape of St. Fillan's Chapel and graveyard. Unfortunately very little of the chapel remains, its ruins lying amidst a pleasant cluster of trees. The graveyard, its brooding edifices still intact, lies nearby. I had already encountered the patron saint of Breadalbane's legacy in the form of the Episcopal Church in Killin and Maurice was intrigued by the missionary's activities in the area during the seventh century.

On a sign by the chapel were depicted two tokens of the Irish monk's mission, given to lay brothers for use in certain rites there, such as taking oaths or treating the sick. These tokens are currently housed in the National Museum of Antiquities in Edinburgh. One is the head of St. Fillan's crozier or staff; an ornately carved piece of silver, inside which was found an older and more simple version. The other, which has humorous connotations, is a bell, supposedly used as a cure for insanity. The poor sufferers were dipped in the Holy Pool in the River Fillan, then taken to the chapel and left overnight tied to a tombstone or the font, depending on the weather, with the bell on their head. The following morning when the bell was removed, they would be supposedly found cured. Maurice had a good laugh over this, saying that it would be a great test for anyone feigning insanity. I had heard about the Holy Pool earlier, for it also had connections with Rob Roy, who seemed to pop up everywhere. He apparently brought a Campbell land agent, who had evicted a family of MacGregors, to the pool and tied him to a wooden frame in the graveyard. Robert the Bruce had also been active in the area, triumphantly elevating the chapel to a priory in 1318, following his victory at Bannockburn. St. Fillan is reputed to have given a miraculous sign of his support to Bruce on the eve of the battle and his arm-bone, encased in silver, was taken to the battlefield as a talisman.

Before leaving we visited the nearby graveyard that perched on a grassy knoll above the valley floor. The sparse and sombre gravestones evoked a feeling of unease. Two gaunt trees spread their eerie branches above us, seemingly sheltering the souls of long-departed mortals. It was a stark reminder of Breadalbane's troubled past.

Our historic diversion provided an opportunity to cool down. We had already felt the effects of the unwavering sun and more perspiration was imminent as we rejoined the track that heads for a bridge at Auchtertyre Farm. Beyond the bridge our route veered towards the River Fillan once more and we passed beneath a ridge of glacial debris deposited during the last Ice Age. Strath Fillan and Glen Dochart form a deep trench that was gouged by the movement of the largest glacier in the British Isles. As it receded, glacial deposits were scattered the length of the valley as far as Killin. Described as the western gateway to the Scottish Highlands, this valley provides access to an array of Perthshire and Argyll mountains, which, on that sunny morning, were vividly etched on a giant canvas.

Our concentration on the superb views was broken by a team of walkers from Cumbria who energetically overtook us. They were tackling the section of the Way that lies between Inverarnan and Bridge of Orchy, which was all their free time would allow. Maurice asked why they had come all this way when there was plenty of fine scenery around their home patch. They assured us that they loved the Lakeland mountains, but occasionally enjoyed different fare, particularly the majestic Highlands.

The A82 road barred our path once more and we hurriedly re-crossed it, keeping a sharp eye out for speeding traffic. A pleasant river-side walk took us past White Bridge which formerly carried the old road over the River Fillan. Here began another stretch of forest walking that was interspersed with views of the sparkling Crom Allt which rises to the north-east of Tyndrum on the slopes of Beinn Odhar. From its gathering grounds beneath Ben Lui and Ben Oss, the nearby River Cononish tumbles past Cononish Farm, that lies beneath one of the disused leadmines that spatter the hill-slopes to the west of Tyndrum. This once-thriving industry originated the building of a crushing and smelting plant which eliminated the dispatching of lead ore to Glasgow by way of Loch Lomond. The plant has long since gone but a scheme is currently underway to establish a gold mine in the locality. An adit has been driven into the flank of Beinn Chuirn with a view to extracting the precious metal.

The area also has associations with Robert the Bruce; for our immediate surroundings - Dalrigh, meaning 'Kings Field', was the scene of his battle with the MacDougalls of Lorn in 1306, which marked a low point in his fortunes. Here he suffered a crushing defeat and ordered his men to throw their weapons into a nearby lochan whilst he tried to cover their retreat. This lochan was given the evocative name Tam an Airm or 'Loch of Weapons'.

As Maurice and I approached the village we broke clear of the ubiquitous trees to be rewarded with a remarkably attractive view of white-walled buildings glistening in the sunshine beneath the contrasting grey mass of Beinn Odhar. Maurice was so impressed that he asked to be photographed leaning against a fence in front of this enticing background. During Wainwright's Coast to Coast walk

Maurice always displayed a superb 'lean' whenever he was photographed, never failing to recline against something. It was obvious that he had not lost his touch. The superb panorama of Tyndrum and its environs has, in my opinion, unfortunately been impaired by the addition of a large hotel complex which overshadows this otherwise delightful community. Formerly one of the main halts on an important cattle-droving route that stretched as far north as Skye, and to Crieff, Falkirk and the English markets to the south, the village has succumbed to mass tourism.

The place was bustling as we entered. Throngs of visitors spewed from car and coach and the village store was awash with walkers replenishing supplies. Here was the last chance for backpackers to stock up, there being no shops on the Way until Kinlochleven, twenty-eight miles away. In the store we met the Glasgow nurses, who seemed much more cheerful than on the previous evening. Evidently the splendid weather and scenery had rejuvenated them and they even joked about their blisters.

On our way out of the village we rejoined the Old Military Road that heads into the pass leading to Bridge of Orchy. It was to become our constant companion, apart from minor deviations, until we were within easy reach of Fort William. Beads of sweat stood out on our foreheads as we climbed the broad track that follows the Crom Allt into the hills. This was formerly the line of the old main road to Glencoe until it was superseded in the early 1930's by the A82 road which heads north from its junction with the A85 Oban road just outside Tyndrum. At the top of the incline we said goodbye to the Crom Allt and entered the pass. The modern road could be seen snaking along the opposite side of the valley, whose slopes were carpeted with familiar forests. A helicopter flew overhead, which, Maurice quipped, was on the lookout for exhausted West Highland Way walkers. My camera was busy capturing the helicopter and Maurice's back view as he strode ahead of me, the top of his head just visible above his bulky rucksack and his sporty red socks adding a distinctive splash of colour. So absorbed was he with the view ahead that he ignored the chance of a 'lean' against one of the reliable Way-markers. His eagerness was fully justified for the pass narrowed to form a shapely valley, scoured by a glacier flowing southwards from Rannoch Moor. Above its forested base mountains sweep upwards to create a dramatic, symmetrical shape. Bolstered by a backdrop of distant Black Mount Hills, it formed one of my most memorable views. It is set deep in Campbell country, for this fearful clan were the hereditary keepers of the surrounding deer forest. The Campbells of Glenorchy, as they were known, were required to supply venison for the royal feasts at the hunting lodge which formerly stood a little way ahead at Auch. James IV in particular loved the area and was known to have spent a week at the lodge in 1506.

The character of the pass changed once more as we contoured the lower slopes of Beinn Odhar (2948 feet) and we were reunited with the West Highland Railway which was heading for Bridge of Orchy station. The A82 road snuggles beside the railway as they squeeze through the narrow channel on their approach to Auch, where the railway departs on a wide sweep into the side valley of Auch Gleann. After crossing a viaduct over the Allt Chonoghlais it returns to the pass beneath the bastion of Beinn Dorain (3524 feet). A good track strikes through Auch Gleann, the old passage to Glen Lyon. This track formed part of the funeral route for the MacGregors of Glen Lyon to their clan burial grounds at Dalmally. I mentioned my earlier journey through the lower region of Glen Lyon to Maurice and its association with the MacGregors, highlighted by Gregor MacGregor's legendary leap across the River Lyon. Its wild upper reaches I knew are accessible by this burial route and when I jokingly suggested a diversion to that desolate area, Maurice questioned my sanity. He suggested that the West Highland Way was quite enough to be going on with.

We were indeed amidst some of the finest scenery of the Way, accentuated by the formidable bulk of Beinn Dorain that towered over the flat valley floor, making us feel minute. Auch seemed a good place to take the weight off our feet and we discarded our rucksacks and perched on a low wall. Don, Derek and Peter came into view. Despite the heat, they were also enjoying themselves, their route-finding difficulties now a thing of the past. Before continuing, Maurice led us to the river where we dangled our feet in the deliciously cool water. Life was good.

Our three friends joined us for the final stretch to Bridge of Orchy, which lay four miles away. Striding beneath Beinn Dorain we crossed numerous bubbling streams that poured from its flanks. Great gullies slashed the fellside above us, seemingly cleaved by giant axes. The crags of its higher reaches, home to the abundant mountain saxifrage, remained tantalisingly out of view. Tiring of the valley floor, the Way crossed the railway and climbed above it. The Allt Chonoghlais meandered below us between alder-strewn banks towards its junction with the River Orchy, within sight of Bridge of Orchy. Maurice and I were full of anticipation as we struck a good pace, spurred on by Don, Derek and Peter who were already relishing a relaxing drink at their destination, the Bridge of Orchy Hotel. They were conveniently staying there that night, but Maurice and I were not so lucky. I was about to lose innumerable Brownie points for we had a further four miles to cover to our accommodation at Achallader Farm. We would also have to retrace our steps on the following morning to rejoin the Way.

At the confluence of the Allt Chonoghlais and the River Orchy the impressive wooded channel of Glen Orchy cuts deep into the hills to the south-west and the railway begins a gradual descent to Bridge of Orchy station before starting an exhausting climb round the eastern fringe of Rannoch Moor to the Corrour summit at nearly 1400 feet. A strategic halt on the West Highland Railway, the station shimmered in the afternoon sunshine as we approached, its slate-grey roof complementing the attractively red platform. It was fringed by a cluster of multi-coloured trees that stood out sharply against surrounding scrubland, curiously peppered with stones. This miniature arboretum displayed a hint of softness amidst the harsher landscape of the snow-tipped hills of Black Mount. We were now in the heart of Glenorchy, that ancient stronghold of the Campbells.

The hamlet of Bridge of Orchy is a tiny oasis of habitation on the fringe of some of the wildest country in Britain. A few dwellings cluster around the distinctive hotel. Accommodation is limited which I discovered to my cost. I had happened to pick the farm sited the farthest from the Way. The bridge from which the place takes its name was built by the military in 1751, which is rather surprising, for although it stands on the military road network, it was not available until after the last Jacobite uprising in 1745. Apart from the hotel and the bridge, possibly the only other thing of note is the annual rainfall which can reach 110 inches per year. Thankfully, Maurice and I were not subjected to any.

As we passed the station our route led through an underpass beneath the railway line and down to the substantial hotel, its entrance beckoning invitingly. Don, Derek and Peter hurriedly made for their watering-hole inviting us to join them for a drink. Maurice and I reluctantly declined as we had a four-mile walk ahead of us. I could sense Maurice's disappointment as we said our goodbyes. We had only gone a few yards when round a corner came two familiar faces. It was surprising to see Reg and Tony who were making remarkable progress. Reg's blisters were doing very nicely, thank you. We discovered that they were also staying at the hotel, which prompted another glare from Maurice amidst their cracks about enjoying our additional exercise and getting lost in the wilderness. It was a relief to escape their banter and head along the A82 road towards Loch Tulla and Achallàder. We agreed that the most direct route lay along the road, where we could eventually pick up a track that leads to the farm. Despite obviating the chance of getting lost we had a particularly uncomfortable end to our day's walk, the tarmac playing havoc with our feet. Sweat flowed, boots chafed in the heat, and Maurice was complaining. I wryly suggested that he booked the accommodation in future. Tremendous views over the blue waters of Loch Tulla took some of the sting from our struggle. Young pine and spruce clothed the roadside, but still permitted distant views of the austere fringe of Rannoch Moor. Silent prayers were offered for the remarkable weather to continue until we had covered the most inhospitable section of the Way that lies over the desolate moor. Three miles of road-walking seemed endless until the eagerly awaited track appeared. Although its surface was rough it was a relief to be in open country once more and the approaching mountains looked friendlier than the wild reaches of Rannoch Moor. Most prominent was Beinn Achaladair, its sleek lower slopes transforming into the grey ruggedness of its indented crest. Fingers of snow clung to the uppermost crevices, hiding from the sun's penetrating rays. Here was peace and tranquillity, away from the intrusion of the traffic that had dogged our steps from Bridge of Orchy. Rounding what proved to be the final bend of the track, I won back a few points from a begrudging Maurice for a breathtaking setting. The farmhouse of Achallader, looking bright as a button, was framed by the formidable mass of Beinn Achaladair. Snow-white walls rose to red gables above vivid-green lawns bedecked with multi-coloured rhododendrons. The buttercups of the surrounding meadows added a further splash of colour. It is logical that any place would seem attractive having walked all day to reach it, but this was exceptional and, in my view, completely vindicated my choice of accommodation. If Maurice agreed he did not concur, merely appearing grateful to take the weight off his sore feet.

An effusive welcome, probably born of relief, awaited us. The farmer's wife, Fiona, had become concerned about our late arrival. Piping-hot tea and delicious cakes were quickly forthcoming as we sank into blissfully comfortable armchairs. Fiona excused herself; the place was full and she had many mouths to feed. Whilst enjoying our refreshment Maurice and I contentedly looked around the tastefully decorated room, its walls covered with family portraits and evocative landscapes, sketched by an obviously talented hand. Resisting the urge to fall asleep we eventually stirred ourselves, not wishing to sit down to supper unkempt and unwashed.

Heads swivelled in our direction as we entered the dining room a little later, minus the dust and sweat and ravenously hungry. Our fellow-guests included a friendly party of five West Highland Way walkers from Aberdeen, three of whom were lively teenagers. The chatter was unbroken as we recounted our respective experiences and they were obviously relishing their walk. Blisters did not seem problem to this party, who were already anticipating the celebration of their arrival at Fort William. A couple sitting nearby interjected that merely listening to our conversation made them feel tired. They preferred four-wheeled travel and were bound for Fort William, Ullapool and eventually Inverness.

Whilst busily keeping us supplied with first-class food, Fiona wickedly suggested that we all climbed Beinn Achaladair after supper to round off our day. The touring couple visibly paled, but the Aberdonians were enthusiastic until they learned that it was all of 3404 feet. Another time perhaps, thought Maurice and I.

As an alternative Fiona recommended a stroll along the nearby Water of Tulla that flows beneath the slopes of Beinn Achaladair, or, if our feet had already suffered sufficient punishment, an inspection of the adjacent ruined fortification. This, we learned, had a chequered history, for in 1692 it housed a detachment of Campbells who marched from there to participate in the infamous massacre of the MacDonalds at Glencoe.

Maurice and I plumped for the fort inspection after supper whilst the Aberdonians strolled along the Water of Tulla. We were keen to see our first manifestation of the massacre. Although little of the original fort remained it did evoke a sense of involvement in a notorious episode of Scottish history. Unfortunately the charm of this relic was marred by an adjacent barn topped with a gaudily-painted corrugated iron roof.

As we strolled around the farm's perimeter the surrounding colours softened in the mellow evening sunlight. The farmhouse looked even more stunning bathed in an orange glow and a photograph was imperative. Thus the final satisfying touch was added to an unforgettable day.

DAY FOURTEEN: ACHALLADER - KINGSHOUSE

This was it; Rannock Moor day. The section that I had been quietly dreading, which involved crossing one of Scotland's bleakest areas. Wainwright describes it as 'a desolation fashioned by nature and right well has she succeeded'. Such a statement did nothing to ease my trepidation. If Maurice had similar worries, he did not divulge them.

Luckily, the weather was on our side as it was another perfect morning. Before breakfast I took my mind off my anxieties by capturing the wonderful views towards Rannock Moor and the distant snow-dressed summits of Stob Gabhar and Clach Leathad that glistened in the sun's welcoming radiance. My photography completed, I found it impossible not to dwell on what the day had in store.

A study of the map of the locality revealed a possible short cut around the north shore of Loch Tulla by means of a good track. This produced a dilemma. Should Maurice and I take advantage of this time-saver, or should we trudge the four miles back to Bridge of Orchy and then circle the west end of the loch? Good boys, for a change, we decided to return to Bridge of Orchy, because the short cut missed out three miles of the Way and also a former drovers' inn at Inveroran.

Our feet were in decent shape after a night's rest and the stretch of road-walking to Bridge of Orchy was completed without undue pain. Our fellow-travellers had departed from the hotel, where all was quiet, apart from a few guests enjoying a leisurely breakfast. We were evidently at the rear of the pack, with no one to turn to if misadventure struck. This predicament was all down to me and I glanced furtively at Maurice, who cuttingly suggested that we got a move on, as there were only eleven hours of daylight remaining. He could not have been overly put out however, for his 'lean' was in fine fettle as he tested the bridge parapet, whilst posing for a photograph, as we crossed the River Orchy. The bridge of Orchy, he declared was still sound after nearly 250 years of wear and tear. His wisecracks were an antidote to our apprehension about what lay ahead. Rannoch Moor had caused me to break into a cold sweat whenever I thought of it, but the approach proved reasonably easy and lay amongst glorious scenery. We said goodbye to the A82 road, which we hoped to rejoin at Kingshouse, and did not expect to see the West Highland Railway again until Fort William. A climb from the river through a plantation on the lower slopes of Beinn Invereigh took us to a cairn at Mam Carraigh, a splendid viewpoint at 1050 feet above Loch Tulla. The loch stretched beneath us, with the tiny island of Eilean Stalcair at its centre. This was probably another of the many such islands used for refuge, because we learned later that it had at one time been shored up with timber and stone. Below our feet nestled a diminutive remnant of Caledonian pine forest, Doire Darach, beneath which passes the old Glen Coe road, now surfaced. This road skirts the loch shore and passes the Inveroran Hotel before deteriorating into a track at Victoria Bridge near the western extremity of the loch.

The view northwards from Mam Carraigh revealed one of the most dramatic panoramas on the West Highland Way and also one of the finest in the Scottish Highlands. The impression created was one of vastness as we overlooked a massive basin in which sat the Inveroran Hotel, dwarfed by its majestic surroundings. This hollow was rimmed by the distant Black Mount Forest, a huge massif topped with snow, and the wild reaches of Rannoch Moor. The only other signs of habitation were the Victorian Lodges of Black Mount, on the far shore of Loch Tulla, and Forest Lodge that squatted near Victoria Bridge. These buildings recalled the importance of Rannoch Moor as a deer forest. Stalking reached its zenith around the turn of the century when the third Marquis of Breadalbane, a great lover of the sport, owned the land.

Maurice was eager to take the track down to the Inveroran Hotel, which convinced me that he must be dying for a drink. I hurried after him feeling overawed by such scenic grandeur. He set a lively pace and we were soon approaching the inviting hotel that appeared a splendid halt for travellers. Maurice shot me a glance that queried why I hadn't obtained accommodation there. Bright and attractive, the place was a far cry from the former eighteenth-century inn that existed when William Wordsworth and his sister Dorothy stayed overnight. They found the food inedible and living conditions basic, but Dorothy was intrigued by the smoky, but harmoniously pleasant, atmosphere of the kitchen. It probably furnished a dash of local colour during the Glen Coe to Bridge of Orchy section of their Scottish tour in 1803. For many years a droving stance, it provided a valuable resting place for cattle and sheep on their way to market. The Scottish Mountaineering Club met there in their early days, for it served as an ideal base for attacking the Black Mount Hills. Maurice was so impressed that he demanded a photograph whilst leaning languidly on a sign in front of the modern version of the hotel.

Under a clear blue sky we joined the old Glen Coe road and skirted Loch Tulla to arrive at Victoria Bridge. Here, roles were reversed as Maurice was instructed to take a shot of me leaning on the side of the bridge whilst enjoying the stunning view of the vibrant Linne Nam Beatach hurrying towards Loch Tulla. Only a short, level stint remained between us and the climb to Rannoch Moor, a prelude to eight miles of the wildest terrain that the Way offers. The old Glen Coe road, now a wide track, leads up the Black Mount Pass with our reliable friend, the Old Military Road, running parallel on a slightly higher line. Feeling the heat and the effort we hauled ourselves up the dusty track, with the fierce sun beating down upon us. At the head of the pass we took a welcome lunch-time breather. Not only did sandwiches appear, but also Maurice's handkerchief, which he carefully knotted and placed on his head. His portrayal of the archetypical Englishman on holiday was not on as far as I was concerned. Despite my threats to abandon him he resolutely stuck to this headgear for five days. Chewing on our packed-lunches, caringly prepared by Fiona, we gazed nostalgically over the placid expanse of Loch Tulla, now far below us, to the distant Grampian Mountains.

John Hillaby likened Rannoch Moor to the opening act of *Macbeth* and the meeting place of the three witches. He had joined the West Highland Way at Crianlarich and made his lone journey over the moor as evening was closing in, half-expecting to see the three sorcerers appear in the twilight. It was now our turn to venture onto this expanse, which boasts sixty square miles of emptiness, with a prodigious annual rainfall. The West Highland Railway tries to avoid it by skirting its eastern edge, but covers ground so boggy that part of it is laid on floating brushwood and another section is roofed to protect against blizzards. Not so timid, the A82 road heads across the heart of the moor amidst what appears more water than land. Its treacherous course threads between the watery expanses of Lochan na h-Achlaise, Loch Ba and Lochan na Stainge. On a hot summer's day it is possible to swim across the moor and on a freezing winter's day, to skate across it. Both these feats have remarkably been accomplished. Maurice and I felt like swimming on that hot day, but nothing was likely to steer us from the lifeline of our track.

Walking became easier as the ground levelled out and we made steady progress for two miles until the Old Military Road rejoined us once more. A further mile brought us to Ba Bridge, the most remote spot on the Way. It proved much less daunting than expected, affording admirable views over the lovely River Ba whose gathering grounds are the slopes of Clach Leathad and Stob Gabhar, the two most prominent Black Mount Hills. The river traces the course of a great glacier that poured from these mountains and scoured the deep depression of Coire Ba, a gigantic corrie whose beauty is undeniable. Our eyes were drawn to its head where snow-dusted, purple peaks presided over the lush green hollow at their feet. The glacier that carved this captivating scene had formerly augmented a massive ice-field that covered the moor during the Ice Age. This isolated, but beautiful setting is also the haunt of red deer that seemed to stay well out of the sight of human intruders. We had seen some wild ducks flee from the heather on our approach and I was keen to discover the greenshanks that supposedly lurked in the mosses that peppered the surrounding moorland. Lacking expertise in bird identification, Maurice and I were unfortunately to miss many of the rarer breeds that frequent the Highlands.

We were now roughly halfway across what we had anticipated would be the most testing part of our walk and the Kinghouse Hotel lay only four miles away. Once again the actual event had turned out much better than the imagined. Our trepidation was receding for we knew that providing we stuck to the reliable track we were home and dry. Rannoch Moor was evidently on its best behaviour, but we realised that conditions would be very different in bad weather, when it is imperative to keep to the Way, for shelter is non-existent.

With lighter hearts we climbed gradually to the ruins of Ba Cottage and onwards to a memorial cairn dedicated to Peter Fleming, the brother of Ian Fleming, author of the James Bond novels. Peter tragically died whilst shooting on the moor and his family and friends provided this simple monument in the surroundings that he had loved. Less famous than his brother, he had nevertheless lived an accomplished and exciting life as an author, traveller, explorer and special correspondent for *The Times*. He visited many countries, in particular Central Asia, South America, and, during service in the Second World War, Norway, Greece and Burma. In the latter three countries he made successive escapes from enemy-held territory. Maurice felt that such an interesting character deserved a 'lean' and thrust one hand against the cairn which did not budge an inch.

The track persevered around the base of Meall a'Buiridh before easing gently into another wide basin through which the streams begin to drain into the River Etive. Our day's toil was nearly over as we coasted into this welcoming arena and obtained our first glimpse of the striking Buachaille Etive Mor. This group of granite peaks stands sentinel over the giant fissures of Glen Etive and Glen Coe. Its crags and crevices offer some of the most popular rock-climbing conditions in Scotland. The best known climb is the dramatic 700 foot ridge that plunges from Crowberry Tower, a projection just below the summit.

Maurice and I burst into celebratory song as we followed the downward track to the A82 road which re-appeared beneath us. We saw a party of walkers approaching our destination, the Kingshouse Hotel, the oldest in Scotland. They were the first group that we had encountered since our late start from Bridge of Orchy and they were fortunately out of earshot of our rendition of *The Road To The Isles*, a great favourite of Maurice's. Our lusty singing, born of relief, was the antidote to earlier fears of extinction on Rannoch Moor. The hotel beckoned from beneath Beinn a'Chrulaiste, presenting the only evidence of habitation in this isolated and compelling amphitheatre, with the exception of nearby Blackrock Cottage. This lone hut, operated by the Ladies' Scottish Climbing Club, crouches beneath a chair lift that serves the ski-slopes of Meall a'Buiridh. Although a smaller ski-centre than Glenshee and Aviemore, it has many keen devotees.

Our pace quickened as we crossed the A82 road once more and began the final half-mile of our day's journey. The ever-faithful Old Military Road led us conveniently to the door of the hotel. Eager to remove our boots and the grime of Rannoch Moor, our singing mercifully faded as we galloped the last few yards. The Kingshouse Hotel looked just as appealing at close quarters and, like the one at

Inveroran, was far removed from its original version of 200 years ago. Sampled by William and Dorothy Wordsworth during their tour, it received a damning write-up from Dorothy, who described it as a miserable and wretched place. Maurice and I hurried inside to give it our own appraisal.

We were not disappointed and a little time later we emerged bathed and refreshed from our comfortable rooms to seek the bar where we found many familiar faces. Don, Derek and Peter invited us to join them for an update on events. They had also experienced no problems in crossing Rannoch Moor and were anticipating a straightforward two-day journey to Fort William. We optimistically agreed to meet in a hotel there for a celebration. The team of nurses were nearby and they told us that their blisters were troublesome, but hopefully would not prevent them from succeeding. This enjoyable interlude was rudely interrupted by my drawing the short straw for the chore of laundry duty. This was a vital necessity if Maurice and I were to keep our friends. Carrying what seemed a mound of dirty clothes, I headed for the launderette and bumped straight into Reg and Tony. Reg's feet were unfettered by bandages, but he was apparently using sticking plasters at an alarming rate. He joked that he now had blisters on his blisters, but was undeterred and still determined not to be beaten.

Obviously used to catering for the needs of walkers, the hotel sported excellent laundering facilities, which thankfully eliminated the alternative of washing your clothing in a mountain stream and beating it on a convenient rock on lonely Rannoch Moor.

My good deed completed, I was able to give my eyeballs a rest from watching our clothing spinning round and join Maurice for a stroll around the hotel before supper. In the softening light of early evening the surroundings were spell-binding. The entrance to Glen Etive beckoned, a ten-mile defile cut by the River Etive, its brown waters flowing into the glen between the Buachaille and Clachet. In the distance lay the portals of Glen Coe, beyond the plantation at Altnafeadh, which marks the foot of the Devil's Staircase, a demanding climb to the highest point of the West Highland Way at 1800 feet. This would be our objective on the following morning and if the weather held we also planned to explore Glen Coe and the scene of the historic massacre.

Supper was an extremely pleasant affair, with good food and stimulating company. Maurice and I shared a table with a Scottish actor, Paul Young, and his wife Jean, who is a journalist. They were enjoying a short holiday by walking part of the Way. A friendly and modest man, he described himself as a jobbing actor who, unlike some better-known stars, managed to stay in regular employment. His description was remarkably accurate, for I have since seen him many times on television in a variety of series and films. He has appeared alongside many notable performers, including Penelope Keith and Gregor Fisher of *Rab C Nesbitt* fame. His portrayal of the devious owner of the indefatigable boat, 'The Vital Spark' in *Tales of Para Handy* displayed an able foil to Gregor Fisher's wily captain. His most recent role was that of Hamish MacBoan in *The Crow Road*.

Relaxing in the television lounge after our most agreeable meal, we noticed an elderly gentleman sitting nearby with a newspaper incongruously folded over the top of his head. He was engrossed in the television programme, seemingly oblivious to the puzzled glances from those around him. No-one had the courage to ask him why he needed a newspaper on his head, there was evidently no danger of sunburn. Eventually he left the room to an outbreak of sniggering and ribald jokes. We thought no more about the incident until the following morning when we saw him depart amidst a cloud of smoke in a clapped-out Volkswagen.

Now that the Rannoch Moor section of our walk lay behind us, there was no longer the nagging fear of losing our way. Consequently I slipped into blissful semi-consciousness until I was shaken by Maurice and told that it was time to turn in and I could not spend the night in that soporific lounge.

DAY FIFTEEN:KINGSHOUSE - KINLOCHLEVEN

The ubiquitous sun beamed upon us as we left the hotel to rejoin the Old Military Road that runs north-west to Altnafeadh and the head of Glen Coe. Our view was dominated by the gaunt triangle of Stob Dearg, (3352 feet) the most impressive peak of Buachaille Etive Mor, looking distinctly like a volcano with solidified lava spattering its wrinkled slopes. The distant hump of the iron bridge that carries the A82 road over the River Etive was dwarfed by its great bulk and appeared incongruous in such a bare landscape.

Boots scuffed the track behind us and we turned to greet two young men who had seemingly appeared from nowhere. We discovered that they were attempting to walk the Way in four days, which meant covering twenty-four miles each day, a formidable task. On target so far, they had apparently set out from Bridge of Orchy that morning and covered the twelve miles to Kingshouse in a remarkable three hours. Maurice and I felt positively pedestrian compared to these high-speed performers. Wishing them luck we watched them forge ahead at a punishing rate. Speed is all very well, but at what price? Records boost the ego, but allow no time for absorbing views or enjoying your surroundings. We pitied those supermen who charged from sight, heads down, with only the ground to contemplate.

Stimulated by the untamed environment we soon arrived at the tiny outpost of Altnafeadh nestling by the A82 road where it enters Glen Coe. In a layby at the bottom of the Devil's Staircase stood the Volkswagen that had torn away from our hotel a little earlier. It's owner was nowhere to be seen, but all his belongings were strewn on the car's seats and covered over with newspapers. Recalling the episode of the previous evening, Maurice and I joked that its owner had to be a frustrated journalist.

The writhing track of the Devil's Staircase snaked above us, certain to demand sweat and toil. Brushing aside our anxiety we turned towards Glen Coe, determined not to miss out on a golden opportunity. Its bold, granite peaks beckoned, inviting us to enter the 'Jaws of Death' as the entrance to the pass itself is known, another reminder of the carnage that was wreaked within it. We left the Old Military Road, to which we would return for our journey to Kinlochleven, and struck across the fellside, where our path traversed the headwaters of the River Coe, passing sparkling streams that congregate in the valley-floor for a journey to Loch Leven. Glen Coe exuded a distinct starkness and lack of vegetation as we approached the pass, where the mountains crowd in on either side, squeezing the road and infant river into an intimidating channel between them. Pausing at 'The Study', a flat-topped rock, we had a grandstand view of the river plunging through the gorge beneath a high waterfall and flowing through a series of pools towards the Meeting of Three Waters.

From our vantage point the dramatic character of the pass was revealed. Formed by a massive ring fault, it is bounded by 3000 foot mountains shaped by millions of years of subsequent erosion. Maurice and I had anticipated an eerie and atmospheric place, heavy with vibrations of evil slaughter, but this was not the case. Our perception was one of austere beauty, enhanced by benevolent sunshine.

Anxious to see as much of the pass as time would allow we descended to the valley floor and hurried to the bridge at the Meeting of Three Waters, where we stared in admiration at the three streams tumbling from the granite corries of the Three Sisters. Now in the heart of the pass we stood by the side of the A82 and watched it snaking through the great defile towards Glencoe village and eventually Ballachulish where it crosses Loch Leven. There was no proper road through the pass at the time of the massacre which occurred in the early hours of a February morning in 1692. If there had been the consequences could have been even more dire. It may have aided the Campbells in taking up their positions at either end of the glen, thereby rendering escape impossible for the MacDonalds. Few are unaware of the Massacre of Glen Coe, even though its butchery was often equalled in the annals of Scottish history. What made this particular carnage unique and unforgivable was the associated political intrigue and the systematic arrangement of mass murder by responsible government figures, supported by the Hanoverian King. It all began when MacIain, the chief of the MacDonalds, was late in swearing allegiance to King William, as all clan leaders were ordered to do. The Secretary of State for Scotland cunningly decided to take advantage of the hatred by other factions for the troublesome MacDonalds and make an example of them. He set the train of events in motion by ordering 120 men of the Argyll's regiment, consisting mainly of Campbells, to billet themselves with the unsuspecting MacDonalds. Led by Campbell of Glenlyon, who was related to MacIain by marriage, they were welcomed as friends. On the day before the massacre, other detachments were dispatched to cordon off the glen, but fortunately for the MacDonalds, they encountered blizzards and were late in arriving.

At five o'clock on the morning of the 13th of February, Glenlyon and his troops stealthily arose and put to the sword any poor victims that they could lay their hands on. Forty MacDonalds were slain, including MacIain and his wife and the remainder fled into the hills, under cover of the violent snowstorm, where many died from exposure. Some escaped through the unsecured end of the pass. The story does end more happily, for the MacDonalds later resettled in the glen and enthusiastically fought for the Stuart Kings in the uprisings of 1715 and 1745.

Keeping a wary eye peeled for any marauding Campbells, Maurice and I beat a hasty retreat from the pass; only because we were short of time, you understand. We hurriedly returned to Altnafeadh where we were confronted by the untamed Devil's Staircase. As we began our tortuous climb we were accompanied by a tourist who trained a Camcorder on us. Maurice flashed a broad smile at the cameraman from beneath his knotted handkerchief, now regular attire, realising that we would be starring in the man's home video. We were haunted by him for quite a distance before the gradient forced him to return to his family. With a farewell wave, Maurice and I battled up the remorseless slope. It proved hot and demanding work and our sweat mingled with the dust of the track. We stopped several times, hands on knees, gulping air. Our torment proved worthwhile, for as we lurched over its crest to collapse onto the summit cairn, a superb panorama was revealed, which wreaked a remarkable transformation in us. The ravages of exhaustion were replaced by wide-eyed wonderment as we recovered our composure. To the north an herculean range of mountains shimmered beyond the colourful green cleft of the Leven valley. White spumes of cloud lazed in a vibrant blue backdrop above the Mamore Forest and the distant Ben Nevis range. Very few days could match this, with air so clear that every detail stood out in stark relief. The snowy crown of Ben Nevis was clearly exposed and the Mamore mountains carved a jagged imprint in the massive canvas. Our interlude on the rough summit cairn proved to be one of the highlights of the West Highland Way; superb weather, cooling drinks and unforgettable views. Rations that day consisted solely of liquid and fruit; solid food had been abandoned. This proved to be a wise decision for the searing heat had made us wringing wet.

Contentedly sipping our revitalising drinks we watched other walkers struggling from the valleys on either side and several stopped to rest and admire the view. Amongst them were two elderly ladies who were walking the Way in the opposite direction. Unlike Maurice and I, who had only a further one and a half days to its completion at Fort William, they had the majority of their traverse ahead of them. Both ladies were slightly built, very thin and remarkably fit. They were in fact relishing their walk and in very optimistic mood. As they disappeared down the Devil's Staircase I remarked to Maurice that neither would be of much use in a cannibal's stewpot.

Greatly refreshed, we began the long descent to Kinlochleven by crossing an expanse of bleak moorland. The featureless terrain was relieved by the Blackwater Dam and Reservoir that lies at the head of the Leven valley. Constructed between 1905 and 1909 it supplies power to the large aluminium works in Kinlochleven. During the building of this vital source of hydro-electric power, an army of navvies was encamped in harsh conditions on the wild moor. Tales are told of workers dying of exposure in the deep snows of winter whilst travelling to, or returning from, the Kingshouse Hotel.

We were jerked from our conversation by a pair of curlews that startled us with their warning cries as they flew overhead. They were obviously wary of any approach to their nest and they circled watchfully at a safe distance. Fortunately they did not resort to the divebombing tactics sometimes employed by lapwings when faced with intruders.

Eventually the barren moorland receded and attractive birchwood coated the steepening valley-sides. Across the valley, the shapely upthrust of the mountains of the Mamore Forest crowned a splendid scene. This was the setting for an episode in Robert Louis Stephenson's *Kidnapped* which features the flight of Alan Breck and David Balfour after the Appin murder.

Beneath us a series of huge pipes hurtled down the valley at an alarming angle, transporting innumerable gallons of water to the factory set in its heart. The huge British Aluminium Works dominates the town of Kinlochleven that is set in otherwise delightful surroundings. The attractive azure waters of Loch Leven lap at its back door and steep, wooded slopes enclose it. The imposition of the sprawling factory buildings on its outskirts represent a necessary evil, for they form the lifeblood of the community, providing an oasis of employment in an otherwise rural area.

As the late afternoon shadows lengthened, Maurice and I entered Kinlochleven and strolled through the outskirts searching for our accommodation. We discovered the pleasant house, evidently undergoing significant renovation, in a quiet, tree-lined road. Building materials littered the front garden, and scaffolding still clung to one of the newly-rendered walls, as we approached the entrance porch to remove our dusty boots. We were welcomed by the friendly mother of the family that had recently taken occupancy and introduced to her husband and children who appeared dour and taciturn by comparison. In fact, they hardly uttered a word during our time there. Luckily we had a couple of fellow-guests, also walkers, for company at mealtimes, otherwise they would have been silent affairs. Flora, the mother, busied herself in the kitchen whilst her husband James waited at table. The food was dumped unceremoniously in front of us in dead silence. Recalling the saying 'If you see someone without a smile, give them one of yours', I deliberately smiled pleasantly at him during one of his forays with our food, but his stern features never moved. This was very uncharacteristic of the hospitality that we normally enjoyed and I charitably imagined that a pleasant person must lurk behind this gruff exterior. Flora, by contrast, chatted freely whenever the opportunity arose, telling us stories of the town and its inhabitants. She recalled some disasters that had occurred during the house renovation, and remarked how glad she was that it was nearing completion. Their pain of enduring upheaval for nine months, instead of the projected four, was just beginning to recede.

After supper Maurice and I wandered around the town amidst some splendid scenery and I was kept busy photographing the surrounding hills which glowed resplendently in the colourful evening light. The town centre was completely deserted, reminiscent of a Western film where nothing moves apart from occasional brushwood rolling lazily across the street and the plaintive howl of a prairie dog shatters the eerie silence. Maurice commented that the local inhabitants must be exhausted after a hard day at the factory and were stretched out in front of the television. Now devoid of all but local traffic the place resembled a ghost town. Apparently it used to be a busier place before the bridge over Loch Leven was built at Ballachulish. At that time traffic passed through Kinlochleven on its way to Fort William, as an alternative to the ferry where the bridge now stands.

DAY SIXTEEN: KINLOCHLEVEN - FORT WILLIAM

The hardest work of our final day on the West Highland Way came at the outset when we grappled with a demanding climb from the Leven valley. Maurice and I tackled this with determination knowing that only fourteen miles lay between us and Fort William. Surprise, surprise, the sun was accompanying us once more. If you are becoming sceptical of my endless accounts of sunny days, believing that no-one can enjoy such weather in Scotland, let me assure you that this remarkable sequence was to last for several more days. The locals were incredulous, shaking their heads in wonder at the lack of the familiar mist and rain.

Birds sang and the sun's searching rays filtered through birchwood and pines as we hauled ourselves, already hot and legs protesting, to the entrance of a gorge, through which jingled the pleasant Alt Nathrach. Here we joined a track that traverses the hillside from Mamore Lodge, a reminder of the sporting attraction of the Mamore Forest, once a very popular deer-stalking area. Stopping to catch our breath we were treated to an invigorating view across Loch Leven, with the magnificent profile of the mountains of Appin and Glencoe towering above the conspicuous and slender blue sheet of water that stretched seawards.

Progress was much easier as we headed through the gorge towards the Lairigmor Pass and the hillsides enveloped us, blotting out further views. To keep him amused, I told Maurice that we were now in the ancient province of Lochaber that was mentioned in his beloved song *The Road to the Isles*. This was a mistake, for I was immediately berated once more with the lusty strains of 'By Tummel and Loch Rannoch and Lochaber I will go .....' Eventually his Kenneth MacKeller impression subsided as he sheepishly confessed that he had always believed Lochaber to be a loch, but could never find it on the map. My laughter was cut short when he burst into song once more. He was obviously in a buoyant mood, so I sent him ahead of me to keep him out of earshot, where he could sing to his heart's content. As the sun became fiercer, out came his knotted handkerchief and, as he was about to don it once more, I suggested that he tied it over his mouth instead. Unabashed, his singing continued to reverberate from the surrounding hillsides as we followed the undulating track towards the head of the pass at Lairigmor, which proved to be nothing more than an abject ruin. Here the glen widened and our track skirted the foot of Meall a'Chaorainn. Rabbits scurried from our sight and a skylark hovered at a safe distance like a feathered helicopter, joining Maurice in joyful song. The occasional grouse flew from the grass indignantly calling 'Go back...go back...' I assured Maurice that they were only protesting at his raucous singing. The itinerant sheep seemed oblivious to his noise and unconcernedly cropped the rough vegetation, casting desultory glances in our direction to ensure that we posed no threat. Formerly they would have shared their upland grazing with the cattle that were brought from the valleys in mid-summer to the numerous sheilings that formerly dotted the hillsides. Very little now remains of those rough stone dwellings where the women and children tended their herds whilst the menfolk looked after the crofts.

An extensive Forestry Commission plantation loomed, but Maurice, undeterred, strode onwards, confident that the Old Military Road would guide us unerringly through it. John Hillaby expresses the hope that 'one day there will be a track through the length of the Highlands'. If his dream was to materialise, I can think of no better basis for such a long-distance route than the Old Military Road network that had served Maurice and me so well since joining it in Glen Falloch. The establishment of a track that traverses the full extent of the Highlands would also bring closer the prospect of a recognised route for walkers that spans the length of Britain.

It was hard to keep pace with Maurice who was evidently spurred on by the culmination of the West Highland Way, that lay tantalisingly within our grasp. The lure of a celebration at Fort William was obviously driving him on. When I suggested that many hours remained before our rendezvous, he merely smiled and wedged his knotted handkerchief, now noticeably damp, more firmly over his head. He did spare the time to stop whilst we spoke to several passing walkers who were roughly halfway through their first day of a north to south traverse of the Way. They were all eager to know what Rannoch Moor was like.

Emerging from the forest we caught sight of the diminutive Lochan Lunn Da Bhra, its waters shining temptingly in the distance. Maurice and I could have killed for a refreshing dip in it. However, we were mindful of the legend concerning the mythical 'waterbull' that supposedly emerges from its waters to drag unsuspecting victims in to drown. Being devout cowards we kept well out of reach. Also according to legend Macbeth was killed in a castle that formerly stood on an island in the loch, which even we knew was inaccurate. There is however, a positive local link with Banquo, his fellow-general. He was Thane of Lochaber and lived at Tor Castle, three miles from Fort William, beside the River Lochy. The adjacent stretch of riverbank is still known as Banquo's Walk.

A gate marked an unfortunate parting of the ways. The Old Military Road deserted us at that point and headed for Fort William by an alternative route, having metamorphosised into a narrow tarmac road. The Way, inflicting a final sting, lured us uphill. As momentary respite from climbing our last gradient of the day I paused to take a shot of the full extent of Lochan Lunn Da Bhra. I was surprised to see the Glasgow nurses, strung out in a long line below us, who were evidently going to finish their stint and hopefully collect a significant amount of sponsorship money. They had obviously been following Maurice and me through the forest, hidden by the all-embracing spruce and alder. We waited for the leader to reach us with slow, but determined, steps. As she stopped to recover her breath and mop her dripping brow she quipped that the fierce sun was keeping her weight down. We admired her tenacity and that of her companions. It was a real test for novice walkers and they had come through with flying colours, despite the continual, intense heat. She was clearly elated that they were about to win their battle against rapacious blisters and fatigue without losing any of their team. Suggesting that we carried on, she sat down to wait for the stragglers with a promise that they would meet us that evening at our planned gathering. The jungle telegraph was obviously alive and well, for they had heard about it from several sources.

Maurice's relief was plain when we began to descend a little time later signifying that the most demanding part of the day's walk was over. We were eager for our first glimpse of Ben Nevis (4418 feet) that we knew from the map lay across the deep furrow of Glen Nevis, but was obscured from view. In a clearing amidst relenting spruce our hopes were fulfilled as the massive khaki dome of the Ben thrust skywards, its summit liberally carpeted with snow. As we gazed at its awesome presence we began to doubt the wisdom of scaling it on the following day. Trying to overcome our anxiety with flippancy, we joked that such a little hill would not defeat us. It happens to be the highest little hill in Britain!

Unable to keep our eyes from the Ben, we broke Wainwright's cardinal rule of watching where we placed our feet, I tripped over a stone, stumbled and collided with Maurice who just managed to stay upright. We agreed to look where we were going in future, having nearly come to grief by searching the enlarging slopes of the mountain for evidence of a path.

A little farther on in another clearing sat Paul and Jean, resting on tree stumps. We chatted about Ben Nevis and the magnificent, but energy-sapping weather, that showed no signs of abating. Paul was quite taken with Maurice's distinctive headgear. He complained of having to constantly mop his dripping brow. A knotted hanky, he reckoned, would be just the thing. Despite a ribbing from me he carefully knotted his own handkerchief and emulated Maurice, who suggested that I take a photograph of their sporty headgear. Jean, not to be outdone, also got in on the act and joined 'The Knotted Handkerchief Club', as I dubbed them. Maurice was over the moon, convinced that his headgear had been completely exonerated by an accomplished actor. I whinged that, as a result, he would never take it off and even wear the wretched thing in bed.

Bidding farewell to the friendly couple we zig-zagged through mature larches, pausing periodically to scrutinise Ben Nevis. Its rugged features were now exposed and great gashes, scoured by the elements, cleaved its enormous crest. A smooth thread was discernible, snaking up its tortuous slopes. This was the elusive path, its alarming gradient demonstrating what the mountain had in store for us.

The Nevis Forest, through which we were walking, stretches to the mouth of Glen Nevis and almost to Fort William, but we dropped out of the trees and down a spur of the Way to the heart of the glen that accommodates Glen Nevis House and a Youth Hostel. The appealing valley seemed a very popular spot for holidaymakers and campers, its lush, green floor providing a pleasant contrast to our miles of forest-walking. We made for the Youth Hostel, which stands conveniently near the path to Ben Nevis and found the starting point of our next day's climb. The shape of the Ben's summit had changed for it now towered over us looking even more unassailable.

Outside the hostel we met one of the rangers responsible for the management of the West Highland Way. He covered the section between Bridge of Orchy and Fort William and was eager to hear our views of it. We told him that the route was well maintained and generally easy to follow and that our accommodation had been good. Indicating that only the extensive forests had marred an immensely enjoyable walk, we cheekily added that we would allow him a few months to clear them. Smiling broadly, he retorted that we were hard taskmasters, but he would see what could be done. We also asked if he laid on such superb weather for all West Highland Way walkers, but he replied that the past week had been exceptional and unfortunately he could take no credit for it. He was very interested to hear of my walk to John O'Groats, and hinted that the section through Wester Ross and Sutherland could be desolate and very lonely. He wished us both well and said that he hoped that the weather held, especially for my lone trip through the wilds of the north-west.

Rather than retreat into the forest again, Maurice and I followed the road that runs through the glen for the final two miles to Fort William. Numerous camping sites and picnic areas flecked the valley, through which scurries the appealing River Nevis, eager to join Loch Linnhe on its journey to the sea. At the mouth of the glen the hills receded and the wide basin at the head of Loch Linnhe spread before us. Amidst this sheltered setting nestles the town itself, bounded by disconcerting industrial sites. The suburbs present an urban sprawl when compared to the smaller settlements found on the Way. At the junction of the Glen Nevis road and the ubiquitous A82 on the outskirts of Fort William, the West Highland Way gracefully bows out, having completed its ninety-five mile journey. Maurice and I pumped each other's hand in celebration. Despite missing out the initial section from Milngarvie to Inversnaid, we were thrilled to complete an extremely satisfying walk through an exhilarating part of the Scottish Highlands. It was a double celebration on my part for the 250 mile point had been passed; almost the halfway mark. Maurice promised me an extra-large drink that evening in recognition of my achievement.

Having time in hand we seized the opportunity to explore the historic town whose name originated from the fort that formerly stood where the River Nevis flows into Loch Linnhe. Built in 1654 by General Monck, it is strategically sited at the south-west end of the Great Glen, which lies along a geological fault line that effectively cuts Scotland in two. Monck constructed garrisons at either end of the glen when he was sent to Lochaber to restore law and order following the covenanting conflicts. The local fort's condition was allowed to decline during the reign of Charles II, but it was repaired at the accession of William of Orange. Grateful townspeople gave it the name Fort William in honour of the Dutch King. The town had originally been named Inverlochy, by Monck, after the nearby castle that still stands in a beautiful setting two miles to the north-east. For anyone wishing to stay at the castle, which has been converted into a splendid hotel, it will set you back well over £100 per person per night. Some may think this is a small price to pay for such luxurious accommodation in stunning surroundings, others may not.

The modern town is a bright, attractive place, plainly accustomed to the hustle and bustle of its many visitors. Maurice and I were lured to its main shopping street, on the lookout for souvenirs and postcards. Its shops cater for a variety of needs and tastes which emphasise the town's importance as the major shopping centre in the west of Scotland, north of Glasgow.

Whilst searching for the hotel, where our rendezvous was planned later that evening, we felt the overwhelming presence of mighty Ben Nevis that rises majestically behind the town. It appeared to follow our every move, taunting us to take up the challenge of its fearsome inclines. A night's rest was thankfully due before we made our assault and time dictated that we hurried to our guesthouse, situated on a quiet outlying street. It offered superb views from its upper windows over the blue waters of Loch Linnhe as it curves towards Corpach.

At supper we were entertained by a gregarious American couple enjoying a tour of the Highlands. They were captivated by their first visit to Scotland and enquired if the weather was always so wonderful. Maurice replied that it did have its moments. By the end of the meal we knew much about their home city of Detroit where the husband, Floyd, was a senior lecturer. His wife, Jane, enthused about their daughter who was taking a sabbatical from college and touring Europe.

Begging the use of an iron, Maurice and I attacked our crumpled casual clothes that had suffered continual crushing in our rucksacks. Looking vaguely presentable we headed for the hotel in the cool of the evening. On our arrival we were delighted to see so many of our friends. Virtually everyone that we had met along the Way had turned up, together with walkers that we did not know. Excitement was at fever pitch amidst much laughter and conviviality. Everyone seemed determined to let their hair down and enjoy themselves. The nurses were in good form, cheekily moving through the throng demanding sponsorship money. Reg, still hobbling, was delighted to be there, but had not yet been given a new pair of feet. I told him to take the weight off his blisters and give them some respite. Don, Derek and Peter were already planning their next long-distance challenge, considering themselves hardened veterans now that they had several successful completions under their belt.

The celebratory mood was bolstered by a sing-song accompanied by an accomplished accordionist. After many Scottish renditions, the Aberdeen lads demanded *Flower of Scotland* which I felt was becoming excessively patriotic. English pride was at stake, so, after being subjected to 'sending proud Edward's army homewards to think again' I bribed the accordionist to play *On Ilkley Moor Bah't At.* Yorkshire's national anthem was belted out with relish by the English contingent, which prompted a taunt that we Sassenachs might consider ourselves good singers, but we were hopeless at dancing. We were dared to participate in some eightsome reels; not in the hotel, but on the pavement outside in the full view of passers by. Undaunted, we took up the challenge, flinging ourselves into the fray much to the amazement of open-mouthed onlookers. It proved an exhilarating experience which bolstered the camaraderie when the Scots saw that we were willing to have a go. The illicit dancing crowned a memorable evening that ended with *Auld Lang Syne* and a horde of weak-kneed walkers staggering away to their beds. A fine preparation for climbing Ben Nevis!

CHAPTER THREE

Ben Nevis, The Great Glen and Glen Shiel

DAY SEVENTEEN: FORT WILLIAM - SPEAN BRIDGE

Not surprisingly, Maurice and I were not at our best the following morning. Throbbing heads and an inability to concentrate plagued us during breakfast. The American couple were full of lively chatter, in stark contrast to our occasional mumblings. What must they have thought of our surliness? Perhaps they attributed it to the characteristic British reticence. Whilst they enthused over their plans for the day, our thoughts were elsewhere; on the forthcoming 4,418 foot climb, God help us!

Ben Nevis marked the start of the second phase of our journey together, which would take us eventually to Shiel Bridge. Many walkers celebrate a successful completion of the West Highland Way by climbing Ben Nevis, but how many live it up on the previous evening and severely jeopardise their chances? Some consolation was gleaned from the thought that a few more aspirants would be feeling just as bad as us on that daunting morning. Floyd was no comfort, for he related some sobering advice given by a clergyman in 1793 to prospective Ben Nevis climbers. It advocated allowing seven hours for the climb, if we wished to take in our surroundings, and declared that we would not escape a feeling of fatigue for a day or two after. Nothing was mentioned about feeling weary before we had even started. One thing turned in our favour, however, for Floyd had helpfully offered to take our rucksacks to Spean Bridge, our final destination that day. They were conveniently driving through the Great Glen to Inverness and would pass our guesthouse that lay on the main road through that village. This manna from heaven relieved us of the burden of cumbersome rucksacks for a whole day and meant that we could climb Ben Nevis unimpeded. Gratefully we packed the day's rations and some weatherproof clothing into a plastic carrier bag.

Despite the weather maintaining its incredible sequence we knew that conditions could easily turn nasty at high altitude. The roof of Ben Nevis, we learned, gets only two hours of bright sunshine per day on average, as atmospheric condensation often causes the summit to be shrouded in cloud when the remainder of the sky is clear.

In pensive mood we retraced our steps of the previous afternoon towards the Youth Hostel in Glen Nevis. Our movement was leaden in the glorious sunshine, but eventually the fresh air began to clear our heads and dispel the lethargy. By the time we had reached the start of the steep path running up the hillside near the hostel we felt ready to rejoin the human race.

The severe gradient hit us with a vengeance, quickly making us breathless and tormenting our limbs. This was not going to be a good day. Here we were on the initial slope and suffering already. Several halts were needed to catch our breath, and ease protesting muscles, until we reached the pony track that ascends from Achintee Farm. This track signifies the main route up the mountain and was originally laid to serve an observatory, situated on the summit, that supplied meteorological data around the turn of the century. We looked apprehensively along the rising track that agonisingly climbed the steep south-west slope of Meall an t-Suidhe. Steeling ourselves, we struck out along its rough surface, baked hard by the late spring sunshine. We had resolved to proceed steadily and to try and conserve what little energy we had; no records would be broken that day. Consequently stops were frequent and drinks were sipped to

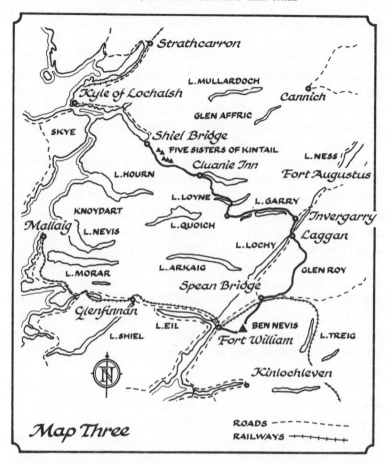

Map Three

ROADS -----------
RAILWAYS ++++++++++

combat the searching sunshine. Resting on one of the tiny iron bridges that crossed the numerous streams hurtling down the mountainside we looked out over Glen Nevis. The green sward of Nevis Forest clothed the hillsides opposite, relenting eventually to reveal a scattering of tiny farms, dwellings and camp-sites set amongst the meadows and cultivated fields of the valley-floor. Standing out clearly beyond the tree-lined ribbon of road that wound lazily through the glen was the Youth Hostel, which already seemed an age away. Above us we were aware of the cascading slope of the mountain, from which we deliberately averted our eyes.

A steady stream of people were climbing the track, in all kinds of attire ranging from light summer wear, to full walking outfits. Ben Nevis was obviously an attraction for holiday-makers as well as walkers and climbers, which pricked our consciences at being passed so easily by sightseers. Our earlier resolve forgotten, we began to pick up the pace and remarkably got our second wind. We made steady progress around the southern shoulder of Meall an t-Suidhe, overtaking some of the people who had recently passed us. Amongst them was a friendly party of Americans who exchanged good-natured banter as we passed. They offered a race to the summit, with free cups of tea as the prize, which would be difficult to claim unless there was a newly built café up there.

The track steepened and clawed its way to the crest of a snug basin in which reclines tiny Lochan Meall an t-Suidhe. Welcome respite came with a short descent into this secluded valley, which brought us to a significant junction of tracks, where we met the alternative northern approach route that we planned to use for our descent to the Great Glen. Here the track nearly doubles back on itself as it eases across the slopes of Carn Dearg before commencing a series of strenuous zigzags towards the summit of Ben Nevis itself. Maurice and I were pleased to note that we had already attained 2000 feet, nearly half of the total ascent, but this was soon forgotten as the ferocity of the gradients began to take their toll. The loose stones that littered the track were a hindrance, frequently causing us to glide backwards.

The plastic carrier bag that Maurice and I were carrying in turn had now aroused considerable interest amongst fellow-strugglers. Several enquired if we were on a shopping trip, or expecting to find a supermarket on the summit. What caught people's eye was the word 'Virgin' emblazoned on the bag, an advertisement for Virgin Airways. We quipped that it wasn't every day that a virgin was carried up Ben Nevis.

In intense heat, despite the altitude, we reached the first snowfield and our steps slowed as we negotiated the soft, white carpet that overlaid the shattered rock fragments littering the mountainside. All vegetation had disappeared. Pausing for breath, we enjoyed a captivating view over Meall an t-Suidhe and its attendant lochan, whose rich blue waters contrasted vividly with the snow beneath our feet. The wide sweep of Loch Linnhe was visible beyond Meall an t-Suidhe, with the minuscule buildings of Fort William and Corpach hugging its ponderous curve. How long ago it seemed since we had left the guesthouse.

As we completed the traverse of the snowfield, its virgin-white surface now stained by a multitude of grey footprints, the jagged teeth of the Mamore summits appeared amidst the distant haze of that sunlit morning. They looked even more majestic from this viewpoint. More tripping and skating over myriad stones brought us within sight of the summit ridge of Ben Nevis, heavily be-decked with snow. This had a galvanising effect as we summoned our remaining strength for the final push.

Conditions underfoot improved, the stones on the path had compacted and Maurice forged ahead as I took a photograph of the approaching summit. He looked resolute, combating the heat with rolled up trouser legs and shirt sleeves, but the knotted handkerchief was conspicuously absent. Was he embarrassed at wearing it in the midst of so many people I wondered?

A final snowfield separated us from the summit plateau and tiny figures tottered across it beneath a huge cloud that was drifting towards us. Alarm bells rang, for above the Mamores a barrage of fleecy-white clouds was also hovering. Was the bubble of good fortune about to burst and make the superb views disappear? Uneasily, I recalled the description that I had read concerning the harsh conditions on the Ben's summit, which included gales for eight months of the year that sometimes reached hurricane force, and the atmospheric condensation mentioned earlier. My worries proved unfounded, for despite a tugging wind, the sun continued to shine merrily, despatching the menacing clouds.

As we plodded through the snowfield I was able to study several structures on the summit, all of which were constructed from the indigenous stones. The rather incongruous red roof of a shelter stood out above the largest configuration, which turned out to be the ruins of the observatory. After its original demise in 1904 it was surprisingly used as a hotel for a period. We thought of an eye-catching advertisement for such a lofty retreat; 'Situated in remote and quiet surroundings at an altitude of a mere 4,418 feet. Superb unimpeded views for two full hours per day. Guests should be physically fit and carry ice axes, ropes and survival kit. No car parking facilities.'

Once the summit plateau was attained the hard work was over. During our ascent the sun had resembled a giant toaster, under which we were roasted, wrung dry and finally ejected on to the roof of the mountain, where it was still amazingly warm. Surely we had no perspiration left as we made the final assault on the beckoning finger of the trig point which was surrounded by an excited crowd.

It perched on a broad, flat cairn, and as we approached many people reclined around us, enjoying the sunshine. Some were clad only in shorts and sweatshirts, despite the snowy surroundings, as they took respite on rocky outcrops. We passed a memorial cairn, Britain's highest, near the remains of the observatory, which displayed a wreath of bright red poppies.

Maurice, who had noticed a Union Jack fluttering proudly on top of the trig point, remarkably leapt up to it for a triumphant 'lean', in anticipation of a celebratory photograph. I quickly obliged and then joined him at the column when a passer-by kindly offered to photograph us both.

Searching for a suitable resting place on the roof of Britain we eventually perched on some rocks that overlooked the sheer north-facing cliffs. The view was probably the most dramatic that the mountain offered, for the ground fell away beneath us for a staggering 2000 feet to the head of the Allt a' Mhuilinn valley. A landscape of rugged mountains, penetrated by yawning valleys peppered with shimmering lochs, stretched as far as the eye could see. Through this awesome panorama cleaved the gigantic gash of the Great Glen.

Whilst ravenously tearing at our rations we conversed with an amiable walker sitting nearby, whose name, we discovered, was Arthur. He was no stranger to the mountain, having scaled it many times. He described some of its other interesting features, which include the intimidating southern approach to the summit, that comprises the longest and steepest hill slope in Britain. Striking upwards from the termination of the Glen Nevis road, it rises relentlessly for 4,000 feet at an incredible angle of thirty-five degrees, virtually reaching the summit. Eat your heart out Ben More, I thought, this makes your most striking gradient seem like a gentle slope.

Arthur enquired how long our ascent had taken and we sheepishly told him, three and a quarter hours. Surprisingly we learned that the average time was three and a half hours. We had not done badly, despite our slow start. As Maurice peered cautiously over the cliff-edge, Arthur jokingly suggested that we took the quickest possible descent, down the precipice. That hazardous challenge was best left to climbers, we said, reeling at the thought. To experienced mountaineers, Arthur ventured, the profusion of tortuous gullies, some of which were still compacted with snow, were well-known territory and most were known by name.

Time and tide wait for no man - sorry ladies - no person, and we grudgingly took our leave; we had to reach Spean Bridge by early evening. Clouds were energetically scudding overhead, but posing no real threat, as we began a fairly rapid, but occasionally heart-stopping, descent. Frequently we were transported, faster than intended, on rafts of loose stones that threatened to launch us into oblivion. Many people were still toiling upwards, some anxiously enquiring how much farther it was to the summit.

In what seemed a remarkably short space of time we arrived at the junction of tracks near Lochan Meall an t-Suidhe, its placid, sheltered waters seeming to welcome our return. Here we changed course, taking the alternative track that contours the northern slopes of Carn Dearg to reach the Mountain Rescue hut at the head of the Allt a'Mhuilinn valley. The burn has cut a deep cleft between Carn Dearg and Carn Beag Dearg, gathering the waters of numerous rushing streams as it plunges towards its rendezvous with the River Lochy, far below. Maurice and I scrambled, as hastily as was prudent, down the valley, stopping occasionally to admire some arresting views over the Great Glen. The unavoidable A82 road coursed beneath the vast Leanachan Forest bound for Spean Bridge and minute Inverlochy Castle snuggled amongst serene surroundings 1000 feet below us. To the north-west, where Loch Linnie and Loch Eil meet at the connecting channel called The Narrows, the dominant Pulp and Paper Mills of Corpach intruded into an otherwise gentle scene. A ferryboat wound lazily from Fort William's pier, bound for the jetty at tiny Camusnagaul on the opposite shore of Loch Linnhe.

Descending to the western fringe of Leanachan Forest, we deserted the Allt a'Mhuilinn to head into its restrictive confines on one of those dire forestry tracks. Landmarks were non-existent as we ploughed through a series of confusing arboreal tunnels, searching for tiny Creag Aoil that lies secreted in the depths of the forest. From the freedom of the heights we had been plunged into an oppressive prison of never-ending trees, where all tracks looked identical. After some cursing and back-tracking we eventually found our objective, whose link with the outside world is the narrow road to Torlundy. Just beyond this isolated outpost we were relieved to find the track that heads north to Tom na Brataich in the Great Glen.

On reaching the Glen the roar of traffic speeding along the nearby A82 road confronted us as we joined the line of General

Wade's road. This formerly traversed the Great Glen, from Fort William to Inverness and the General embarked on this demanding venture with a 500 strong road-building squad in 1726. It took several arduous years before the project was completed and some parts of the glen posed severe problems. A typical example was the precipitous rocks at Inverfarigaig, by the shore of Loch Ness, which necessitated blasting. Sections of his Old Military Road still remain, but much of it has been obliterated by the modern A82 road.

Our strength was beginning to ebb away as we pushed towards Spean Bridge, with three miles still remaining. The combined effect of our mountain climb and the struggle through the forest was taking its toll. Tired legs and protesting bodies forced us to take a breather. Our condition was hardly surprising when we discovered that we had already completed sixteen tough miles. I was chastised for over ambitious route-planning by Maurice who had expected a short day's walk in mileage terms. I assured him that we would be in good time for supper and after a night's rest we would be as fit as fleas. He didn't seem convinced.

There is a saying that the longest mile of any journey is the last one and this proved very apt as we struggled to keep walking. Afternoon dissolved into evening as we dragged ourselves over the final interminable mile and entered Spean Bridge with profound relief. We barely noticed the attractive stone bridge straddling the lively River Spean that gave the village its name. Our attention was rooted on the guesthouse that lay beyond it; sightseeing could wait.

We were solicitously ushered into the entrance hall by Mary, who ran the place with her sister Betty. She confirmed that our rucksacks had been delivered that morning, courtesy of Floyd, who had indicated that we were on our way. Concerned by our weariness she enquired if we were feeling alright as she shepherded us to the lounge. Maurice assured her that a refreshing bath and a good meal would put us in fine fettle. As we sank into comfortable armchairs, she bustled away, to return promptly with welcome tea and biscuits. Apologising for relegating us to the attic floor of the house, due to an overflow of guests, she hoped that we would not be inconvenienced. I foolishly retorted that all we required was a bed to sleep on. This rash statement rebounded on me when, after leading us up several flights of stairs, she entered a cramped attic room, whose effect was claustrophobic. The sun had obviously beaten upon the single window of the sloping ceiling all day and the heat was stifling. Space was at a premium around the twin beds and it was difficult to move about the room. After a struggle I managed to open the small window, its hinges creaking in protest, but it did not provide much relief. The low, sloping ceiling made it virtually impossible to remain upright and our heads were frequently bumped. Maurice escaped to the bathroom and returned with a broad grin on his face. The place, he said, was fit only for hunch-backed Quasimodo, the bathroom being even more cramped than the bedroom. He joked that he could not even sit upright in the bath. From then onwards, as we moved awkwardly around those deadly attic rooms, there were mutterings of 'The Bells' and 'Esmarelda' and we christened the house 'Notre Dame'.

Whimpishly, we did not complain, because we were otherwise treated with the utmost kindness by the well-intentioned sisters. There were obviously no spare rooms and we were not disposed to seek accommodation elsewhere. We kept our peace and hoped that we would not develop permanent humps on our backs.

After a hearty supper we did a spot of local sightseeing. Dusk was falling as we gazed over the broad stone parapet of the bridge along the River Spean, its ripples dancing in the moonlight and casting silvery shimmers into the darkness of the surrounding pines. Feeling tired, but thankfull that Ben Nevis was now behind us, we needed no persuasion to return to our cramped garret. Hopes of a sound sleep were unfortunately ruined by the hot and airless conditions. Bed clothes were flung off in desperation as we tossed and turned, until exhaustion mercifully overtook us in the early hours.

DAY EIGHTEEN: SPEAN BRIDGE - INVERGARRY

For the second morning running we were not at our best. Exhausted by our fitful sleep we stumbled around the attic rooms in a semi-stupor. At breakfast we spoke little amidst the general hum of conversation.

On our departure we were handed substantial packed-lunches by the caring sisters. Not having the heart to voice our complaints we viewed the previous night's discomfort as an experience that would be amusing to look back on. It did provide some humorous interludes later, for in secluded places, away from watching eyes, we mimicked Quasimodo as we lurched along with rolling eyes and lolling tongues.

The initial section of our day's walk lay to the east along Glen Spean, as my route-plan ignored the more direct approach to Invergarry by way of the Great Glen and the shore of Loch Lochy. My reason for this deviation was to escape the hurly-burly of the A82 road that we would be obliged to follow on the direct route. We were seeking the sanctuary of the quiet Glen Roy, that branches from Glen Spean at the village of Roy Bridge, as we set out on yet another sun-drenched morning.

An hour's walking brought us to this pleasant village and judging by the presence of numerous camping and caravan sites, many other people had evidently discovered the attractiveness of verdant Glen Spean. Along the way we met the West Highland Railway again that takes a circuitous route from Rannoch Moor to Fort William in order to avoid the Ben Nevis range. There are several stations on this line within Glen Spean where expectant walkers alight to enjoy journeys into the surrounding foothills or to take a well-trodden path through the mountains from Inverroy to the head of Loch Treig.

Beside a tiny church, a narrow road begins its twisting journey into Glen Roy, which runs parallel to the Great Glen. The good news was that this road would guide us to the head of the eight-mile long glen. The downside was that it terminates at that point, thereby forcing us to take an uncharted route over encircling fells to Laggan that lies deep in the Great Glen. Thrusting this unsavoury prospect to the back of our minds we embarked upon what proved to be a delightful exploration of the secluded glen which was virtually devoid of traffic.

Its lower reaches revealed the quiet and unspoiled beauty of a wide valley coated with colourful meadows interspersed with variegated woodland. Having the area to ourselves rendered us free to perform Quasimodo impressions and sing to our heart's content. The only annoyance in that idyllic setting was the searing heat which became so intense, that, despite my previous chastisement of Maurice's headgear, I relented and donned a knotted handkerchief. The laugh was now on me.

The playful road seemed to snake into infinity ahead of us, its tarmac surface shimmering in the sun's powerful rays. Frequent stops were made to admire retrospective views of the receding Ben Nevis range which jutted into a perfect sky. The only intrusion into this vivid blue canopy was the occasional velvet cloud. A lone car overtook us, heading up the glen, as we passed the tiny settlement of Bohuntinville. Here Maurice enjoyed a luxuriating 'lean' on the long, tubular legs of a signpost whilst he cooled down.

As the glen narrowed it acquired a vastly different aspect. The fells began to crowd in on either side and the green vegetation of the lower slopes ended abruptly and evenly, part-way up their flanks. This remarkable phenomenon stems from the time when spectacular glaciers covered parts of Lochaber. 10,000 years ago a huge glacier dammed the entrance to Glen Roy and waters flowing from the surrounding hills submerged the glen and formed a loch. As the great glacier in the main valley melted the Glen Roy water level dropped and new beaches formed in stages with a resulting series of demarcation lines or 'roads' showing the various water levels as melting took place. These 'roads' could be clearly seen as they scoured the mountain sides in dead straight lines. What we were witnessing were the 'parallel roads', as they have become known, that encircle the upper ends of Glen Roy and its neighbour Glen Gloy.

Through the narrowing valley flows the lively River Roy that rises in the foothills of the Corrieyairack Forest, the old country of the MacDonalds of Keppoch. Its bubbling waters beckoned, a promise of refreshing coolness in every ripple. This was too good an opportunity to miss so we hastened to its bank for a lunch-stop. The bliss of removing red-hot boots and plunging swollen feet into the soothing river was a highlight of our day. Beneath the shady foliage of an accommodating tree we enjoyed a relaxing lunch as our feet dangled in the swirling waters.

When we reached the lonely head of the Glen we found it deserted and the pervading silence was broken only by melodic bird song, a reminder that the area is a Nature Reserve in the care of the Nature Conservancy Council. The moment of truth had arrived. A suitable escape route had to be found over the mountainous barrier that encircled us. Fortune took a hand in the form of a path that wormed its way up a valley that conveniently headed in the required direction.

With only the birds for company Maurice and I began what proved to be an exhausting climb. Initially, all went well as we ascended the gradually sloping path into the foothills, our knotted handkerchiefs thankfully discarded, for the heat was mercifully subsiding. Elation turned to anxiety for the path was merely a false dawn. It soon swung in the wrong direction up a side-valley that had not been visible from the glen. We were forced to abandon it and clamber up a rapidly steepening gully. What had appeared a reasonable climb from below was becoming distinctly uncomfortable. Maurice and I grabbed at the tussocky grass to haul ourselves up the fierce incline. His face was grim as we struggled with this disagreeable turn of events. Progress was painfully slow and our breathing laboured as we forced ourselves to the head of the hostile cleft. At the top we were forced to rest and as we gasped for breath we threw off our rucksacks. The prospect before us was not inviting, for a steep, boggy slope led up to bleak moorland that forms the watershed between the Great Glen and Glen Roy. This climb was certainly no picnic. Leaden legs were dragged through clinging peat as we edged upwards towards the barren and windswept crest that was all of 2000 feet. Maurice's dour features made me regret eschewing the easier and more direct route along the Great Glen. Not a word was uttered during our struggle, Maurice's expression said it all.

At long last we mounted the crest with tortured limbs protesting and lungs heaving. As we began to recover and take in our surroundings we had the compensation of extensive views on either side of us. Ben Nevis and its satellites were still clearly visible beyond Glen Spean, but our attentions were drawn to the beckoning Great Glen that lay to the north-west. My confidence surged at the sight of an oasis of habitation nestling in the glen directly beneath us. This signified that we were dead on course for Laggan. Elated, I tried to reassure Maurice that the worst was over, but once again I was to be proved wrong.

The only visible obstacle on our descent appeared in the form of an ominous band of dense forest that coated the lower mountainside. We made better progress with gravity now in our favour and we were soon approaching the dark velvet curtain of trees. Fixing our position on the map, I hunted for signs of a track through this annoying barrier. There appeared to be a convenient one not far from us, but it unfortunately started within the forest. Taking a compass bearing towards this hopeful lifeline, we descended to the forest's upper boundary where our progress was halted by a wire fence. No stiles were evident and the diffident track was nowhere in sight, so we had to make a decision. We could wander along the fence and search for an opening or a stile, which demanded additional time and distance, or we could climb the fence and hunt for the elusive track. We foolishly chose the latter and risked incurring the wrath of the Forestry Commission. The nightmare events which followed provided a just punishment for our misdemeanour.

We blundered into the mature forest which was carpeted with dense undergrowth. Maurice quipped that he should have brought along his machete as wild briars tore at our legs and we were plagued by swathes of inhospitable bracken. A few minutes of struggling through this crippling assault course wiped the smiles from our faces and reduced us to near exhaustion. Concealed tree roots wickedly added to our discomfort by frequently tripping us and we only narrowly escaped being sent sprawling. There was no sign of a track and after twenty minutes of struggle and sweat I began to despair of ever finding one. We had several false alarms, fighting our way into blind alleys in vain attempts to release ourselves from the energy-sapping foliage. Laggan, that had appeared so reassuringly close a little earlier, had disappeared, beyond an all-pervading green blanket. Eventually we came upon a stream that plunged through a rock-strewn gully. Reckoning that this channel would at least lead us to lower ground and was preferable to grappling with infuriating vegetation, we began to clamber over its mossy boulders. This did little to relieve our tormented limbs and in our exhaustion we began to resign ourselves to never escaping from this arboreal hell-hole.

Unexpectedly, salvation suddenly appeared in the shape of a bridge that carried a track over our tortuous channel. Our delight was tempered by the sight of a dour-looking man leaning on the parapet and observing our antics with keen interest. Too tired to try and avoid him we lurched and stumbled over the remaining rocks that brought us to the bridge. Our worst fears were justified as we clambered onto it. 'What the blazes are you supposed to be doing?' This terse enquiry had us abjectly mumbling about being lost and our hearts sank even lower when we learned that he was employed by the Forestry Commission. He informed us that his organisation didn't take kindly to idiots roaming all over their property and despoiling it. In a pitiful attempt to placate him I profusely apologised. Omitting to tell him how we came to be in the forest, or of our clandestine climb over the fence, I explained that we were heading for Laggan and were searching for a convenient track. Mercifully he did not ask why we had been so far from one, but gave us a lecture on irresponsible behaviour and the necessity of keeping to authorised routes. He demanded to know what would happen if everyone blundered around their forests like rampaging bulls. Feeling like wretched school children being chastised by their teacher we assured him that we would be more careful in the future. Having vented his ire the man indicated the direction that we should take and bade us a curt goodbye. We heaved a huge sigh of relief and although very tired, we scurried away, extremely glad to escape. It was comforting to know that we were back on course and had firm ground beneath our feet.

The track, although easy to follow, frustratingly embarked on a series of broad loops as it descended the steep valley-side and it seemed an eternity before we emerged from cover into an area of recently felled trees. We were still at a sufficient height to enjoy good views along the Great Glen. The head of Loch Lochy lay below us with the tiny settlement of Laggan nestling nearby. In both directions, as far as the eye could see, sparkling blue water covered the valley floor, broken only by the short strip of land that links Loch Lochy and Loch Oich. A line of remarkably symmetrical mountains, pale grey in the distant haze, stood sentinel over Loch Lochy, their lower slopes careering into its deep waters. They provided our first view of Glengarry Forest that dominates the area between Loch Archaig to the south and Loch Garry to the north. A section of the Caledonian Canal was visible, its course closely followed by the A82 road, which we were shortly to cross for the last time.

Beautiful as the views were, Maurice and I were in no mood for hanging around. Our supply of liquid had run out and the dust from the track was irritating our parched throats. Maurice declared that he could murder a pint, but wondered if he had the energy left to find an inn. We were both nearly dead- beat and Maurice didn't think that he could go much further. I began to feel concerned for him, he certainly looked all-in and it was my fault. Shepherding him down to the A82 road, I tried to encourage him with the promise of finding a convenient watering-hole. Too tired to look for a path we tottered along the roadside, our eyes peeled for a pub or café. Just as Maurice reached the end of his tether deliverance materialised in the form of a Watersports Centre just beyond Laggan. By our reckoning, there would be a bar or cafeteria within the complex and we barged in, ignoring the possibility that admission may be for participants only. In no mood for tiresome restrictions we found a bar and tumbled in. I sat Maurice down before he could fall down and quickly obtained two pints of beer from the barman who thankfully asked no questions. Maurice raised the glass to his dry lips and gulped ...and gulped ...and gulped, barely allowing the reviving nectar to touch the sides of his throat. I had barely tasted my drink before Maurice's glass was drained. Still worried about him, I hurried to the bar for another pint which he demolished with consummate ease. Immediately his empty glass touched the table, it was whipped away and replenished. Although the cure was drastic, it seemed to be working, but there was a strong possibility that I would get him blind drunk. His third pint, lovingly savoured, was consumed more slowly and he began to talk between draughts. He had obviously been seriously dehydrated, but I would not recommend my remedy as a normal cure. It would have been prudent to carry more liquid with us and nip any such problems in the bud.

Our hectic interlude had evidently been enjoyed by a couple sitting nearby, to whom I had not given a second glance. The young man, whose face seemed vaguely familiar, said that he had been intrigued by our antics and that Maurice had the makings of a beer-drinking champion. He asked if I recognised him from his visits to the company where I was employed. The realisation dawned that I had done business on a couple of occasions with this smiling sales representative, whose name, I recalled, was John. He introduced his wife, Hazel, who, despite expecting their first baby, was acting as first mate on the canal boat that they had hired for the week. They were travelling from Fort Augustus to Fort William and were apparently enjoying their trip through the Great Glen. John certainly was, but Hazel complained of exhaustion, whereupon Maurice said that he knew exactly how she felt.

We chatted for a while which allowed Maurice further recovery. As he drained his third pint he declared his thirst well and truly quenched and that if he had any more he would not be able to walk at all. It was a relief to see that his sense of humour had returned.

Delaying our restart for as long as I felt prudent, I eventually suggested to Maurice that we made the final push to Invergarry. Bidding goodbye to John and Hazel we emerged into the late-afternoon sunlight determined to reach our destination, a farmhouse on the outskirts of Invergarry, by the most direct route possible, which appeared to be by road.

We rejoined the A82 road near to where it crosses the Caledonian

Canal at Laggan Bridge. The construction of this significant waterway was begun during the age of sail and its completion in 1822 permitted a traverse for boats through the breadth of the country from the Atlantic Ocean to the North Sea. The engineer was the renowned Thomas Telford who was required to construct it to a depth of only twelve feet, instead of the twenty feet, as originally intended for naval vessels. Industrial development then overtook it and vessels became too large to pass through. It never fulfilled its original potential due to the arrival of the railways and the improvement of road communications. In the late nineteenth century the West Highland Railway arrived at Fort William and plans were made to build a branch line through the Great Glen, from Spean Bridge to Inverness. Thus the Invergarry and Fort Augustus Railway was instigated and the construction of viaducts, tunnels and cuttings commenced. It opened in 1903, but the section to link it with Inverness was never built due to rivalry between the railway companies and it sadly closed in 1911 to a storm of protest. So vociferous was the outcry that the line re-opened in 1913 and unprofitable passenger services survived until 1933. Its final demise came in 1946, well before the Beeching axe of the 1960's, when it was closed to all traffic. The overgrown embankments and viaducts are virtually all that remain of this sad relic, which reminded me of the redundant railway that I had followed through Glen Ogle and Glen Dochart.

To the north of the bridge we passed a monument, named the Well of Heads, that was erected on the shore of Loch Oich in 1812 by the Chief of Glengarry. It carries a gruesome cluster of seven heads on its lichen-encrusted apex, which commemorate the vengeful action taken against seven local murderers. Their heads were presented to the outraged chief in Glengarry Castle, after being washed in what became known as the Well of the Heads, as reprisal for the slaying of two young members of the Keppoch family. The monument marks the site of the well, which is now buried under the A82 road.

Anxious to reach the sanctuary of the farm, with its promise of a hot meal and a cool bed, we gave only a cursory glance to this gory reminder of a local feud. Protesting limbs were dragged as speedily as possible towards Invergarry. Even the sight of Glengarry Castle on flat ground between Loch Oich and the road could not distract us. We could see that the former mansion has been converted into a fashionable country house hotel and stands in close proximity to the ruins of the old Glen Garry Castle that sheltered Bonnie Prince Charlie before and after the debacle of Culloden.

Our strenuous journey presented a final hurdle, for to our dismay, we discovered that our accommodation lay some distance beyond the village. It was torment to plod a further mile when we desperately wanted to throw off our rucksacks and relax.

The welcome was friendly and warm when we finally arrived at our destination. The farmer's wife, Jean, remarked how tired we looked; was our condition that obvious? A soothing bath was followed by a typical farmhouse meal of gigantic proportions. Maurice and I ate what we could, but were too tired to really do justice to it. I was worried that Maurice might fall asleep and bury his face in the main course. It was late evening when our meal was completed, whereupon we immediately crawled upstairs to our beds. My weary brain prophesied that an earthquake would not keep me from sleeping that night, as I sank into the blissful comfort of a soft bed. However, fate still had a cruel blow in store. We suffered our first attack by rapacious Scottish midges that don't merely bite, they devour. The cool bed that I had been deliciously anticipating did not materialise despite the open window, which unfortunately provided an invitation to the squadron of rampaging insects that invaded the room. I leapt out of bed and closed the window but it was too late. We had not been seriously troubled by these monsters up to that stage as it was still early in June. They had obviously decided to make up for lost time as they attacked Maurice and I with a ferocity that had us writhing in our beds as they gleefully bit lumps out of us. Sleep became impossible for we were stinging all over and the air was cloying. Thus we were forced to endure a brutal climax to an exhausting day.

DAY NINETEEN: INVERGARRY - LOCH CLUANIE

Over breakfast Maurice and I were bemoaning the trial by midges that had ruined our nights sleep. Jean listened sympathetically and apologised for our discomfort, although it was hardly her fault. She promised to rid our bedroom of those pests as soon as breakfast was over and hoped that we could still enjoy our day's walk. Maurice told her that we were aiming for the inn that stands at the west end of Loch Cluanie, near the entrance to Glen Shiel. Helpfully, she suggested a convenient route to the inn, by quiet roads that were in places now little more than tracks. We were advised to leave the A87 road, the modern main road from Invergarry to Glen Shiel, after three miles and take the older and much narrower one that follows the north shore of Loch Garry. On reaching the hotel at Tomdoun we were to change course and walk across Loch Loyne. This prospect puzzled us, never having walked on water before. Jean read our thoughts and laughingly indicated that there would be no problem. Our route would follow the old Road to the Isles, which swings north at Tomdoun to carry us over Loch Loyne, conveniently very shallow at that time of year. From thereon we would simply follow the old and partially overgrown road to the Cluanie Inn and Glen Shiel.

True to her word, Jean went to our bedroom a little later, armed with a vacuum cleaner fitted with a flexible hose. She ran the cleaner nozzle along the window ledges that were overlain with layer upon layer of ugly midges whilst Maurice and I looked on in amazement at her regular routine of sucking up writhing black heaps. No wonder we had been whipped into a frenzy the previous night, there were hundreds of the beasts.

We left the farm with Jean's good wishes and provisions that could supply an army for several days. After a short distance Glen Garry began to open out and the expanse of Loch Garry appeared. Lochaber's northern boundary is marked by the glen which stretches west for twenty-six miles to the isolated peninsula of Knoydart. The average annual rainfall for the area is reputedly a mighty 120 inches, but we caught it on a good day for the sun was still resolutely shining from a cloudless sky. Skirting the eastern tip of Loch Garry the A87 road runs very close to the water in places and protective barriers have been erected on these sections to prevent careless motorists from taking an unscheduled swim. Across the loch we could see the mountains of Glengarry Forest once more, their shapes strikingly altered from when we had first viewed them over the Great Glen. The morning air was still refreshingly cool and a light mist lingered over the water, but these ideal conditions would change once the sun attained full-bore.

Traffic was still thankfully light as we forged along the main road to reach the point where the old road, that Jean had recommended, branched off. A road sign indicated that Tomdoun lay six miles along this now deserted road and that Kinloch Hourn could be reached at its termination twenty-two miles away. Maurice had fond memories of that secluded settlement, having explored the wild country that surrounds it many years before. He had been captivated by Loch Hourn, one of several lochs that slash the rugged west coastline and flow into the Sound of Sleat that separates the mainland from the Isle of Skye. The area, he said, appeared to be solely inhabited by red deer that only occasionally show themselves. He did see several impressive stags, which in that mountainous setting reminded him of the famous painting *The Monarch of the Glen*.

Our journey along the quiet backwater was delightful, for the leafy lane that it had become meanders along the north shore of Loch Garry, fringed by a splendid mixture of rowan and birch. The squadrons of midges must have been having a lie-in after their exertions of the previous night for they were not troubling us that morning. Life was improving. I had shrugged off my initial tiredness and the tribulations of the previous day. It was pleasing to see that Maurice was back to his usual form as he lustily sang *Lochaber No More*, a timely reminder that we were soon to leave the ancient province. Today, I thought, would be less frenetic, but I still had reservations about walking across Loch Loyne. These I kept to myself as we marched jauntily by the lochside. Butterflies cavorted amongst surrounding foliage, some proudly displaying exquisite colours. Above a background of birdsong rose a disconcerting sound resembling screeches of laughter. Was someone laughing at our singing, I wondered? Maurice explained that the culprit was probably a Laughing Jay Thrush and though we scanned the trees, the perpetrator remained frustratingly hidden. At one point an enthusiastic red setter surprised Maurice by seemingly emerging from nowhere and resting its paws on his chest whilst playfully trying to lick his face. Narrowly avoiding being bowled over, he managed to calm it down with a few soothing words. As he began stroking its luxurious coat it furiously wagged a flowing tail. We could have made use of that wonderful appendage as a fan, for the mist had evaporated and the sun was beating down. The dog, its curiosity satisfied, bounded into the woods to disappear as abruptly as it had arrived. Where its owner was remained a mystery for we saw no signs of life. As the friendly animal departed Maurice donned his knotted handkerchief, which was a sign that we were in for another roasting.

This section of our journey, amidst agreeable lochside scenery, came to an end as we approached the appealing Tomdoun Hotel, conveniently around lunchtime. This old inn is constructed from attractive red sandstone and is made even more impressive by an imposing arch over the entrance which is covered with emerald-green ivy. A shaded porch extends along the front of the building and a convenient bench seat occupies this cool haven. Here I sat down next to a couple who were enjoying a mid-day drink. Maurice, eager to repay me for reviving him on the previous day, disappeared inside. My talkative companions revealed that they were touring the north of Scotland and had taken the opportunity to escape the main roads and explore Glen Garry.

Maurice soon returned with cooling drinks and the couple asked how far we had travelled. I suddenly realised that I had completed more than half my journey. It had slipped my mind to celebrate whilst we were at Invergarry, for obvious reasons, so now was a good time to make amends. Maurice and I proposed a toast to the successful completion of our respective walks. His would be over in two days, whereas I had a further twelve to survive. John O'Groats still lay many miles away.

As we looked over the narrowing loch the couple remarked on the splendid outline of the mountains surrounding Loch Quoich that dominate the view to the west. They had driven that morning to the point where the River Garry flows from that lonely loch which lies beneath the jagged mountain barrier that guards the western seaboard. I told them that the area evoked memories of John Hillaby's epic cross-country marathon, for he had skirted the west end of Loch Quoich as he headed for Kinloch Hourn. The track that he had been following inconsiderately disappeared into the loch, I related, which, along with its tributaries has been converted into a large hydro-electric scheme incorporating several dams and the submerging of much of the valley.

Not to be outdone, Maurice related his experience of visiting Knoydart, which, he reckoned, would have altered little in the intervening years. As he did so my thoughts returned to John Hillaby and his evocative description of its wild, but inspiring, landscape. At the time he was existing on a diet of oatmeal and raisins, similar rations to those carried by the clans during the old campaigns. I admired his guts and determination in tackling such wilderness areas alone, but reading of his escapades, such as wading through treacherous bogs, filled me with trepidation. I felt glad of

Maurice's company and John Hillaby's exploits made me realise that our route-finding problems were insignificant when compared to his.

It was soon time to strike north from the hotel along the old Road to the Isles and head for Loch Loyne. We had over twenty miles to cover that day so there was no time to waste. The road, little wider than a track, twisted between brutal wire fences that bordered forests of fledgling pines. As we strode purposefully along it my apprehension grew as I wondered what Loch Loyne held in store. I endured two miles of uncertainty, plagued by disturbing visions of finding our way barred by unfriendly water. Another detour over rough country was too dreadful to contemplate.

At the point where the forests relented we entered a large basin, devoid of cover, in which lay what could only be described as the dregs of Loch Loyne. Jean's prophecy was absolutely correct for the water had shrunk to a mere quarter of its normal level, exposing great tracts of stony shoreline overlaid with mosses, lichen and soils of various hues. Across the centre of the parched loch coursed our road, barely recognisable as such, its surface shattered by weather and erosion into little more than an embankment of fractured tarmac, edged with rubble. Despite its dereliction, it represented a comforting lifeline and I said a silent prayer for our deliverance from another stumbling detour. I happily took a photograph of Maurice, complete with knotted handkerchief, surveying the shrivelled loch from the crumbling walkway.

As we reached the far bank the road turned west skirting the foothills of Bunloinn Forest that separates Loch Loyne from Loch Cluanie. Now partially grass-covered, it toiled up a steady incline to a pass between Bunloinn Forest and the neighbouring mountains of Cluanie Forest. The sun's fiery heat continued to hamper us as we stopped at intervals to cool ourselves. Before entering the pass, we turned for a last look at Lochaber and the shapely peaks of Glengarry Forest, now almost a distant memory.

The view as we emerged from the rocky channel was a revelation. Loch Cluanie's seven miles of deep-blue water spread beneath us. Despite being fuller that Loch Loyne it still displayed a sandy fringe around its curvaceous perimeter that glowed in the sunshine. Glen Cluanie looked resplendent on that clear afternoon, its encircling mountains carving a magnificent skyline. Seven Munros surround the loch, their adjoining summits an obvious attraction for ridge-walkers and Munro-baggers. I thought of the two young men from

Manchester that I had met on the summit of Ben More, who would relish the challenge of climbing them all in one day.

Maurice and I felt much better than we had on the previous afternoon when we struggled out of Glen Roy. We were now enjoying scenery of the highest order and were happy in the knowledge that journey's end lay not far away. Although we couldn't make out the Cluanie Inn, its location, near the west end of the loch, was in sight. As we strode down the gentle slope towards the lochside we were treated to a splendid backdrop of mountains that guard the entrance to Glen Shiel. On the far side of the loch traffic was hastening along the A87 road. The uncharitable thought that, cocooned in their cars, those travellers would have a far more restrictive view than we lucky walkers, was impossible to dismiss.

As we descended towards the loch we met a farmer, who, with the aid of his energetic dog, was trying to round up some sheep. Despite the dog dashing hither and thither, the sheep weren't having any of it and darted in all directions. We had obviously interrupted his arduous task, but he didn't complain and joked about the weather, which he said was remarkable. He added a warning that the forecast was not good and that rain was on the way. The pendulum was bound to swing sometime.

The farmer raised the familiar query as to where we had walked from and where we were heading. Our answer was now well-rehearsed. His eyes widened as he listened intently and it was soon evident that he had spent his entire life in the glen. Inheriting the farm from his father, he had only left the area on rare occasions and had never ventured further than Fort William. 'All I ever wanted is here', he said simply, indicating that he had no inclination to travel. As we gazed around the tranquil glen, it was easy to see why. How refreshing it was to meet someone genuinely content with his lot. When we mentioned that we were staying at the Cluanie Inn he replied that we could do a lot worse. It was a very popular place, he told us and had been for many years, providing an excellent base for shooting, fishing and fell-walking. There are apparently many deer in the area and the loch is well- stocked with fish, eagerly waiting to jump on to dangling hooks.

The sheep had been taking advantage of the farmer's distraction by galloping away and searching for juicy vegetation. His faithful dog, which had been called to heel, sat patiently by him during our conversation, with a pleading look in its eyes. If the dog had been able to speak it would have expressed annoyance at having its work interrupted by two strangers. His master said apologetically that he must chase his flock or he would be out there until nightfall. The very affable farmer seemed genuinely sorry to leave us. We watched the dog bound away at his command to take up the chase once more, much to the chagrin of the recalcitrant sheep.

The inn itself eventually materialised, standing some distance away on the far side of the loch. At its west end the water narrows almost to a point and a convenient bridge carries the slender road towards the inn. There was no doubting the strategic position of the Cluanie Inn, at the head of Glen Shiel, as an important halt on the Road to the Isles. The glen splits the mountain barrier that stands between the traveller and the romantic Isle of Skye.

The farmer's weather prediction came true remarkably quickly and with a vengeance. Menacing clouds rolled across the sky as we approached the bridge and the benevolent blue ceiling that had watched over us for so long was obliterated. The glen was plunged into dark shadow, warning drops of rain already falling as we crossed the bridge and ran, as fast as our rucksacks would allow, towards the inn to escape a drenching. Welcoming lights beamed from its windows as they would have done in the days when travel-weary passengers tumbled stiffly from their coaches and tired drovers brought their herds to a thankful halt.

We rushed into the entrance porch and hastily removed our rucksacks and boots as the rain hurtled down. Maurice echoed my relief at not being caught in open country during the deluge. Our hearts went out to the poor farmer who would still be out there bearing the brunt of the storm with only his jacket for protection.

A very pleasant receptionist greeted us, remarking on the sudden change in the weather. She smiled when we told her that we couldn't complain after enjoying nearly two weeks of continuous sunshine. As we were guided to our room, rain lashed the windows, making us wonder what the following day held in store weatherwise. As though reading our thoughts, the receptionist comforted us by saying that according to the local forecast the heavy rain would abate by morning. That was a relief.

Emerging later from our comfortable quarters we made a beeline for the dining room, appetites honed by the sweet Highland air. Our expectations were well-founded, for the food was delicious and the service admirable. One note of sadness did prevail however, during the meal. The realisation that the following day would see the culmination of our walk together had dawned upon us. We agreed that even if the last day proved a washout, we would still have enjoyed an unforgettable journey through some of the finest scenery that Britain has to offer.

There was no shortage of good company in the lounge after supper and we struck up what turned out to be a one-sided conversation with three friendly Scotsmen whose very broad accents were difficult to decipher. We kept nodding our heads in reply whilst barely deciphering that they were keen fishermen who came frequently to fish the loch, which, according to them, was well-stocked with brown trout. They enthusiastically related what we understood to be shaggy fish stories about monsters they had captured, or had just eluded them. Maurice and I refrained from telling them that dangling a bent pin into water for hours on end wasn't our idea of fun. This was a wise move for we could well have found ourselves thrown into Loch Cluanie amidst cries of 'Philistine bloody foreigners'!

DAY TWENTY: LOCH CLUANIE - SHIEL BRIDGE

Our mood at breakfast was a mixture of reflection and anticipation. We recalled some highlights of our journey, such as humbling Ben Nevis and dancing in Fort William. The debacle of Rob Roy's cave and our flounderings through the forest above Laggan were unsurprisingly omitted. Having greatly enjoyed travelling more than 130 miles together we were poised to embark on separate adventures. At Shiel Bridge Maurice planned to turn west and head for the Isle of Skye, whilst I would steer north through Wester Ross and Sutherland. I reminded him that our joint venture was not yet over and that a treat still lay in store. Following his earlier expedition to Knoydart, Maurice had completed the superb ridge walk over the Five Sisters of Kintail. They overlook Glen Shiel and Maurice's wish to see them again, albeit from low level, was about to be granted. An added bonus, I remarked, was the fact that we would be walking downhill for the whole day; a rare treat. This was by courtesy of the twelve-mile corridor of Glen Shiel which descends unerringly between 3000 foot high mountains to Shiel Bridge, thus ensuring that even we could not get lost.

The weather, despite an improvement, still looked threatening. A melancholy drizzle from an overcast sky began to coat the windows bringing the ominous thought that the Five Sisters could yet elude us. Stepping from the hotel into a fresh morning breeze we cast a parting glance at Loch Cluanie, whose name means Loch of the Meadows. Very few meadows are in fact visible for they were swallowed up when the loch was dammed. I was beginning to feel that very few natural lochs remain in Scotland, for so many of those passed were now gigantic water tanks, throttled at the neck and grossly distended, their original characters distorted.

Our initial task was to find a footpath as an alternative to the A87 road that passes by the inn before wriggling through the depths of Glen Shiel. Road and river are bosom companions on this journey. The River Shiel, rich with salmon, is inextricably bound to the modern carriageway as they squeeze through the constricting valley, which in parts leaves very little room for manoeuvre. After an abortive attempt to find permitted access across the foothills we resigned ourselves to using the road, much to our consternation. Help was at hand however, for we had gone a mere quarter of a mile when we found the remains of another Old Military Road that led in the right direction. This particular road is attributed to Major Caulfield, the unsung hero and successor to General Wade. He built it between 1750 and 1784 to link Fort Augustus with the military barracks at Bernera on the west coast.

The irksome drizzle had fortunately melted away and the cloud cover was perceptibly lifting. Not only did we now have a track to follow through the valley-floor, but the stately mountain ranges that bordered the glen began to reveal themselves, minus their peaks, which remained resolutely buried in cloud. A quick burst of song was called for as we ventured into the open arms of Glen Shiel at a lively pace. The head of the glen lies just below 900 feet and heralds the gathering grounds of the River Shiel, which ultimately expends itself into Loch Duich. At this point we were crossing the backbone of Scotland, the great ridge of Drum Albyn, which, if it were a human spine, would deform its owner because it is way off-centre. It lies mainly to the west of the country, nearly touching the west coast in places. Many lochs intrude deep into the coastline hereabouts. Loch Alsh divides at Dornie and projects two probing fingers, Loch Long and Loch Duich into the interior. Loch Long heads north-east to Killilan whilst Loch Duich thrusts south-east to the mouth of

Glen Shiel, burying itself in a mountain cordon that surrounds it like a snugly-fitting collar. The land enclosed by these two sea-lochs and their continuing glens is Kintail, which adds its name to the Five Sisters.

Time was plentiful during the relatively short day's walk, which allowed us to relax, take stock of our surroundings and to stop and admire some of the wild flowers that flourish in the valley. Particularly colourful were the tall hollyhocks that swayed rhythmically in the breeze. As we rested beneath a small outcrop of trees we were scrutinised by inquisitive sparrows that flitted amongst the overhanging branches. Floating on the wind came a low-pitched and monotonous bird-call that resembled the sound of a car engine ticking over. Maurice and I looked enquiringly at each other, mystified as to what the culprit might be, but we were immediately goaded into action by a posse of marauding midges. Recalling the voracity of their relatives at the farm in Invergarry we beat a hasty retreat. The incident brought to mind a recent advertisement in a magazine that had caught my eye. I explained to Maurice that it was headed 'Midgebusters of Skye', which was guaranteed to attract attention, for most summer visitors to Scotland have yet to find an entirely successful repellent to those horrible insects that are the western version of the yellow peril. The infallible device in question was an anti-midge hood, invaluable to walkers, campers and gardeners. No details were supplied, but Maurice laughed and said that he had no wish to walk the countryside looking like a beekeeper. He quipped that a cheaper version could be made from a pair of ladies tights, or a rolled- down woollen hat, with holes cut in for the eyes, provided that you didn't mind being arrested. Maurice promised to keep a look out for signs of unusual headgear when he reached Skye.

Roughly halfway down the glen its narrow floor begins to widen and here stands the Bridge of Shiel which transfers the road to the opposite side of the river and also denotes the entrance to Kintail. Nearby we found a sign marking the site of the Battle of Glen Shiel that took place in 1719. This conflict was one of many between Jacobite sympathisers and Hanoverian troops. Immediately prior to the battle, exiled Jacobite leaders of the 1715 rebellion had returned from Spain and their forces had taken Eilean Donan castle, the proud fortress whose modern version stands on a promontory that juts into the water where lochs Alsh, Duich and Long meet. They were soon ousted by three English frigates which sailed into Loch Alsh and reduced the castle to ruins. The embattled Jacobites and a company of Spaniards fled and took up positions on the hill-slopes to either side of the Bridge of Shiel in order to defend themselves. They were joined by a party of MacGregors and also by Rob Roy who seemed never far away. I told Maurice that I could not evade him for long and that, like Robin Hood, he had reputedly been everywhere. In the ensuing battle the Hanoverians won the day and many Jacobites were slain as they tried to flee into the mountains. The name of the mountain that stands above the battle site is Sgurr nan Spainteach - The Peak of the Spaniards. This is the peak at the east end of the Five Sisters and its name relates to the Spaniards who took part in the battle.

As we stood by the battle sign we were passed by three young ladies who had struggled from the hills, borne down by enormous back-packs. Maurice and I greeted them as they passed but we received no reply from the beleaguered and exhausted trio. They resembled rucksacks with legs when seen from behind and we wondered where they were heading. I don't think they knew either, for a few minutes later they passed us in silence once more and returned by the way that they had come. Our mouths gaped and Maurice muttered something about the Grand Old Duke of York. They were the only walkers that we met that day and it was unfortunate that they could not even stop to say hello.

The military road appeared to peter out at that point, so Maurice and I crossed over the bridge to see if conditions were better underfoot on the other side of the river. As we did so a car crawled towards us, travelling so slowly that it seemed to be free-wheeling. However, the throb of its engine could be heard as it approached and the man and woman inside, sporting voluminous sun hats, gazed around as though mesmerised. The driver was jerked from his reverie as the bridge loomed before him and they waved to us as they passed. We could see them staring at their surroundings once more as they disappeared. Some people never learn. Maurice remarked that those ridiculous sun hats made them resemble flower-pot men and were surely not necessary in a car.

The temperature was, we conceded, rising steadily and off came our sweaters as the clouds fragmented, exposing patches of pale-blue sky. From our vantage point we got our first good view of the Five Sisters. Three of the peaks were visible, protruding above the indented ridge, including the tallest of the range, Sgurr Fhuaran at just over 3500 feet. Maurice was thrilled to see the scene of his high-level traverse once more. The views on that occasion were magnificent, he said, encompassing much of the western seaboard and the Hebridean Islands.

We spent the next part of our walk meandering along the floor of the glen, alternating between spells of road-walking and hugging the river bank. During frequent stops we scoured the River Shiel for signs of fish, particularly the elusive salmon, without success. A pleasant interlude of unpressured walking was very welcome after several hard days. It was no hardship to occasionally amble along tarmac, laid upon the old road to the Isles. This evocative route terminates at Glenelg, by the Sound of Sleet, the narrow, swift-flowing channel that separates Skye from the mainland. If the remainder of the Western Isles are to be included, it can be argued that the Road to the Isles also branches north and heads for Cape Wrath on the north-west tip of Scotland.

As we neared the mouth of the glen the river widened into a tiny lochan. On its banks a splendid display of yellow flags lit up the glen's lower reaches. Despite our leisurely pace we had worked up quite a lather and Maurice stopped to dry himself with a towel. For one agonising moment I visualised him reverting to that disgusting appendage, his knotted handkerchief. Luckily the sun, that had made spasmodic appearances, hid behind a drifting cloud and his temptation passed. I said that I would not accompany him into Shiel Bridge if he wore that degrading headgear. With a wicked smile he retorted that I should be glad that he didn't put the towel over his head and really embarrass me.

The River Shiel narrows once more for the last half-mile of its journey. As it prepares to enter Loch Duich it passes under Shiel Bridge that gives the adjacent village its name. Here we encountered a backdrop of grey, furrowed hills, with tentacles of vegetation creeping into the corries of their upper reaches, surrounding the historic high-arched bridge, its uniquely patterned stonework resembling a giant jigsaw puzzle. The bridge stands strategically at the gateway to Loch Duich and the west coast. It carries the A87 road across the river once more as it begins the final stage of its journey to Kyle of Lochalsh. The road's terminus is now a place of controversy for the long-standing ferry from Kyle of Lochalsh to Kyleakin on Skye has been replaced by a bridge that links the island to the mainland. Angry local residents and opponents of this recent scheme declare that the modern structure, another sop to the demands of the motor car, destroys the natural beauty of its surroundings.

At one time, Shiel Bridge probably shouldered the Old Military Road from Fort Augustus as it turned west to the Bernera barracks. The ruins of this former outpost, where Hanoverian troops were stationed for a period of seventy years from 1722, still remain by the Sound of Sleet near Glenelg village. Maurice planned to take the same route, along what is now a modern metalled road, and cross the Sound of Sleet on the small ferryboat that operates between Glenelg and Kylerhea. This one-man concern was in the news some years ago when the boat's owner was featured on television and asked for potential buyers to come forward and purchase his business for £150,000.

We strolled from the bridge past a caravan site that squatted outside the village and found a convenient shop and café. We spent a relaxing half-hour over some welcome refreshment, which made a pleasant change from the strenuous episodes of some afternoons. Maurice kept me entertained with stories of his previous visit to Kintail, adding that he was happy to have paid his respects to the Five Sisters once more. He was eagerly anticipating his visit to Skye and he intended staying for two nights on the island to allow a first-hand view of the Black Cuillin. Pictures of the dramatic horseshoe of the Cuillin ridge, that towers above Glen Brittle and Loch Coriusk, near to Skye's jagged west coast, had never ceased to thrill him. Few people conquer the ridge, he said, but many admire it. Its splintered apex, he believed, was accessible to only the brave and the skillful and he preferred to admire it from ground level.

We searched later for the farm where we were to spend the night and found it tucked beneath the hills that overlook Loch Duich. The road to Glenelg passes by the entrance, which would be handy for Maurice the following morning. As we approached the farmhouse we were set upon by two lively Border collies that leapt at us with gusto. Fortunately they were friendly and only wished to lick our hands and faces. A curt command from the farmer's wife, who had appeared at the doorway, sent them scampering to a nearby barn. Their excited yelping had virtually drowned the straight-faced welcome from Margaret, our host, who hoped that we were not put out by the over-enthusiastic dogs. We were eventually invited into the kitchen and treated to a huge pot of tea and an assortment of home-made cakes, despite our protestations that we had been in the café a little earlier. Margaret seemed friendly but rather stern; a person not to be argued with. Whilst Maurice and I munched her delicious cakes I got my first view of a salmon, albeit a dead one. A man entered clutching a monster of a fish that he had obviously just pulled out of the loch. It transpired that he was a helpful neighbour who had brought the massive salmon for our meal that evening. When our benefactor left we had intermittent spasms of conversation with Margaret, who was not over-talkative, before being taken to our room. It was made clear that we were expected to be prompt for supper which, she said, would be at seven o'clock precisely.

We bathed and changed and reported to the dining room five minutes early, not wishing to incur Margaret's wrath. Seated obediently at the table were a middle-aged couple who whispered that they dared not be late for one of Margaret's meals. As we sat patiently awaiting the first course our whispered conversation revealed that the couple lived in Bradford, not far from my home village, and were using the farm as a base for touring the area by car. They were full of praise for Plockton which lies at the south-west tip of Loch Carron, declaring it to be the highlight of their visit so far. They were in good company for Wainwright describes the place as a little paradise. 'Throughout the 1970's, this delightful village was the priority holiday venue of my wife and myself, a kind friend providing her cottage for our annual visits: always we arrived in eager anticipation and departed with reluctance. By common consent, it is the prettiest of Scotland's west coast villages'. Maurice and I should not miss it, they said, and we had to explain that we were parting company the next morning. Loch Carron was on my route, I told them, but unfortunately only its north end.

To the casual observer, our whispering would have appeared comical, as though we were afraid of being overheard by Margaret. To us it seemed a natural caution, for she could appear at any time. In fact on the stroke of seven o'clock she entered with a voluminous dish of soup. We each had several helpings, reluctant to offend her by leaving some uneaten. The main course, when placed in front of us, was a revelation. On each of our large, oval plates lay a quarter of the enormous salmon, surrounded by a jungle of salad, that barely left any available space for the potatoes and vegetables heaped in expansive dishes in the centre of the table. We wrestled manfully with our intimidating portions and everyone but Maurice managed to make significant in-roads into them. He was ruing the cakes and other goodies that we had eaten earlier and failed miserably. When Margaret came to collect our plates he looked crestfallen as she snatched his away and tight-lipped, slammed a huge slice of fresh cream gateau in front of him. This proved too much for my friend who humbly declared that he could not eat another thing. Margaret stared incredulously at him and demanded to know what was wrong with her food. His apology was met with a cold stare and she grabbed his sweet and stormed out of the room amidst an embarrassed silence.

Conversation was understandably sparse for the remainder of the meal, but when we were back in the privacy of our room, Maurice brightened and even managed to joke about the incident. He christened our angry host Dawn, because, he said, she had come up like thunder when he had rejected her prized gateau.

CHAPTER FOUR

Wester Ross and Sutherland

DAY TWENTY-ONE : SHIEL BRIDGE - STRATHCARRON

Maurice and I parted company at the farm entrance and I watched him set out for Glenelg, his red socks shining vividly as he disappeared down the road. At one point he had turned and waved, whilst I vigorously waved back, realising with some trepidation that I was on my own once more with much wild country ahead of me.

The day would not be easy, as it involved an eighteen-mile crossing of outer Kintail, that stretches north from Loch Duich and is bounded by Loch Long to the west and Strath Croe to the east. Much of it is mountainous, riven by deep valleys which are scoured by fast-flowing rivers. My intention was to aim for Attadale that lies near the head of Loch Carron. When that was reached the hardest part of my journey would be over, for only two miles of level walking separate it from Strathcarron.

My journey began by circling the east end of Loch Duich and then heading along its north shore towards the village of Inverinate.

My spirits were dampened by the weather which had turned decidedly nasty. Angry clouds marshalled themselves for a downpour and I donned my waterproofs in anticipation of a soaking. I had been very lucky with the weather thus far, but unbeknown to me, nature had wickedly decided to redress the balance. The impending storm was a prelude to the vile conditions that I would suffer during many of the remaining days of my walk.

Reputedly, the finest view of the Five Sisters is from Ratagan, that unfortunately lay off my route, on the southern edge of Loch Duich. I was nevertheless treated to a fairly dramatic view of them before the weather closed in. As I turned for a final look at their majestic outline, they disappeared in the mist that was insidiously rolling towards me. Rain began to fall with a vengeance and I was not relishing the challenge of leaving the security of the A87 road which had guided me from Shiel Bridge. It would soon be time to stumble across-country as I trudged apprehensively past the string of gloomy roadside buildings that lay beyond Inverinate. I was on the lookout for the valley of the Coire Dhuinnid that cleaves a gap between Sgurr an Uillt Tharsuinn and Boc Beag. Its entrance finally appeared out of the murk and I left the comforting tarmac to join a path that snaked upwards alongside the tumbling burn and soon vanished into a thickening mist. I climbed past several small waterfalls that frothed and churned in a frenzy of activity. A couple of miles of squelching along the sodden path brought me to its junction with a more daunting one that rose sharply into the hills of Inverinate Forest. Only the sound of my laboured breath broke the eerie silence as I struggled upwards cocooned in swirling mist. The path was indistinct and I was following its line with the aid of my compass, determined not to stray off course. I was occasionally startled by the appearance of ghostly sheep that gazed at me with pity in their eyes, incredulous that idiot walkers should be wandering their hills in such foul weather. The angry calls of disturbed grouse, as they took flight, did nothing for my peace of mind. An anxious hour was spent with my head down, eyes straining for signs of the fickle path.

As many walkers will know, if you are on your own and apparently isolated by mist from the outside world, your imagination goes into overdrive. To dispel fearful thoughts of my rigid corpse being found sometime later by a local shepherd, my mind conjured up the tantalising image of climbing a challenging mountain in perfect weather, with superb views all around me. This is akin to the

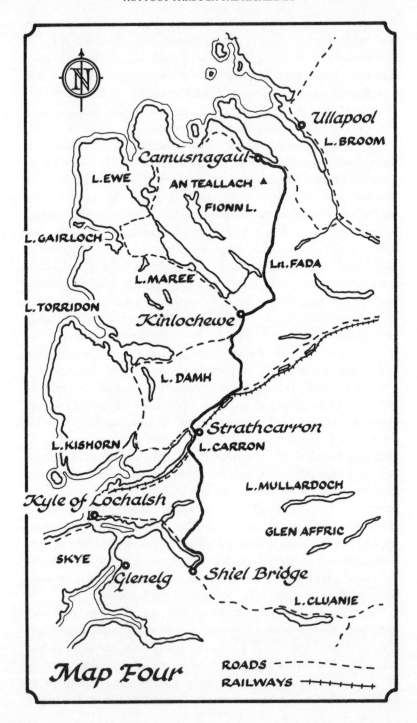

Ullapool

L.BROOM

Camusnagaul

L.EWE

AN TEALLACH ▲

FIONN L.

L.GAIRLOCH

Ln.FADA

L.MAREE

L.TORRIDON

Kinlochewe

L. DAMH

Strathcarron

L.KISHORN

L.CARRON

L.MULLARDOCH

Kyle of Lochalsh

GLEN AFFRIC

SKYE

Glenelg

Shiel Bridge

L.CLUANIE

Map Four

ROADS - - - - -

RAILWAYS +++++++++

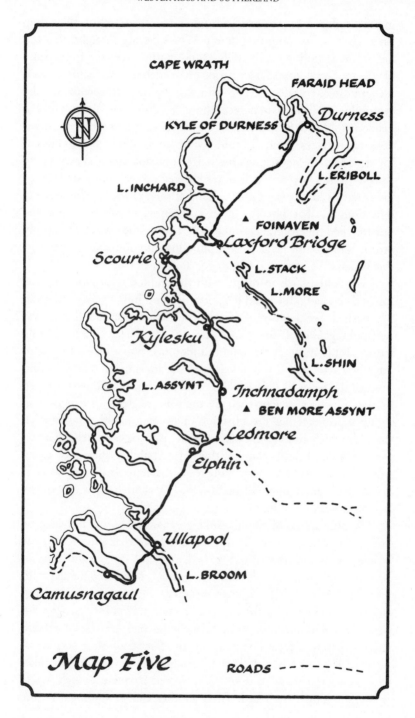

CAPE WRATH

FARAID HEAD

Durness

KYLE OF DURNESS

L. ERIBOLL

L. INCHARD

▲ FOINAVEN

Laxford Bridge

Scourie

L. STACK

L. MORE

Kylesku

L. SHIN

L. ASSYNT

Inchnadamph

▲ BEN MORE ASSYNT

Ledmore

Elphin

Ullapool

L. BROOM

Camusnagaul

Map Five

ROADS - - - - - -

mirage suffered by stranded, thirst-crazed travellers as they drag themselves across a burning desert. The sobering thought, that my demise in dense fog on the hills would hardly make the front pages of the national newspapers, was unavoidable. To achieve such recognition I needed to be clinging by my fingertips to the crumbling edge of a precipice above a 3000 foot drop, whilst a helicopter, teams of rescuers and a slobbering Saint Bernard tried desperately to reach me. I could vividly imagine myself hanging on, for dear life, to an inaccessible ledge, my fingernails slowly being ripped off as a hovering helicopter lowered a keen young reporter to my side. As he thrusts a microphone at me in order to discover my sensations at that horrific time, I absentmindedly reach for the outstretched microphone, intent on telling the world about my ordeal, and lose my grip. Whilst plunging into oblivion I think, boy, this is news. If you are going to go, do it in style!

I was jolted back to reality with the sudden realisation that the mist was clearing, for I had begun to descend into a valley. Beneath me nestled the hamlet of Killilan, which confirmed that I was overlooking Glen Elchaig and directly on course. Despite being barely visible through the rain and gloom it was a reassuring sight. Eagerly I dropped down towards the scattering of buildings and reached the River Elchaig which is conveniently crossed by a wooden bridge. I cast a glance up the grey and sombre glen. Tucked away in its upper reaches lies the offshoot valley of the Allt à Ghlomaich through which tumble the magnificent Falls of Glomach. Known as the Hidden Falls, because of their inaccessibility, they draw many would-be visitors, but few actually reach this remarkable spectacle. It is not the highest waterfall in Britain, but at its head is one of the longest drops at 350 feet.

The only splash of colour in the grey landscape was provided by bright yellow flowers on the thickets of broom that sheltered by the bridge. Crossing the river I passed a school on the outskirts of Killilan and turned north into Glen Ling. Here I coincided with John Hillaby's route for a short distance. He, apparently, had not enjoyed a good day by the time he reached this point. Setting out that particular morning from Glenelg he had travelled by boat, chartered from a local boatman, up the Sound of Sleat and across Loch Alsh to Ardelve. Part way through the voyage the boatman treacherously demanded double the agreed payment, which nearly resulted in a fight on board. After another violent argument on the quayside at Ardelve, he paid an inflated fee before setting out along the shore of Loch Long. When he reached Nonach, near Killilan, he was promptly bitten on the calf by a dog. Things went from bad to worse as he entered Glen Ling and found that his map had fallen from a torn pocket of his jacket, rendering him rudderless. As a consequence he blindly followed the River Ling for miles in thick mist before ending up in a quagmire of peat at its remote source. My worries were as nothing when compared to his.

Determined not to make the same mistake that he had, I kept my eyes peeled for a path that diverges from the main one about a mile up the glen and climbs into the Attadale Hills. According to my map this path would eventually reach Attadale and the shore of Loch Carron. I found the path in question and began to climb from the glen, pausing as I did so to survey the upper reaches of the River Ling that had lured John Hillaby into difficulties. The sinister river wound, beneath tentacles of mist, through a scene of pure desolation, the kind that scares the pants off you in a horror film. You are always treated to such a scene just before the blood-curdling baying of a werewolf rivets you to your seat. My heart went out to John Hillaby.

I ascended into the pea-soup of a mist once more which returned me to my eerie and disturbingly silent world. My sole objective was to stick to the path at all costs, but this time I was unsuccessful. Somewhere on those shrouded hills I lost it and all my attempts to re-locate it failed. I was doomed to blunder through inhospitable country with only my compass to guide me and to make matters worse I twisted my ankle in a bog. Feeling sorry for myself I tottered over the rough ground until a forest loomed out of the mist. This cheered me a little for I knew that one lay on my route, but there was no track at my point of entry, as there should have been. Thankfully there were frequent breaks in the tree cover, but I still spent an uncomfortable half-hour lumbering through it.

As I escaped from the forest, the ground began to plunge sharply downwards and soon extracted me from the mist to find Loch Carron lying 1000 feet below. What a joyous sight it was, with the Kyle of Lochalsh to Inverness railway line hugging its south-east shore and Attadale lying right beside it. Elation turned to frustration, for despite being able to see my goal, as I had when above Laggan, I had great difficulty in attaining it. My descent was halted by a deep gorge, which demanded a detour and I then had to tangle with dense bracken, frustrating woodland and numerous fences. I was just about exhausted when I finally reached the lochside road.

Loch Carron marks the demarcation between the softer country to its south, which is more open to the Atlantic Drift, and the harder land to the north. It lay calmly beside me as I approached Attadale, enfolded by hills that give way to gaunt mountains that surround its head. All around were ash, alder and conifer plantations, whose dark sprawl was punctuated with bright green meadows. Loch Carron and its environs displayed a tranquil beauty.

The most notable building in the small settlement of Attadale is Attadale House that stands in a lovely situation not far from the loch. It hosts the annual Lochcarron Highland Games; not on the same scale as those at Braemar, but nevertheless a source of splendid entertainment. The skirl of pipes and the thrill of competition are guaranteed to delight whatever the setting.

As I passed the grounds of that fine country house, the lure of Strathcarron, with its promise of a meal and relaxation was strong. I was feeling the effects of tussling with the Attadale Hills and was eager to put my feet up. The realisation dawned that, so far, I hadn't met a soul that day. Those hills were hardly buzzing with walkers and I was learning that Wester Ross is empty, apart from pockets of habitation.

During the final two miles of my day's journey I had a close companion; the railway that I had observed from my high-level vantage point above Attadale. Wainwright expresses his regard for this impressive line in the following manner. 'The people of Wester Ross depend greatly on the trains for travel and supplies and would be even more isolated without them; moreover, the railway proves a most enjoyable crossing of the Highlands scenically and is very popular with visitors. The last time I travelled on it there was standing room only. Closing it would be a criminal folly'. His final sentence is a reference to the threatened closure and subsequent reprieve of this vital link between Kyle of Lochalsh and Inverness. I passed Attadale station, which lies on the line and could have been built for the convenience of the residents of Attadale House, for they stand adjacent to each other. I was gratified to see that the station had not suffered the same fate as the one at Luib.

The broad head of Loch Carron fragments into a series of watery tentacles that intrude into the surrounding pastureland as though striving to swamp Strathcarron that lies a mere half-mile beyond.

Into this lacerated shoreline squirms the River Carron, which is immediately confronted by two small islands that threaten to block its mouth. This watery scene provided an introduction to Glen Carron, which would form the early part of my following day's walk. My thoughts, however, were on more immediate tasks. As I passed through Achintee, a near-neighbour of Strathcarron, I studied the directions that would hopefully lead me to my night's refuge. It was a great relief when Strathcarron Station came into view, for journey's end was near. A short search amongst nearby cottages that lie under the shadow of Carn Mor, a great dome that towers over the village, resulted in a very cordial welcome at the home of Jimmy and Jennifer, with whom I had booked accommodation. It was a great relief to remove my boots and enter that most hospitable household, where everyone was chatting like old friends from the outset. As I lay in the steaming bath a little later the strain of the day's adventures began to melt away in the caress of soothing hot water. I could look back on my antics in the hills with a mixture of relief and amusement.

At supper the conversation was lively, particularly from Jimmy who possessed a fund of anecdotes. He kept me and my fellow-guest, a pianist who was on holiday, entertained throughout the meal and for several hours afterwards. The young piano player, I discovered, had visited many parts of the world with the small orchestra to which he belonged. He related many adventures, which made mine seem mundane by comparison. Unlike him and other members of his orchestra I have not had to endure extremes of climate and geography, for many of their venues were in far-flung locations, remote from the more grandiose facilities on the major concert circuit. In some instances it was a triumph of logistics just to get the players and their instruments to the right place at the right time.

My walking exploits were made to appear even more trivial when Jimmy mentioned his accomplished neighbour, Martin Moran, a formidable mountain guide who is equally at home in the Himalayas, the Alps, or the Scottish Highlands. One of his outstanding achievements is conquering all the 277 Scottish Munros in one continuous circuit, in the depths of winter. It took him eighty-three days to complete this marathon, a remarkable length of time when you consider that it takes many fell-walkers the best part of their lives. Another of his feats, which I find incredible, is crossing the Cuillin Ridge on Skye in three hours and thirty-three minutes. This is all the more amazing when you learn that it includes eleven Munros.

I was quite overcome with such tales of derring-do and crept up to bed feeling decidedly inferior. My night's sleep was invaded by a recurring nightmare in which I was hauling a piano across the Cuillin Ridge.

DAY TWENTY-TWO: STRATHCARRON - KINLOCHEWE

My fitful slumber was broken by the drumming of rain on the bedroom window. I yawned and tumbled from my bed. Not a good start to the day, which promised 'more of the same' as far as the weather was concerned. I hoped that the wet clothes that Jennifer had taken away to dry were ready to wear,despite the likelihood that they were in for another dousing. My concern was unfounded because they were laid out for me, when I got downstairs, perfectly dry. My shirt had been washed and ironed. What wonderful service, I thought, so typical of the warm Scottish hospitality.

During breakfast Jimmy enquired where I was heading that day. When I told him Kinlochewe, by way of the Coulin Pass, he said that I had made a wise choice. In his opinion, a walk through the pass was essential for it epitomises the true character of Wester Ross. All I needed, he said, was a break in the weather.

The young pianist had been listening intently to our conversation. He volunteered his plan for the day, which involved driving to Kyle of Lochalsh and crossing to Skye for a tour of the island. Walking, he said, was not for him. I suggested that he kept a lookout for Maurice who should be on his expedition to the Cuillins. This reminded me that I must ring my friend that evening to discover how he had fared.

As we said our goodbyes I reluctantly ventured into the pelting rain. Another soaking was definitely in prospect. I often have to steel myself at the outset of a day's walk because a relaxing night's stay amidst good company makes me lazy. This state usually abates after the first mile, but in bad weather I find it harder to get into my stride. Just as on the previous morning when faced with the misty hills above Loch Duich, I was reluctant to knuckle down and get going. I hauled myself from Strathcarron, uneager to attack the mist and rain that permeated the glen. Not a glimmer of brightness did

Glen Carron reveal for the whole of the six-mile journey through it to Achnashellach.

Crossing the River Carron near New Kelso Farm I joined a track that accompanies the languidly meandering river through the wide valley floor. A pine forest emerged from the gloom like a dark, shimmering curtain, its shadowy inhabitants resolutely hovering at my side for the next mile. Then I made an enforced diversion through the forest to the A890 road, for Jimmy had warned that the riverside track was fenced off a little farther along and, even if I was reckless enough to climb the fence, I would be confronted by the wide Fionn Abhainn burn that spills into the River Carron. Grateful for his advice I joined the road and crossed a bridge over the burn which funnelled through a deep cleft in the grey hills above me, as it neared the end of its three-mile journey from the tiny and secluded Loch Coire Fionnaraich.

I returned to the riverside and passed under the railway which veered across my path in order to avoid the impending Loch Dughaill, out of which the River Carron flows. It fills the valley-bottom and forces the road and railway to squeeze side by side between the steep valley-side and its north-west shore. The low-lying land was saturated with the incessant rain and I endured a boot-filling couple of miles until I was forced onto the A890 road once more by the constricting Loch Dughaill. In contrast to the beautiful photograph of the loch that I had seen earlier, in which it lay amongst striking autumn colour, it was a great disappointment to see it in darker mode with rain lashing its tortured surface.

Such miserable conditions generate the head down and get it over with approach. I ploughed along the A890 road, occasionally leaping aside to avoid a drenching from passing vehicles and tore into Achnashellach on the lookout for shelter. The downpour had intensified and rain bounced gleefully from the tarmac as I at last found refuge at the tiny station. I scurried into a brick-built shelter, which unfortunately had no door, but at least provided some respite. The deluge beat ferociously on the roof as I gazed through the doorway at a solid sheet of water. Frustration gripped me, for further progress seemed impossible unless I dispensed with my clothes and walked naked.

There I cowered for twenty minutes before the torrent abated slightly, but showed no sign of stopping. Torn by indecision I teetered in the doorway, reluctant to brave the elements. Five agonising minutes elapsed without any sign of improvement. As I dithered I thought of John Hillaby and his unsettling experience near Achnashellach. Extricating himself from the wilderness around the head of the River Ling he went by way of the lonely Loch an Laoigh and the mountain range to the south-east of Glen Carron. It was well into the evening when he climbed the crest of Sgurr na Feartaig, from which, hampered by thick cloud, there appeared to be no way down. Eventually a merciful break in the cloud revealed a track that took him some way down the mountain, until visibility disappeared once more. Unable to tell what lay below and imagining fearsome drops on all sides, he camped at the spot for the night. He awoke next morning to find that he had slept on a track that leads towards Achnashellach station. His troubles, however, were not over, for he had to wade across the River Carron that lay in his path.

The thought of the tribulations that he had overcome made me feel cowardly by comparison. Stung into action, I tore myself from my refuge and climbed through an extensive plantation. Fortune favours the brave, for as I reached the edge of the forest the rain remarkably ceased. The sun appeared, to my great relief, and shone on a series of bubbling waterfalls that punctuated a nearby jingling burn. In a remarkable transformation the sky turned a startling blue and there was colour all around me. Out came my camera to capture a mosaic of dark heather, rusty-coloured bracken and emerald grassland, enfolded by garlands of watchful spruce. Through this idyllic scene cavorted white cascades of playful water.

Now that Glen Carron had been relieved of its mantle I could look over the valley and see Sgurr na Feartaig, that had caused John Hillaby so much heartache, towering above it. The more distant Attadale Hills were emerging from a shifting bank of cloud to arouse memories of my own struggles in the high places above Loch Carron.

I gratefully removed my waterproofs and with a lighter heart completed the climb to the crest of the hill in glorious sunshine. Here I was treated to a panoramic view over the Coulin Forest, which in common with many others in Scotland is a deer, not a tree, forest. It stretches to Glen Torridon that lies eight miles to the north of Glen Carron, revealing an area of unrivalled appeal. Jimmy's promise of an outstanding walk was no exaggeration. Surrounded by majestic mountains, the Coulin Pass steers through a unique landscape. It portrays the true character of Wester Ross - vast tracts of land with a peerless colouring of vegetation. I stood spell-bound, for it was so different to all that had gone before. Here was another world, where heather and heath hugged the land like a giant brown carpet beneath an array of purple mountains, their rocks remorselessly exposed. A dead vast is how John Hillaby described the area around Glen Dessary, which precisely sums up much of Wester Ross. I was surveying a vista formerly clothed by the great Caledonian Forest that once covered most of the Highlands and was destroyed by man, who burned it and left a great wilderness.

The Torridonian sandstone that overlays the landscape was introduced a staggering 800 million years ago; a combination of shales and deposits washed from the bed of Lewisian Gneiss by pre-historic seas. On the highest summits, such as Beinn Eighe and Liatach that lie beyond Glen Torridon, the bright Cambrian quartzite, a mere 600 million years old, glints like silver in the sunshine.

I gazed on this superficially empty landscape in wonder, for it was difficult to comprehend the origins of its age-old rocks. It appeared empty to my untrained eye, which could only pick out the occasional bird. To a naturalist there is intriguing activity on even the most bare and exposed ground. John Hillaby discovered an infinite variety of tiny plants and insects that frequent such wastelands during his journey. How I envied his powers of observation and recognition.

I entered the Coulin Pass determined to be more vigilant, but my resolution soon waned as I became infatuated with the beautiful scenery. The majestic summits of Sgurr Ruadh and Beinn Liath Mhor lay to the west; home territory to Martin Moran. I recalled a photograph that Jimmy had shown me of Martin's wife Joy on a winter expedition in those mountains, courageously carrying their young child in a harness on her back.

Pangs of hunger demanded a lunch-stop in the heart of the pass at the opportune point where the River Coulin was joined by the Eason Dorcha burn which rushed over its stony bed through a scene of sheer delight. I eagerly removed my rucksack and found a convenient viewpoint beside the rippling stream. A dramatic transformation had occurred since my previous waterlogged respite in the shelter at Achnashellach. Life felt much sweeter now as I basked in sunshine amidst an oasis of undisturbed tranquillity. The prospect upstream, where the burn emerged from a scattering of graceful trees was riveting. Reflections in the water gave it a soft-purple hue, which subtly blended with the backdrop of shapely peaks. The crests of the Coulin Forest mountains were themselves presided over by the distant crown of mighty Liatach.

It was a short journey to Loch Coulin and its neighbour Loch Clair that occupy the north end of the Coulin valley. The ashen surface of Loch Coulin was barely rippled by a taunting breeze that hurried through colourful shrubs and a cluster of gently-waving birches on its bank. An occasional decapitated tree added austerity to the scene, its trunk standing erect like a gnarled flag pole.

Progress was good as I followed a wide bridle-path along the shores of the lochs. It was overlaid with shale that had been scoured from the surrounding hillsides. Its slate-grey surface complemented an attractive archway of silver birches that enclosed it. Emerging from the tree-lined tunnel I saw the massive bulk of Beinn Eighe thrusting skywards beyond Loch Clair. The mountain oozed character, from its long and dramatically indented summit ridges down to the vivid quartzite outcrops on its angular slopes. Wainwright describes Beinn Eighe as the 'great cornerstone of Torridon', and goes on to say, 'It is more a range than a single mountain, having nine peaks linked by the graceful curves of supporting ridges'. Determined not to be overshadowed, the giant arrowhead of Sgurr Dubh beckoned from across the loch. From my viewpoint its shape was reminiscent of Schiehallion, as I had seen it from the Tummel Valley.

There was so much to admire, I could have lingered by the lochside for the whole afternoon, but Kinlochewe beckoned. The track had become a metalled private road as I passed Coulin Lodge and I marched at a good pace until I arrived in Glen Torridon and joined the A896 road that traverses it. I realised that walkers had again been conspicuous by their absence and, unless I could escape that road, which covers the remaining three miles to Kinlochewe, it was unlikely that I would enjoy any company at all. No convenient paths were evident so I struggled along the stony bank of the nearby River A'Ghairbhe. The river scenery was splendid, but short-lived, for I was eventually beaten back by thickets of broom and an impenetrable wood that stood in my way. Accepting defeat, I rested on a riverside rock and enjoyed a final view of the river. It was pleasing to see the occasional coot and moorhen, with their distinctly coloured foreheads, gracefully skim above the water. The river looked inviting for travel-weary feet, but the water felt ice-cold, so I lazed in the sunshine instead.

As I rejoined the road for the final two miles of my day's journey

I had a clear view of Beinn Eighe protruding from the undulating heathland of a National Nature Reserve. In the care of the Conservancy Council, the Reserve encompasses 10,500 acres and includes a mountain trail on Beinn Eighe itself. At the end of the last Ice Age the area was clothed with pine and birch, which formed part of the great Caledonian Forest, whose sad remnants are isolated pockets of Caledonian Pine. Deer and wildcat now roam the land which was formerly the home of bear, wild pig and wolf. Majestic golden eagles keep watch from lofty corries.

Beinn Eighe occupied my thoughts until I approached a road junction on the outskirts of Kinlochewe where the A896 road meets the A832 which leaves Gairloch on the west coast to traverse the south-west shore of Loch Maree before heading for Kinlochewe and eventually Fortrose. The junction is overlooked by the mountain wall of the Letterewe ridge that guards the north-east flank of Loch Maree and forms the southern boundary of Letterewe Forest. A little colour was added to this grey canvas of grizzled mountains by the brightly-flowering broom that flourishes in the valley beneath.

I followed the A832 road into Kinlochewe and easily found my accommodation; an attractive bungalow that stood by the roadside. It belonged to the local District Nurse, Ivy, and her husband Brian; very beneficial for walkers suffering aches and pains or troublesome blisters. Brian seemed keen to talk about the area whilst I enjoyed some refreshment. He told me that, despite its size, Kinlochewe had been an important staging post on the old packhorse routes. If the Kyle of Lochalsh to Inverness railway had not avoided the village in favour of Achnasheen, he said, it may well have grown in prominence. However, he reckoned that it was currently doing very nicely as a halt for tourists, many on their way to Gairloch or Inverewe Gardens. Admittedly not a walker or climber, he said that mountaineering opportunities were limitless in the surrounding heights and you could walk for miles through uncluttered countryside without meeting a soul. I could attest to that, I told him, having walked for the previous two days in complete isolation. Brian's preferred recreation was pulling salmon from Loch Maree or shooting deer in the surrounding hills. Many of the locals he said, enjoyed the same pastimes, but were sometimes scathing about incomers who often made idiots of themselves by disturbing the fish or blundering over the surrounding moorland scaring anything that moved.

After supper I wandered from the village towards Loch Maree, along the Letterewe track, as it is known, that traverses its north-east shore. This splendid loch is one of the most highly-rated in Scotland, surrounded as it is by magnificent wild country for the whole of its twelve-mile length. Long before Wainwright devised his English Coast to Coast Walk and prior to the advent of the Inverness to Lochalsh railway, postmen carried mail on a Scottish cross-country route between Dingwall on the east coast and Poolewe on the west. This remarkable 'post-round' took a week to complete on foot and part of it, from Kinlochewe to Poolewe, lay along the track that I was on. All the mail for the Outer Islands was carried along the shore of Loch Maree, beneath the Letterewe ridge; an apt name, for it could have been devised by the Royal Mail. In the glow of a fine evening I enjoyed a close inspection of the ridge's towering mountain chain that once yielded many veins of iron ore from its lower slopes. As I looked along the blue expanse of Kinlochewe River the pointed peak of Slioch, meaning spear, protruded above its neighbours into a perfect evening sky. The ubiquitous broom lined the riverbank as far as Loch Maree, to complete an unforgettable picture.

Returning to the bungalow, I rang Maurice who had thoughtfully given me the telephone number of his lodgings on Skye. His surprisingly disgruntled voice greeted me, but it brightened when he learned who his caller was. Apparently he had not had a good day. His journey to Broadford on the previous day had gone smoothly, but his attempt to reach the Cuillins had been a disaster. He had waited for three frustrating hours that morning for a bus to Elgol, where, he had been advised, there was a superb view of them across Loch Scavaig. The problem was that only one bus plied between Broadford and Elgol, which also acted as post-van. It had departed on time in the early morning from Broadford, to find on reaching Elgol that the mail had been delayed. At mid-day Maurice was told that it would not arrive back in Broadford until one o'clock. The even worse news was that due to the delay its return trip to Elgol would be its last of the day and that it would have to turn round there and immediately return to Broadford. Whereupon, an exasperated Maurice told the inspector just what he thought of his bus service. When he had cooled down he caught a bus to Portree and spent the afternoon there.

DAY TWENTY THREE: KINLOCHEWE - CAMUSNAGAUL

Another long day was in prospect. Twenty-four hard miles lay between me and my destination, Camusnagaul, a scattering of dwellings on the shore of Little Loch Broom. This sea-loch is one of many that bite into the dissipated west coastline which borders the Designated Area of Natural Beauty that encompasses much of Wester Ross. Today I planned to cross the desolate and wild region of austere mountains and rampant peat that is sandwiched between Loch Maree and Little Loch Broom.

As I lay pondering the challenges of the coming day, an activity I normally try to avoid, I recalled Wainwright's warning to those attempting such a journey. 'It is an expedition only for the very fit, weaklings and novices must expect to perish. Once committed, there is no escape. It is just about the roughest terrain that can be encountered'. This chilling prospect propelled me from my bed and I busied myself with ablutions and sorting my kit in an effort to keep such disquieting thoughts at bay.

Things always appear rosier when you are fortified with a good breakfast and so it was on that morning, when, with enough cholesterol inside me to block every artery, I looked from the dining-room window upon a garden bathed in sunshine. Emboldened with false courage I felt ready to tackle anything that nature could throw at me. In expectation of a late completion of my day's walk I had purchased milk and biscuits the previous evening, at the village store, in order to supplement my packed-lunch. As events turned out, it was a wise move.

I was thankful for excellent visibility as I followed the valley of the Abhainn Bruachaig which leads towards Kinlochewe Forest; the last thing that I needed as I approached open, rugged country was mist. Walking was remarkably easy along a good level track that wound alongside the burn. All was at peace as I covered the three miles to the Heights of Kinlochewe at a good pace. The occasional warning cry of the protective curlew floated on the breeze and timid squirrels and rabbits scurried from my path. I turned periodically to enjoy a splendid retrospective view of the snow-spattered Ben Eighe that was attractively framed by the foothills of Carn à Ghlinne and Kinlochewe Forest.

The tiny cluster of buildings that comprise the augustly named Heights of Kinlochewe appeared to be no higher than Kinlochewe itself. Where were the dramatic rocks that its name suggested? All around were lush meadows in which Highland cattle quietly grazed; a serene amphitheatre, ringed by steep, heather-clad hillsides, with not a formidable rock-formation in sight.

As I pondered who had bestowed such a misleading name on the locality, I swung north into the valley of the Gleann na Muice. Here I passed a daunting notice bearing a rampant stag and a similar message to the one I had seen at Inverlochlarig. It warned me that deer are shot in the surrounding hills from mid-August to February, for sport meat, in accordance with government control policy. Around four percent of deer stocks are apparently culled to maintain a balance. Walkers were advised not to venture onto high ground during the stalking season for it could be dangerous. Kinlochewe Forest is rich with red deer, which are more prolific than the roe deer that only survive in the remnants of the Caledonian Forest and older Lake District woodland. Red deer, the largest native mammal to be found amongst mountain and woodland, inhabit most upland moors in the Highlands and the Lake District and are even living as far south as Exmoor. They display an intriguing social pattern based on small family groups, all of which are probably descendants of the oldest hind, which acts as leader. Each group keeps to its own territory, but in high summer, when flies become a pest, they move to communes on the mountain summits. In autumn they forsake the high ground and return to their own territory. The stags form their own small groups, often on different territory and break up when they join the hinds for the rut in October.

The sweat and toil was about to begin, for I could see the track unravelling before me as it twisted through the steepening valley in search of lonely Lochan Fada. There was nothing for it but to grit my teeth and tackle a four-mile climb to the loch that lay hidden a thousand feet above me. The track appeared to snake into infinity each time I hopefully gazed along it to check on my progress. I climbed steadily until the gaunt features of distant mountains appeared beyond the head of the valley. They beckoned me towards an isolation into which few people venture. When I finally emerged from the valley to gaze over the serene indigo waters of Lochan Fada, it heralded a scene of untamed splendour. The loch lies in a long and narrow basin surrounded by a galaxy of impressive peaks that portray nature in the raw. It was a haven of tranquillity that has remained undisturbed for an eternity. The Letterewe ridge looms over the south shore of the loch, its furrowed north face exposed. Slioch's distinctively sharp peak once again dominated the ridge, overshadowing the more rounded summits of Beinn Làir and Meall Mhèinnidh. It is a mountain that impresses when viewed from all angles. The north shore rises gracefully towards the foothills of a softer mountain range whose pinnacle is Mullach Coire Mhic Fhearchair that was obscured from my view by its outlying hills.

For the third day running I nurtured the vain hope of meeting other walkers and I thought that my wish had been granted when I noticed a small tent by the loch. It looked tiny and incongruous in such a boundless landscape, but I hurried eagerly towards it anticipating some welcome company. There was sadly no sign of its occupants who were probably exploring the surrounding mountains.

My hopes dashed I returned to the point where the track from Heights of Kinlochewe ended. From there I had to rely on map and compass to guide me, for there would be no paths until I reached Loch an Nid that lay tantalisingly several miles to the north. Searching for a landmark on my map I discovered the minuscule Loch Meallan an Fhudair which formed a useful initial objective. Secreted a mile above me amongst the hills, it has a convenient stream issuing from it that tumbles almost exactly to the point where I was standing. All I needed to do was follow the stream, or so I thought, but it did not turn out to be that simple.

At first all went well as I began a stiff climb up the rough fellside, guided by the lively stream. Perversely it soon decided to disappear underground, much to my consternation. It was not far from the surface for I could hear it gurgling merrily. This indicated that, despite its disappearance, I could follow its sound and still use it as a navigator. I renewed my struggle up the testing slope, keeping one ear as close to the ground as possible, a feat that necessitated bending almost double. It was fortunate that I was completely alone as I staggered up the incline, lurching from side to side whilst desperately trying to follow the meandering stream. How ridiculous I must have appeared. I was reminded of Maurice and our Quasimodo impressions as we stumbled around the attic room in Spean Bridge. How I wished that he was with me now, his sense of humour would have been a great asset.

With back aching and ears straining I reached the crest of the hill to come face to face with the diminutive loch, that is nothing more than a large pond. It was a gratifying sight enhanced by a beautiful setting. The garland of rounded hills that encompass it resemble the rolling waves of a jade ocean and they compelled me to pause and enjoy the thrill of this vast emptiness. I eventually turned towards distant Torridon, beyond Slioch, which now exhibited pockets of snow that glistened in the sunshine. Beinn Eighe and Liatach shimmered in a distant haze, bidding me a final farewell, for I would not see them again. I felt privileged to enjoy the grandeur of such surroundings and could happily have remained there for the rest of the day. This solitary corner of Wester Ross is a heaven on earth, a place of riches that money cannot buy.

I still had many challenges ahead of me and if I did not wish to spend the night under the stars it was time to extract my finger. On the move once more, my admiration for that appealing wilderness quickly waned. How fickle I became when faced with the savage adversary of cloying peat. All romantic thoughts vanished as I leapt in and out of peat-groughs that would severely test the metal of an Olympic steeplechaser. Having conquered the glutinous peat-bogs of Kinder Scout and the Cheviots that threaten to swallow Pennine Way walkers, I reckoned that I could deal with any kind of terrain. Nothing, however, had prepared me for this hostile country, which made Kinder pale into insignificance. The quivering mass of peat threatened to engulf me and I was convinced that I was about to disappear without trace. Wainwright's words of warning echoed in my brain - 'It is just about the roughest terrain that can be encountered'. How right he was and how stupid was I to have ignored them.

Observing my struggles from aloft was a large bird that soared gracefully on currents of warm, clear air. Could it be a vulture waiting for a meal, in the likely event that I became marooned? The realisation dawned that I was still in a popular domain of eagles and this was probably an inquisitive one bent on scrutinising a rare human intruder. As it floated effortlessly above me I hoped that it wasn't hungry and fervently wished that it could metamorphose into a helicopter, lower a rope and pluck me from this mass of brown treacle. Sadly I could only gaze upwards and wonder what it thought of my antics. Was it a sea-eagle, I asked myself? Their last reputed breeding-place was the cliffs above Loch Broom that lay only sixteen miles away as the crow, or eagle, flies. These majestic birds have been in the news recently through the policy of re-introducing them into the Highlands, from whence they disappeared eighty years ago due to extensive hunting. Ten more pairs have just been released from the Western Isles, where they have been bred, much to the chagrin of many Highland farmers. They report incidents of these predators picking up lambs and carrying them to their nests. One farmer tells of finding the carcasses of twelve lambs in one eagle's nest. I sincerely hoped that the bird circling above me had not mistaken me for a lamb. Thankfully it became bored with my performance and flew away.

My tussle with the hostile environment reduced me to a state of near-exhaustion and I began to ask myself what on earth I was doing. Was it the challenge, I wondered, or an irrepressible desire to escape the materialism and sedentary life-style of modern society? Too tired to rack my brain I settled for avoidance of the mother-in-law. After all, out there I merely had the elements to fight and only myself to argue with.

I ploughed through the mire, my spirits flagging and understanding exactly how the soldiers had fared in the Battle of the Somme. My compass was gripped tightly and my eyes were glued to it lest I lose my bearing. I was soon confronted with a selection of valleys and hoped that I had identified the correct one, for tucked away beyond it was Loch an Nid and I had no desire to search them all. Mercifully the going became easier as I descended into the chosen valley and I took the opportunity to rest and gather my strength. The mountain of peat that I scraped from my boots would not be missed. My surroundings appeared dull and featureless in the confines of the valley when compared to the broad canvas that I had recently enjoyed. Although I was now ploughing through scrub and heather it was relatively easy going after the morass of the higher ground. If my course was correct I expected to find a path that crossed the mouth of the valley and I kept my eyes peeled as the hills on either side of me began to recede. I swung into another valley that lay across my path and led me in the intended direction, due north. My anxiety soon disappeared when I discovered a path running through it, and heaved a sigh of relief. My heart sang as Loch an Nid appeared, directly on cue. A study of my map confirmed that I could follow my new-found path, which eventually joined a track, right to the road that runs to Little Loch Broom. Celebration would be premature, for I still had many miles to cover and it was already mid-afternoon. However, I was able to relax and enjoy the view along the wide valley. What an inspiring one it was.

The sun beamed upon the grassy south shore of the loch, imparting a subtle yellow tone to the short-cropped grass. It reminded me of the rich colour of the banks of the Dee near White Bridge. How long ago it seemed since I had set out from Linn of Dee on the long day's march to Blair Atholl. My eye was drawn to the silvery gleam of the Cambrian quartzite that coated the lower slopes of Meallan an Laoigh that soars from the west shore of the loch. I had not seen this bright rock at such close quarters and its dazzle made the attendant mountains appear sombre by comparison. There was, however, nothing undramatic about the magnificent outline of the famous An Teallach ridge that fills the horizon to the north. I could not take my eyes from it as I buoyantly strode through the valley.

Once Loch an Nid was left behind I was accompanied by the energetic Abhainn Loch an Nid that romped beside me in its stony channel. As I walked I recalled what I had read about An Teallach; of its eleven pinnacles and its barbed, three mile-long main ridge. Crossing this dramatic ridge is said to be a fearsome prospect and so it looked as I gazed at its intimidating teeth. The huge bulk of the mountain covers a wide area and its northern slopes career right down to the sea beyond Camusnagaul.

The exciting surroundings kept weariness at bay, but eventually my strength began to ebb and I decided to rest beside a gushing waterfall. I found a convenient rock on which to perch and searched my rucksack for food. My packed-lunch had been devoured, but I found the life-saving biscuits and milk that I had wisely obtained. As I leisurely chewed my favourite custard-creams, in the welcome shade provided by a cluster of shapely larches, I realised that they were the first trees that I had seen since leaving Heights of Kinlochewe. Looking back along the valley I could see the dark dome of Mullach Coire Mhic Fhearchair, the inkiness of its upper reaches relieved by broad patches of milky snow. Despite it being early June, many of the mountains retained traces of their winter coats; a warning to walkers and climbers that it can be bitterly cold on their summits throughout the year.

I stared at the foaming burn as though I could draw strength from it. My bog-hopping exploits were leaving their mark and it was an effort to rouse myself. With a heavy sigh I got to my feet and hoisted my rucksack, that seemed to weigh a ton, onto my back. I struggled to regain my momentum, so easily lost whenever you stop, and my feet began to protest. Thankfully I had not been seriously troubled by blisters, but the patches of hard skin that had developed - I had been walking for over three weeks - were determined not to be ignored. A mental note was made to give them some attention when I reached Camasnagaul.

The path, that would shortly transform itself into a stony track, stretched for what seemed many miles in front of me. At least I no longer needed to scratch my head over map and compass; merely keep myself moving. The great mass of An Teallach drew closer and I could make out many of its other features, including its fickle colour, which had become chocolate brown. My eye ranged along its massive spine, the vertebrae transforming from rounded humps at the base into ragged teeth on its higher reaches. What a thrill it would be to walk along that remarkable backbone. I had carried a mental image of it in my mind since seeing an aerial photograph of its summit ridge, resembling a giant chocolate bar, disfigured by great teeth marks, protruding through a furry blanket of cloud into a startling aquamarine sky. How I wished that I could have stood on its 3484 feet summit in such memorable conditions.

The track steepens as it skirts the base of the mountain bringing into view the distant peaks of Inverleal Forest that lie to the east. This spiky range is crowned by mighty Beinn Dearg that rises over 3500 feet. During the Ice Age it was one of several mountains in the locality that were covered by an ice-cap thousands of feet thick, from which glaciers flowed to the Atlantic Ocean. When the ice-cap melted it carved the huge gorge of Corrieshalloch as its waters rushed towards Loch Broom.

I trudged wearily to the brow of a hill, where I removed my rucksack and took a breather as I surveyed the final descent of the day into the Dundonnell Valley. The distinctive grey of the track was clearly visible as it squirmed through a sepia-coloured landscape. Overlooking the valley stands the handsome dome of Carn à Bhreabadair, its summit disclosing patches of grizzled rock and its lower slopes flecked with stunted trees.

The early-evening sun coated the scene with a lustrous veneer as I hauled on my rucksack and tottered down the track. I was now on automatic pilot, a state that many walkers find themselves in towards the end of a gruelling day. My arms and legs no longer belonged to me and moved instinctively. Even the sight of waterfalls, dancing in the nearby Gleann Chaorachain failed to lure me from the track. I was beyond struggling through heather for a closer look. Another feast of views was unfolding before my tired eyes and although I was unable to see Little Loch Broom itself, the mountains of the Cailleach Head peninsula that lie to the north of it were clearly visible. The shadows were lengthening on their rugged flanks, an indication that time was rapidly slipping away. I was too exhausted to increase my pace and I could only hope that I would get some supper that night.

My spirits enjoyed a boost when I met the first walkers that I had seen since leaving Shiel Bridge. I was approaching the Dundonnell River when I saw two sprightly, middle-aged ladies coming towards me, accompanied by a splendid golden Labrador. These ladies believed in sharing their load, for not only were they each bearing a rucksack, the dog also had one strapped to its back. When I laughingly commented on this unusual sight, I was told that the animal was regularly made to carry his food and blanket. The ladies asked where I was heading and listened intently to a brief account of my day. It was not until we said goodbye and I watched them striding up the track that I realised I had forgotten to ask where they were going at that time of the evening. I must have been more tired than I realised.

The remainder of my journey was completed almost mechanically, my sole objectives being to get a meal and put my feet up. Thankfully there was no more climbing and I soon joined 'Destitution Road', as it is known, for the last few miles. It led me down to Little Loch Broom and its name is a reference to its construction during the potato famine of 1851, thus providing work for destitute and starving men. Dundonnell River came alongside occasionally as it wound through the widening Strath Beag. The river is the haunt of the merganser duck that goes up it to breed and I managed to observe a group of those tousle-headed creatures. They swam low in the water, their distinctive coloured crests bristling in the breeze; chestnut-brown for the females and bottle-green for the males.

At last Little Loch Broom appeared, stretching serenely towards the open sea. I only had a further two miles to complete. Desperately tired now, I summoned my remaining strength as I passed the Dundonnell Hotel, reposing at the south-east corner of the loch. Aching limbs were dragged along the pleasant lochside road. The sun was beginning to wane when I finally reached my objective, an attractive dormer-bungalow overlooking the water's edge.

My first question to Anne, as she opened the door to greet me, concerned my anxiety about supper. I need not have worried, for after a hurried shower, I was treated to an admirable meal. Considerately she made no mention of my late arrival nor complained that the other guests had already eaten. These I discovered were four young men, all doctors, who were staying for a few nights. I was very interested to learn that they had scaled the An Teallach ridge that day and I eagerly asked how they had fared. Exhilarating and exhausting was their judgment. In fact they were so tired that they went to bed at nine o'clock and I wasn't far behind them. We all slept like logs.

DAY TWENTY-FOUR : CAMUSNAGAUL - ULLAPOOL

I awoke greatly refreshed. This was remarkable, considering that I had been dragged from my bed during the night in order to lead a rescue party onto the An Teallach ridge in pitch darkness. Delighted to call upon the services of a seasoned traveller and heroic mountaineer, the local mountain rescue team had begged me to master-mind the daring recovery of four young doctors who were at that very moment clinging for dear life to one of the pinnacles of the mountain's great backbone. My initial reaction had been one of disbelief. I indicated that the only young doctors I had encountered were on television. Was this a hoax, I wondered? Eventually realising that their request was deadly serious, I agreed to accompany them with the proviso that I could take my faithful Labrador which would carry all the necessary ropes and equipment in a rucksack strapped to its back. After a record-breaking night-time ascent of the ridge, the piercing beam of my torch revealed the four protagonists, who had been reduced to jibbering wretches. Their white knuckles were radiant in the shaft of light; glowing fingers clung to slivers of rock poised tantalisingly above the black void that separated rescuers and potential victims. Screams of anguish rent the air, alternating with desperate pleas for me to pluck them from their predicament. Their agonising cries rose to a crescendo as I reached out for the nearest petrified figure. My outstretched hand clutched the air a taunting foot away from him. Summoning every ounce of courage and strength I stretched as far across the terrifying chasm as I dared and flung out my hand once more. I was straining, straining with every fibre of my being .... then I woke up and realised that it was all a dream.

My agenda for the day would be far more mundane than the fantasy that I had just experienced. I was going to treat myself to a seven-mile stroll to Ullapool; provided that things went according to plan. Success hinged on the small ferry that crosses Loch Broom, from Altnaharrie to my destination. If it was operating my day would be easy; if it wasn't a seventeen-mile walk was in prospect, something that I did not relish after three long days in the hills. Only the three-mile wide Cailleach Head peninsula separates Little Loch Broom from Loch Broom, but the latter is the longest sea-loch in the north-west Highlands and thrusts twenty-one miles inland. It would be a long walk around its head, for Ullapool stands seven miles from it on the north-east shore.

I had no wish to suffer the same fate as John Hillaby when he tried to cross Loch Broom. He reached Allt na h-Airbhe at dusk to discover that the ferry was not operating, but was helpfully put up for the night in a partly-completed house that a man was building for his sick wife. The following morning he managed to cross the loch in the boat that carried the workmen, who were building the house, from Ullapool.

My concern over the ferry was the only cloud on the horizon as I joined the doctors for breakfast. They were greatly amused when I told them about my dream. They swore not to go near An Teallach again and showed me their knuckles, which were far from white.

Whilst we were finishing coffee after breakfast I asked to use the telephone in order to set my mind at rest. I rang the inn at Altnaharrie and anxiously enquired if the ferry was available. A cheerful male voice told me that he would take me across and asked what time I would arrive. We settled on a rendezvous at one o'clock, much to my relief. I returned to give the good news to the doctors who were preparing to spend the day in the mountains of Inverleal Forest. Now that there was no need to hurry I had another cup of coffee to celebrate.

Retracing my steps along the shore of Little Loch Broom I felt much fitter and took the opportunity to study a locality that I had barely noticed the previous evening. The loch appeared to be aptly named, for its banks were ablaze with colourful broom which almost glowed in the morning sunshine. When I tired of road-walking I ventured onto the narrow strip of springy turf that separates it from the rock-strewn loch side. Visibility was as clear as a bell and when

I took a backward look down the placid loch I could see the outline of Cailleach Head jutting into the open sea.

As I passed the Dundonnell Hotel I found it worth a second look; its shapely frontage had style, that is often lacking in modern hotels. What a pleasant contrast it was to the concrete monstrosities often found in urban areas, or beside motorways; rectangular blocks, permeated with functional detachment. Dundonnell Hotel had character and a well-manicured appearance. Its pristine walls were a brilliant white, in keeping with the buildings in nearby Camusnagaul. The local painters were obviously never idle.

I veered from the road onto a track that took me through verdant meadows around the head of the loch. The sun beamed, birds twittered; everything seemed idyllic until I came to Dundonnell River. Stepping onto the convenient footbridge in sprightly fashion I felt it lurch disconcertingly. Memories of the bouncing bridge that had threatened to throw me into the Falls of Tarf came flooding back. Clinging grimly to the flimsy hand-rails I edged across the intimidating span that lurched gaily with each step. It was a great relief to regain solid ground without a drenching.

The surrounding countryside was so appealing that I seized every opportunity to use my camera. As I turned to capture the hump of Glas Mheall Mor, an outlying buttress of An Teallach that was visible across the valley, an inquisitive cow wandered into shot and nearly stuck its nose into my face. I retreated and took a quick photograph with the friendly cow in the foreground, which I entitled 'Cow and An Teallach'.

It was soon time to leave the comfort of the valley and begin the 800 feet climb over the Cailleach Head peninsula. I joined a narrow, unfenced road that climbs steeply through a forest, which afforded some welcome shade, for it was hot work. As it breaks out into open country the road becomes less steep, but it was still a hard pull, on the warm tarmac, to the peninsula's crest. I did not spare myself as I rounded Beinn nam Ban, for despite having plenty of time until my rendezvous with the ferry, I was still concerned about missing the boat, as it were. A brief stop was taken to have a last look over Little Loch Broom to the mountains beyond. The white oases of Camasnagaul and the Dundonnell Hotel looked minuscule beneath the towering northern slopes of An Teallach. It was an indelible scene, crowned by a vault of unclouded blue.

Its hard work done, the road abruptly turns and heads west, for the isolated hamlet of Badrallach. I was obliged to join a rough track which continues north and provides the sole access by land to Allt na h-Airbhe. Residents, and guests at the inn, can only reach it by four-wheel-drive vehicle or boat. I allowed myself a short respite beside a secluded lochan that relieved the monotony of undulating moorland. Eager for my first view of Ullapool I was soon striding along the now-descending track and hadn't gone very far before the ground began to drop steeply down to the south-west shore of Loch Broom. A wide expanse of water lay below me, with a sprawling landscape beyond. Ullapool seemed close enough to reach out and touch as it beckoned from the far side of the mile-wide loch. Its pier and harbour, clearly visible, form the focal point of the popular village that seemed a bustling metropolis when compared to the isolation of the previous three days. It shelters beneath rolling hills that surge north towards the distant rock formations of Inverpolly Forest and the Cromalt Hills. What a thrill it was to see the next stage of my journey spread before me like a giant relief map.

I fought the urge to gallop down the abrupt incline, for many pitfalls lay in wait on the rutted track to trap careless feet. Wainwright's sound advice of always watching where you place them when descending came to mind. It was better to lose a few minutes than break a limb. I still arrived at the loch side at mid-day, one hour ahead of schedule; my impatience earning me a long wait. A narrow jetty stood nearby to which a small launch was moored. This, I assumed, was the ferry. It swayed lazily in the rippling water and in my cowardly way I hoped that it was sea-worthy. Ullapool was frustratingly so near, yet so far, and its cluster of buildings, all of which were coloured the indigenous white, looked appealing, even from a mile away. The white paint manufacturers have had a field-day in this part of Wester Ross. They have adapted the Henry Ford edict - you can have any colour you like, providing it is white.

Sitting down on the jetty I took off my boots and socks and dangled my feet in the deliciously cool water. I took out my packed-lunch, happy that walking was over for the day. As I sat contentedly eating my sandwiches I thought of the old saying - cast your bread upon the waters and it will come back buttered - so I threw some pieces into the loch to see what happened. They were swiftly snatched by circling gulls who knew a soft touch when they saw one. I received nothing in return, but hopefully my generosity would ensure a safe passage to Ullapool. The hour passed sluggishly as I waited, breathing the remarkably pure air, typical of the sub-arctic lands of the Western Isles, and continually checking my watch.

True to his word the ferryman appeared at one o'clock and told me that I was his only passenger. He cast off and the tiny craft chugged from the shore towards the flesh-pots of Ullapool. The water, which had appeared calm from the jetty, became quite choppy and we were soon bobbing to and fro like a cork. My benefactor chatted unconcernedly, oblivious to such conditions, but I became quite concerned as I did not fancy a swim. I struggled to concentrate on the emerging features of the harbour to keep my worried mind occupied. The wooden ramparts of the pier were clearly visible and several anglers were perched on them, lines dangling expectantly into the loch. Behind the harbour a line of bright, unblemished buildings overlooked a shingle beach. Their white walls positively gleamed.

Immediately after depositing me on the harbour jetty, the boatman sped away with a friendly wave, leaving me to enjoy the view towards the head of Loch Broom. A ring of mountains encircle it, looming above fertile Strath More which narrows into the dramatic gorge of Corrieshalloch. Superimposed on this mélange of mountains and water was a flotilla of yachts dancing daintily near the harbour entrance. Above the ragged contours of Inverleal Forest and neighbouring Braemore Forest I caught sight of Beinn Dearg once more and I could visualise the doctors dangling from its challenging summit. I wondered how they were really faring.

The afternoon was spent enjoying the delights of Ullapool and I could appreciate why it is such a popular resort, and halting place on Highland excursions. There was a carefree, bustling air about the place, as there had been in Pitlochry and visitors were welcomed with open arms. During its early days the village was predominantly a fishing port and owed its emergent prosperity in the late eighteenth century to herring. Fishing has sadly declined, a fact cruelly demonstrated when I later returned to the harbour to watch the boats landing their catches. How meagre they looked; sad remnants of a once-thriving industry. However, Ullapool refuses to be despondent and offers unlimited outdoor activities to the thousands of visitors who flock there each year. Sea and fresh-water angling is a speciality and for those who prefer countryside pursuits, pony-trekking, walking and climbing are conveniently on the doorstep. Inverpolly Forest draws many visitors. Serious walkers and climbers explore Cul Mor (2786 feet) and Cul Beag (2525 feet) but most people are attracted by the lowest of the trio of its peaks, Stac Polly that stands just over 2000 feet. It is the unique shape of this mountain that makes it one of the most visited in the country. The shattered outline of this multi-turreted bastion of red sandstone is greatly sought after by photographers and is easily accessible, lying a mere ten miles to the north-west of the village, as the crow flies. For anyone interested in a sea voyage, the summer ferry is on hand to Stornaway on the Outer Hebridean Island of Lewis. For those less venturesome, a short trip to the Summer Isles, situated in the wide bay at the mouth of Outer Loch Broom is readily available.

A friendly greeting awaited me at the Tourist Information Office, where I enquired about accommodation beyond Kylesku. The reason for breaking my normal rule of booking ahead on a long-distance walk was two-fold. Firstly, I did not know at the outset if I would get that far, for my previously longest trek had been the Pennine Way, less than half the distance of the one that I was attempting. Secondly, my route across the north-west corner of Scotland was not finalised due to its remoteness and possible harsh weather conditions. I had learned that accommodation was very sparse beyond Kylesku and its availability would also influence my final choice of route. The helpful assistant tried very hard to help me, but after several abortive telephone calls she had to admit defeat. She could only suggest that I make further enquiries on reaching Kylesku.

Around five o'clock I went to the local Youth Hostel where I was staying that night. It was bulging, appearing more like a cosmopolitan hotel than a hostel. There were hostellers of many nationalities, some having arrived by car and coach. Conditions were fully acceptable, but I longed for that special atmosphere of smaller and more traditional hostels. The warden was friendly and not without a sense of humour, which must help when dealing with hoards of visitors. On the reception desk he had placed a cryptic notice which read, 'Ring TWICE for slow service'.

Whilst enjoying supper in the crowded dining room I encountered an entertaining young couple, Brian and Stella, who, I discovered had recently graduated from strollers to their local pub into keen long-distance walkers. Ullapool was their current base for exploring the wilder areas of Wester Ross. Like myself, they were drawn to its remote and sometimes intimidating landscape. Away from its sparse network of roads, they said, you could walk all day in complete isolation. How true. I told them how, after leaving Shiel Bridge, I had walked for three days before meeting another soul.

Our mutual feelings expanded to the cordiality shown by other walkers. We agreed that their greeting often depended on the location. The lonelier the meeting-place, the more friendly the reaction. This we attributed to the pleasure of actually meeting someone in the wilds of Wester Ross or similar untamed settings.

One of my pet hates, I told the like-minded couple, is the unfriendly or superior type of walker who reacts to your cheery salutation with a blank stare or an arrogant sniff. Such a rejoinder makes me check that my flies are not undone or the remains of my last meal are not plastered around my mouth. A smile or a simple 'hello' never goes amiss. Walking is supposed to be a great leveller and an enjoyable social activity. Isn't it?

I easily warmed to the likable couple who obviously enjoyed their food and seemed to share my opinions. When I admitted my aversion to terse walkers, they responded with their dislike of the macho ones who completely ignore what other people have to say, wishing purely to brag about their own accomplishments. Such people, they said, are deservedly served 'soft-soap', which they haven't the gumption to detect, as they are so full of themselves. A funny expression - 'soft soap'. It ranks alongside 'flannel', and apparently is a substance that was often used for removing external tumours from animals. Irate vets might argue that I am misinformed, but I understand that the soap was smeared onto twine which was then tied around the offending growth, eventually eating through it. I mentioned its use to Brian and Stella, adding that I had no idea why the word was used in its modern context. Neither had they.

At the end of the meal I excused myself, explaining that I had work to do, and enquired at reception if I might be allocated my job that evening. A quick get-away on the following morning was needed. The practice may have ceased whereby hostellers perform a cleaning, or other useful task, but at that time you were expected to do your bit towards the efficient running of the hostel. My particular chore that evening was crushing aluminium drink cans under a small hand-press for subsequent re-cycling. Friends of the Earth rejoice.

Later I rejoined my two acquaintances for a walk around the still-busy streets and we were treated to the most glorious sunset over the Summer Isles. Such fiery evening skies are apparently a regular occurrence, and evening cruises will take you to Outer Loch Broom to view them at close quarters.

DAY TWENTY-FIVE: ULLAPOOL - ELPHIN

The day began poorly and went downhill. I left an Ullapool that scowled under heavy skies and spitting rain, cursing the weather pendulum for swinging once more. As I followed the road out of the village my eyes were skinned for the path that would lead me into the hills that overlook Strath Kanaird. This particular route had looked promising on the map for it cuts out a broad loop in the only road running north from Ullapool, the A 835.

I found the coveted path about a mile from the village, which was a signal for the rain to switch into overdrive and a thick pea-souper to obliterate any landmarks. In a few minutes I was wet through and annoyingly, was to remain so all day. With visibility down to a few yards I struggled to keep sight of the inconspicuous path, frequently resorting to my compass in order to keep on its line. How disorientating mist can be. I suffered some anxious moments until I met the track for which I was aiming. Relief flooded through me for I now had a lifeline and would soon be in Strath Kanaird, or so I thought. My pace quickened as I ventured through a silent, ethereal world with only the sound of my boots, scuffing the undulating track, for company. Imagine my shock and dismay when it abruptly disappeared into an expanse of water that lay across my path. I anxiously scanned the map to try and pin-point my position, only to find that Sod's law had prevailed. I had walked off one map and nearly onto the next one, which unfortunately did not exactly correspond. Two miles of my route were missing and I had no idea what lay directly ahead. How far the water extended was impossible to assess, because of the murk, and I had no map to show me. I cursed my bad luck and tried to think of a way out of my dilemma. It seemed risky to try and walk round my obstruction for I might have to travel for miles to circumnavigate it and even worse I could lose my bearings in the fog. The awful realisation dawned that the only sensible solution was to back-track several miles to the A835 road and take the longer route to Strath Kanaird. Angrily I turned on my heel and did just that, seething with frustration.

I rejoined the A835 road a mere mile farther on than where I had left it over two hours previously. A double disappointment was that John Hillaby had successfully negotiated a cross-country route to Strath Kanaird and I had failed. One crumb of comfort was that Wainwright had walked by road from Ullapool to Strath Kanaird,whilst making for Lochinver. He had arrived at Ullapool by bus in mid-afternoon planning to stay that night in the Drumrunie Hotel, beyond Strath Kanaird, only to discover that it had been inconveniently burnt down. He walked along the A835 road hoping to find accommodation, but was unsuccessful and finally resorted to spending the night in the shell of the burned-out hotel.

I was walking in Wainwright's footsteps along the road which careers round the headland to Ardmair where it overlooks Isle Martin squatting in Loch Kanaird, a bay of outer Loch Broom. This road, like many in north-west Scotland, is far from sedate as it cavorts and bounces into the Moine Thrust which extends north to the long ridge of Breabag. It is a land where limestone intrudes into the indigenous sandstone and schists, revealing caves, potholes and vanishing streams. During its passage the road weaves through Strath Kanaird and onwards to Drumrunie and Elphin, my day's destination. As I trudged along it I became acquainted with a strategic tourist corridor that extends for over sixty miles to Durness that lies on the north coast. It searches out the gaps in the hills and glides over a rocky bed through the arid desert that is Sutherland.

Eight miles of tarmac-crunching brought me to Drumrunie and almost to the border of Britain's farthest-flung county that boasts over three hundred lochs and to the casual observer, consists merely of water interspersed with deserts of barren gneiss. Closer inspection, however, reveals that despite its apparent solitude there is organisation and management, demonstrated by deer estates and regimented forests. With apologies to the more enlightened traveller, the popular motorists' view of the tourist corridor is a swathe of tarmac that cannot be abandoned at any cost, for unknown terrors lurk on all sides. If an effort is made to leave the shackles of the car and explore the more accessible parts of this ancient wilderness, a unique area of awesome beauty and tranquillity can be unearthed. One word of warning, do not venture from the road in thick mist as I had done.

A scourge of modern society is beginning to disfigure the corridor; litter thrown from passing cars or discarded at roadside picnics. I followed this trail of drink cans, plastic containers and waste paper all the way to Durness, by which time I had become well versed in the eating and drinking habits of its uncaring visitors. Anyone involved in market research in the food and drink industries would benefit from a journey along the littered roadside verges, for they could quickly assess the popularity of their products and get a few pounds back on the empties. For what it is worth, I found that the most popular brands of soft drink were unsurprisingly Irn Bru and Coca Cola. Scotland's national drink, made from 'gir-r-r-der-r-rs' - steel stanchions to us Sassenachs - just eclipsed the international flavour of Cola. The helpful information on the distinctive can assured me that the actual iron content of this most sought-after beverage is low enough to ensure that it will not rust my insides.

Drumrunie nestles between Coigach and the Cromalt Hills. It is a tiny settlement that clusters around a road junction where an animated unfenced road leaves the A 835 and circles the mountains of Coigach. This lonely road provides the only link with the Rhuba Mor peninsula and isolated outposts such as Achiltibuie that looks out over Badentarbat Bay to the Summer Isles. It also skirts the southern fringe of Inverpoly Forrest and delivers you to the foot of Stac Polly. Wainwright took this road after a night without sleep in the blackened remains of the Drumrunie Hotel. Four miles beyond Stac Polly he took another tortuous road that wriggles round tiny lochs and jinks across bleak moorland in a perilous journey to Lochinver. By mid-afternoon he reached Inverkirkaig, some miles short of his destination, exhausted and famished, having gone without sleep, or food, for thirty hours. He had not met a soul, or been passed by a car on his day's march, which was not surprising, for I too found people thin on the ground. Staggering to a cottage he asked for some refreshment and was taken in by a kindly couple who took pity on him. He was given food, for which no payment would be accepted. This amazing hospitality was repeated a little later that day when he stumbled into a B and B, exhausted once more. The elderly lady who ran the place saw his predicament and walked the five miles to Lochinver and back in order to buy fish for his supper.

I was not exhausted as I tramped through Drumrunie, but I was thoroughly drenched by the incessant downpour and not in the best of moods. At the road junction I glanced along the narrow one that Wainwright had taken to Inverkirkaig and I thought of Stac Polly hiding in the wretched mist, aloof and unassailable in such weather. It did, however, remind me of Bruce Sandison, who had endured a frustrating episode on the mountain a few years earlier. It arose over his quest for an impressive photograph to feature on the cover of his book *The Hill-Walker's Guide to Scotland*. He decided to pose for a self-portrait on its summit, which involved humping a tripod and self-focusing camera up the mountain. He positioned camera and tripod and dashed around the summit rocks taking photographs of himself from all angles with the aid of the self-timer. Unfortunately, as the end of the reel of film approached, the camera and tripod were blown over by a fierce gust of wind. When the camera hit the rocks its back flew open, ruining the film that he had painstakingly taken. The camera was so badly damaged that he had to abort his mission. The following day he returned at the crack of dawn with his wife for another attempt. She was to act as cameraman to avoid further disasters. They sat for hours in their car at the foot of the mountain in torrential rain and thick mist. When the weather showed no sign of improvement the attempt was finally aborted. They decided to await a good day, make the 130 mile dash from their home and hope that the weather held. A few days later their chance came and it proved to be third time lucky. Everything went perfectly, apart from waiting around for the sun to attain the most advantageous position. He and his wife kept themselves warm during their long wait by going up and down Stac Polly like yo-yo's. It kept them as warm as toast, but at the end of their exertions Bruce was completely exhausted.

I visualised his exploits as I squelched from Drumrunie through a gap in the hills towards Sasunnaich. It relieved the drudgery of rain-soaked miles to allow memory and imagination to fill my mind. '*Reach For The Sky*', its well-thumbed pages one of my favourite reads, took over from Bruce Sandison. I became immersed in the exciting world of its subject, Douglas Bader, the legless air-ace of the Battle of Britain. His story enthrals me each time I read of his struggle to overcome horrendous injuries sustained in a reckless bout of low-level aerobatics. What courage and sheer guts the man possessed to walk on artificial legs unaided by sticks and to eventually become one of the heroes of the Second World War. He drove a car, played golf and squash with boundless enthusiasm and tackled many other things that the able-bodied take for granted. I was proud just to see him from afar when he paid a brief visit to RAF Duxford, in his own aeroplane, whilst I was stationed there during my National Service. It was the wartime aerodrome where he had cut his teeth as a fighter pilot. His natural leadership blossomed with the responsibility of leading squadrons of the famous Duxford Wing into battle with the Luftwaffe. He instigated air-battle tactics that became invaluable against superior enemy numbers.

I was mentally flailing around the skies, shooting down enemy aircraft with reckless courage, as he had done, when I was jerked from my day-dreams by a screech of brakes. A Landrover lurched to a stop beside me and a cheery young farmer shouted through the open window to enquire if I wanted a lift. What a temptation. Here was a golden opportunity to speed through the mire and gobble up the remaining miles. Then I thought of Bader. He would not have taken the soft option. Stoically I declined the man's invitation, which prompted a retort that I must be mad; a logical conclusion when your kindness is rebuffed by a bedraggled walker dripping water from every pore. He roared away in a cloud of spray leaving me to savour a solitary crumb of comfort; Bader would have been proud of me. What an entertaining companion he would have been, but even he could not walk such a distance on tin legs. Nevertheless he was a companion in spirit, alongside Wainwright, Hillaby and Sandison.

On this section of his journey John Hillaby had taken the A 835 road from Strath Kanaird to Inchnadamph from where he cut across country to Strathnaver. He reckoned that you can't avoid this highway which in his words 'takes advantage of all the available gaps in the range'. He experienced heavy traffic; lines of coaches, cars and caravans clogging the road. I found the road extremely quiet, which I put down to the awful weather. In fact I would have even welcomed traffic in order to break the monotony.

I laboured through the defile, its floor peppered with a multitude of tiny lochs. Only the roadside ones were visible; iron-grey expanses that provided a chilling reminder of my earlier unfortunate incident in the hills. How I longed for those tenacious clouds to depart. I was heartily fed up with staring at a cheerless landscape. According to Bruce Sandison the west-coast weather changes very quickly, which did give some cause for optimism.

On the wettest ground the road coasts over embankments and hovers on rafts of concrete that prevent it from being submerged. Drumrunie Forest became a lingering smudge on an ashen canvas as I passed its south-east fringe, oblivious to its crowning glory Cul Mor, whose craggy faces guard its 2785 feet high quartzite summit. At tiny Sasunnaich I entered the penultimate county of my walk; Sutherland. Only Caithness remained, many miles ahead. I found myself wishing the remaining miles away, which is futile, for it makes a journey more tiresome.

Sutherland looked no different to Wester Ross under its mantle of mist. The weather was hardly conducive to a clear-cut impression of this wild and untamed land. The remaining miles steadily dwindled beneath my feet and I was soon following the lurching road into Knochan, a near-neighbour of Elphin. I was anticipating a night's rest as I passed a sprinkling of buildings that shelter beneath the foot of the Cromalt Hills. The rain was finally easing now that my destination was almost in sight. In the retreating mist the landscape came into sharper focus and I hoped that Bruce Sandison's weather prediction was about to be proved accurate.

The bridge over the Abhainn a'Chrocain burn links Knochan with the first of the scattered dwellings of Elphin. They dotted the surrounding hillsides as I galloped over the bridge, their white walls gleaming beneath a pall of persistent grey cloud, poised over their rooftops like a giant wad of soiled cotton wool. The painters of Ullapool had evidently been active in the area with their mega-litres of white paint.

The Birchbank Holiday Lodge was my destination and after a short search I walked expectantly up a winding driveway to be confronted by a brand new building. It rose amidst surrounding rubble and debris that normally litters a building site. Some of the exterior paintwork remained unfinished and the solid front door had yet to be varnished. Carefully avoiding the obstacles left by the builders I approached the entrance and rang the bell. Nothing happened. I knocked two or three times, praying that the place was occupied. A harassed-looking man opened the door and seemed surprised to see a walker on his doorstep. I introduced myself and said that I had made a reservation over the telephone with Tom Strang. With a sharp intake of breath he indicated that he was Tom and had completely forgotten that I was coming. Apologetically inviting me inside he showed me around a spacious and impressive interior that combined taste and comfort. Some of the fittings had still to be finished and Tom seemed in turmoil. He was fighting an onerous deadline; to have the place ship-shape for his first group of guests who were due the following week. He had been battling with tradesmen for days but things were still not complete and he was beginning to flag.

There had been no indication of his plight when I telephoned to book accommodation and he admitted that his venture was becoming a nightmare. As proprietor of Assynt Guided Holidays his plan was to entertain parties of walkers, climbers and anglers. They would hopefully enjoy their particular pursuits with Tom acting as guide and instructor. I later discovered that he is a well-known walker and mountaineer, a fact that he modestly omitted to mention, and is also an author.

Amongst his numerous books are two that were commissioned by the Sutherland Tourist Board; *The Hillwalker's Guide to Sutherland* and *Walk Sutherland.* He has also written The Scottish Mountaineering Club District Guide, *The Northern Highlands.* These volumes demonstrate his intimate knowledge of northern Scotland and its mountains, but his rich store of information did, on one occasion, disturb a house-guest. When the traveller Ivan Rowan stayed with Tom during a journey from Cape Wrath to Fort William he was rather alarmed by Tom's disheartening tales about the rigours of life and climate in that area of Sutherland. Several local crofters, he was informed, had succumbed to melancholy and eventually suicide.

His worries temporarily thrust aside by the intervention of a tired and hungry walker, Tom grabbed the phone. He promptly arranged for a lady to come from the village, prepare supper for me and make up a bed. He insisted that I made myself at home, indicating that the television and his collection of tapes and CD's were at my disposal.

Whilst I showered and changed he renewed his battle with the wayward contractors over the telephone, insisting that they extract their digits. Supper was well in hand when I emerged from my room and I was soon enjoying a splendid meal with personal service by the helpful lady who obligingly promised to come again the following morning and cook breakfast for me.

A little later Tom and the lady departed leaving me to enjoy a superbly relaxing evening. I was serenaded by Pavarotti and soothed by the strings of Mantovani until tiredness overtook me and I retired contentedly to bed.

DAY TWENTY-SIX: ELPHIN - KYLESKU

The layer of cotton wool cloud hovered stubbornly over the landscape as I peered anxiously through the curtains of my room for a quick weather check. Thankfully it was dry and optimistically I reasoned that the sun could eventually destroy the fruits of the cloud factory that had been annoyingly working overtime. I was becoming desperate for any photographic record of the latest stages of my journey. The previous day had been a complete wash-out, as had the section from Shiel Bridge to Attadale. It was time to even the score and I was determined to take advantage of any reasonable weather conditions that day.

Next on the early morning agenda was another inspection; of my hard-pressed feet. Not the best of topics to start the day, but, nevertheless very important. Extensive road walking can be their worst enemy, often causing them to swell with the heat that is generated. They were poised for another bashing, for I intended to follow the road to Kylesku that day and I was worried that they might mutiny. To my relief they looked in reasonable shape; one or two red patches indicating mild chafing. If those maltreated feet could speak I could imagine their heartfelt complaints to each other. Left foot - 'I hope we are not in for another bout of tarmac-bashing today, I'm getting brassed-off with it. Why can't he treat us like normal feet, or better still, become a couch potato?' Right foot - 'At the very least he could pamper us with cream or powder. What do we get? Sweet nothing. How would he like being buried in a hairy sock and flung around all day with nothing to soothe him?' Trusting that rebellion was not imminent I thrust my un-pampered feet into their hairy blindfolds and padded into the dining room to find everything laid out for breakfast and the sound of spitting fat coming from the kitchen. Despite Tom's predicament I could not fault the hospitality and service.

Replete with a few thousand calories, which I would hopefully purge with a day's toil, I settled back to enjoy my third cup of coffee. Entirely the wrong thing to do of course, for I had a long way to go and should not have hung around. What the heck, I thought, a few minutes relaxation never hurt anyone. Was my battery running down after walking more than 420 miles? My resolve, I am sad to say, was weakening. I did not know then that it was to be more severely tested on the following day.

Tom arrived whilst I was procrastinating and said that I looked very relaxed. His harassed expression had not faded with a night's rest and he clearly did not relish another day's in-fighting. He enquired if I had been comfortable and had slept well. I assured him that things had been first class and once he was over his teething problems the walking, climbing and fishing fraternity would agree. It brought the first smile, that I had seen, to his lips.

When he discovered that I was bound for Kylesku he explained a little about Assynt, which I would enter at Cam Loch. Measuring only fourteen miles by twelve miles it displays a remarkable geological structure, he explained. Terminating at Kylesku, its indigenous bedrock of Lewisian gneiss is overlaid in places by virtually horizontal layers of Torridonian sandstone. Great masses of this ancient rock, such as Suilven and Canisp, bulge from the choppy expanse of gneiss and, according to Tom, would be plainly visible if the cloud lifted. He said that I could not mistake Suilven, for it resembles a stranded whale lying in shallow, rippling waters. I had already gleaned from my maps that the further north I travelled the more exposed and spasmodic the mountains would become. Bad news for Munro-baggers.

Tom warned that it could be arduous walking over Assynt's inhospitable surface and I was forced to admit that I was unadventurously planning to keep to tarmac in the prevailing conditions. He agreed that this was a sensible strategy, but unfortunately I would miss much of the true character of the area.

The sound of an approaching vehicle interrupted our conversation. Tom rushed to the door to find one of the reluctant contractors' lorries putting in a welcome appearance. Wishing Tom all speed with his preparations I gathered up my belongings and left. On my way out I told him that in a few years time he would look back on his current turmoil with amusement. Tom did not appear convinced.

Back on the road once more, I came upon another group of dwellings that comprise the remainder of straggling Elphin, where, I assumed, life was not easy for this small crofting community. A sign at a roadside farm indicated that it has been put to a more lucrative use as the Scottish Farm Animal Visitor Centre which offers a display of animals as an attraction for passing visitors' children. According to the sign it features over 300 breeds, ancient and modern, to see, stroke and feed.In a nearby compound I could see some piglets rooting enthusiastically in the dark earth. Prepared to point my camera at anything, moving or inert, I took a shot of them and also of the nearby Elphin Tearooms, a small cottage with tables and colourful parasols arranged outside. Visitors were invited to sample delicious home-baking in a countryside setting. Alongside the cottage stands a large modern bungalow that offers B and B accommodation. Together they form an attractive partnership for passing trade. When tired travellers have had their fill they can stroll next-door and sleep, exactly as they can in motorway services with motor lodges attached.

The road swung east, skirting the south shore of Cam Loch, the gateway to Assynt. Low cloud, at around 500 feet, ensured that I saw nothing of distant Suilven, only the stumps of nearby hills. The wooded island of Eilean na Gartaig squatted in the loch, its rich vegetation seemingly out of place amongst a denuded landscape. Habitation disappeared as I strode through the silent valley occupied only by a Bronze Age burial cairn, one of several that I was to pass on my way to Inchnadamph.

A further two miles brought me to Ledmore Junction where the A 835 road, that I was following, comes to an abrupt halt. Here it meets the A837 road that runs north-west through Strath Oykell, which gives passage to the east coast by way of Bonar Bridge. At Ledmore it heads north to Inchnadamph, turns west at Loch Assynt and provides the only main road link with the coastal village of Lochinver. At this important road junction began my push for Inchnadamph, which I hoped to reach by lunchtime. The countryside remained bleak and uninviting beneath its cottonwool hood. Decapitated Canisp rose to the north-west beyond the placid waters of Loch Awe, emphasising the poor photogenic conditions. In desperation I captured some wild ponies grazing near the road, their dapple-grey colouring a perfect camouflage amidst their dull surroundings. Not ideal camera material.

Apart from the occasional passing vehicle, the isolated crofts of Ledbeg and Lyne were the sole signs of life, their presence marked by crude wooden post-boxes standing conspicuously by the roadside. A time-saver for postmen, who were not required to venture along their access tracks, they also demonstrated the trusting nature of remote farming communities. Once again clutching at photographic straws I took a shot of the post-box and any roadside flowers that I came across.

For the next few miles the River Loanan, that flows from Loch Awe, wriggled beside me with youthful energy. It was to keep close company with the road until it mingled with the wide expanse of Loch Assynt. One of its tributaries emerged from the slopes of

Breabag, that also lay hidden in cloud to the east. The Allt nan Uamh, as the burn is known, inhabits a distinctive valley, wherein lie three caves which were excavated by the noted geologists, Peach and Horne. There they discovered the bones of ancient tundra animals and two human skeletons reputed to be 6000 years old. A simple stone memorial, dedicated to Peach and Horne in 1930, stands on the shore of Loch Assynt. It provides a lasting tribute to their major involvement in unravelling the complex geological structure of the north-west Highlands towards the end of the last century.

As my boots pounded away the miles I fully expected rebellion from my feet, but remarkably they did not complain. It was a lonely walk that morning, and, from the few vehicles that passed, eyes stared incredulously at me, their owners amazed that anyone would choose to make such a solitary journey on foot. It was reminiscent of those startled faces peering from the windows of the coaches that bounced towards Inversnaid.

Birds also flew overhead to inspect the lone walker and the liquid warble of several curlews drifted across the still, morning air. Eventually they seemed satisfied that I would not wander from the highway onto their territory, so they did not resort to their shrill warning cries. I was having difficulty finding suitable flowers to photograph, as most were small and hid amongst the foliage of the grass verges. Rooting around those verdant borders reminded me of notices which are sometimes posted on them warning of 'Soft Verges'. I cannot understand the relevance of such notices, which are akin to the one featured on *Monty Python's Flying Circus* that read 'Do not throw stones at this notice'. With my warped sense of humour they conjure up the vision of men dressed in black cassocks frolicking dementedly by the roadside.

My introduction to the hamlet of Inchnadamph, a collection of crofts at the head of Loch Assynt, was the sight of the Inchnadamph Hotel that stands in dignified seclusion at its entrance. A magnet for visitors, judging by its bulging car park, it offers the only accommodation of any magnitude in Assynt. Its conflicting outward appearance indicated that the original building had become too cramped and considerable extensions had been added. Lying near the foot of Ben More Assynt, Sutherland's highest mountain at 3273 feet, it provides an ideal base for sportsmen and geologists. Nearby Loch Assynt bristles with salmon and brown trout and the Cambrian limestone of Ben More Assynt's lower reaches, now a National

Nature Reserve, abounds with caves and underground streams.

Above this band of limestone lies the indigenous gneiss, crowned with the mountain's quartzite tip. Unfortunately these intriguing features remained lost in the mist and I was reminded of Wainwright's astute comment that the only way to know a mountain is to put your feet on it. I would have to wait awhile before knowing Ben More Assynt.

The hotel looked enticing and as it was lunchtime I ventured inside for a refreshing drink. I struck up a conversation with two elderly and distinguished gents who believed that walking should be sedate and have an air of sophistication. They were touring the area on foot, covering a comfortable eight or nine miles per day. Their route wherever possible passed a convenient watering-hole where they could enjoy a good meal, washed down with gin and tonic. I suggested that such places might be a little thin on the ground in Sutherland.

Their morning had been a disappointment for, by their own admission, they had been over-adventurous. After staying overnight in the hotel they had set out with a good breakfast inside them to tackle the arduous path that leaves Inchnadamph and winds for six miles through bleak mountains to the head of Eas Coul Aulin waterfall. Their objective, Britain's highest cascade, proved elusive, for they were severely tested by harsh terrain and finally defeated by the steep climb to the pass that separates Glas Bheinn and Beinn Uidhe. Sensibly they turned back, conscious that such a hard twelve-mile trek was beyond their capabilities. With hindsight they agreed that a better means of approach to the 658 feet high falls would be along Loch Glencoul; but they did not know if a boat and boatman can still be hired at Kylesku Hotel. A short walk then reveals the full extent of the magnificent cataract, a far better view than the one they would have obtained after their six-mile journey overland. That particular path crosses the head of the falls, where the outlook is much more limited. Refusing to be downhearted, they felt it wise to know their limitations. There was also the prospect of a ramble around the base of Ben More Assynt, with its striking limestone features, that afternoon.

John Hillaby's name arose in conversation and I mentioned my fascination with his journey through Scotland. Neville, the older of the pair, had read several of his books and warned me not to make the same mistake as Hillaby had when he left Inchnadamph.

Striking across wild, inhospitable country in a quest to reach Strathnaver, a deep valley that intrudes from the north coast at Bettyhill, he completely lost his bearings. His plan was to follow an appropriate line between the Inchnadamph Hotel and the north-west corner of Loch Shin, a distance of around nine miles, with few landmarks to guide him. What little identification there was disappeared in thick mist shortly after his departure and a few hours of floundering brought him to the south-east tip of Loch Glencoul, many miles off course. It took three further hours of anxious toil until he finally reached Loch Shin.

I assured Neville and his partner Harry, that I would be keeping to the road, certainly as far as Kylesku. The thought of following John Hillaby's cross-country route had previously crossed my mind, but was discounted after seeing an episode of *Wainwright in Scotland* on television, in which Wainwright and his companion, Eric Robson, had gazed from Kylesku Bridge along Loch Cairnbawn. That scene was captivating and I vowed not to miss it. I told Neville and Harry that when I reached Kylesku I would decide whether or not to cut across country.

The affable pair were about to enjoy a leisurely lunch as I left the hotel. Crossing the bridge that spans the River Traligill, I could not help admiring some cottages built from the local 'white marble' - crystalline limestone. Approaching Loch Assynt, I searched for a pleasant spot to eat my sandwiches. I found one at the entrance to the churchyard that nestles on the shore of the loch. Surrounded by gravestones stands the tiny church that looks out over its silvery waters. Seating myself on the base of a modest stone memorial I read its inscription that is a poignant reminder of the Second World War. The edifice has been erected in memory of the crew of an RAF aircraft that crashed on Ben More Assynt in 1941.

As I enjoyed my lunch, hair tousled by the freshening wind, several birds circled above me, watchful for scraps. I recognised oyster-catchers, with their prominent orange beaks, jockeying for position with some vigilant sandpipers. Unfortunately for those feathered scavengers I was ravenously hungry. My sandwiches were quickly demolished and I was soon back on the road once more.

I began to skirt the north-east shore of Loch Assynt. An extensive view of its six-mile length lay before me. Dark hills lined its edges but beyond them the overhanging cloud was at last relenting. It looked quite bright over the coast, which lies a few miles to the west of the loch; a familiar situation where the sky is clear over the sea whilst the mountains draw the clouds inland.

The road unwound before me, hugging the indented lochside as it heads for Lochinver and the coast. I was rather puzzled to see, a hundred yards ahead of me, a woman walking in the same direction. A quick glance at my map revealed that, apart from an isolated farm, there was no habitation for six miles. Surely she wasn't walking the twelve miles to Lochinver. I soon overtook her and she asked where I was headed. She smiled when I said that I was about to ask her the same question. It transpired that she was returning to Calda House, a ruin that stands on the lochside, a mile farther on. It was apparently the site of a clay-pigeon shoot in which her husband was participating. He often took his wife to such events and then left her to amuse herself. Male chauvinism still flourishes, I thought. I wondered how he would fare if his wife took him on an extensive shopping trip with her friends. The neglected lady had wandered into Inchnadamph to kill an hour or two, having no inclination to watch the men-folk shooting at hurtling black discs for a whole day.

In the distance a small white marquee and an accompanying group of cars could be discerned in a lochside field. As we drew closer I could see the missile-launcher, as she called it, with a man standing alongside, shotgun poised. A row of other keen participants sat on a nearby bench, eagerly awaiting their turn. A small crowd of onlookers peered expectantly at the man wielding the gun, eagerly waiting to shout 'Well done!' when he smashed the flying disc to pieces. Rather disturbingly, several young children romped around the field, fortunately out of the line of fire.

I said goodbye to the lady when we reached the field and wished her a pleasant afternoon. This was probably superfluous, because I imagined a boring few hours lay ahead of her. She gave me a wry smile, remarking that the surroundings were thankfully attractive. This was no exaggeration for the sun had broken through to accentuate the colour of the rippling water and turn the surrounding vegetation a luscious green. Cloud still lingered over the mountains but the beauty of the countryside was now revealed. A short distance along the loch stood the remains of tiny Ardvreck Castle, perched on a grassy headland that juts forcefully into the water. Little more than a gnarled fortified tower, it is a former stronghold of the MacLeods of Assynt, built in the late sixteenth century. The Marquess of Montrose, a distinguished general who had been victorious in many battles against the Covenanters, was imprisoned there by Neill MacLeod, after his defeat near Bonar Bridge. He was later taken to Edinburgh and hanged in 1650. MacLeod reputedly gave up Montrose for £20,000, which was never actually paid, plus a consignment of sub-standard meat. The first known occurrence of BSE I wondered?

Adjacent to the shooting site stood the sad ruin of Calda House, surrounded by a protective wire fence. Crumbling stonework was all that remained of a once-proud dwelling. One of the end walls stood in isolation, a broad finger of stone that threatened to topple over at any moment. The other end of this former mansion, built in 1660 for the third Earl of Seaforth and destroyed by fire in the eighteenth century, was marginally more intact. From the top of this ravaged structure sprouted a small rowan tree that brought to fruition a remarkable prediction, made by a seer before the disastrous fire, that one day such a tree would issue from the top of the house.

I left Calda House to its memories and walked a further mile to Skiag Bridge where I abandoned the A837 road and turned north along the A 894 towards Kylesku. This road rises sharply from Loch Assynt to the pass between Glas Bheinn and Quinag. It proved a strenuous ascent, relieved only by the vivid colour of the gorse that lined the roadside. Quinag, its seven tops lurking under retreating cloud, merely revealed slopes of smooth pipe-rock and quartzite.

If I had been more astute I could have given my feet a rest from tarmac for a few miles. So engrossed was I in Calda House and Ardvreck Castle that I had failed to notice a track which leaves the A 837 road near the castle to join a path that would have brought me to Loch na Gainmhich, that lies at the head of the pass, by a more convenient route. I eventually reached the small loch via the metalled road, tired and thirsty after my exertion. It snuggles in a rocky amphitheatre and weather-beaten boulders litter its banks. Bands of barren quartzite glittered in the sunshine. As I rested on a convenient boulder and enjoyed a reviving drink from my flask the evocative surroundings seemed to encapsulate the very nature of Sutherland - wild, barren and beautiful.

It only remained for me to follow the contorted road on a protracted descent to Kylesku. As I began the last leg of my day's journey, a mountain top at last revealed itself. The rugged dome of Sail Gharbh, the highest of the seven tops of Quinag at 2653 feet, appeared through strands of feathery cloud dancing around its summit. Its Gaelic name means Rough Heel, an accurate description, for the mountain clearly resembled an upturned heel from my viewpoint. Its cliffs mark the end of one of Quinag's shapely ridges, which form a clover-leaf pattern when seen from the air.

The view towards Kylesku was formidable, its centrepiece the writhing band of tarmac that wound towards Loch Gencoul. Stretching seemingly for miles, it was flanked by bare countryside, speckled with numerous pockets of water. From several tiny lochans streams tumbled towards Loch Glencoul and Loch Cairnbawn. Passing cars were reduced to miniature models before disappearing round a distant bend on their final approach to Kylesku. The village itself stands on a narrow strip of land that virtually severs Loch Cairnbawn, the main sea-loch that runs inland from Eddrachillis Bay. East of Kylesku it forks into Loch Glendhu and Loch Glencoul, which are only accessible through a confined straight which is now crossed by Kylesku bridge. Originally the crossing was by a time-consuming ferry.

As often happens when you can see your destination from some miles away, it takes an age to cover the distance on foot. I breathed a sigh of relief when I eventually reached the Kylesku Hotel. A welcoming sign advertised bar meals and a restaurant that serves local sea food, conveniently brought from the nearby tiny harbour. A row of small fishing boats hugged the jetty in the sheltered inlet where the catches are landed, but their paintwork was the only thing of brightness to be seen. The sun had disappeared from a relentlessly grey landscape. Water, sky and the hills encircling Loch Glencoul, their colours intermingled, had assumed an angry appearance. A wretched drizzle drew a veil over the harbour as I left to find my accommodation.

The miserable weather was forgotten when I received an enthusiastic welcome at the B and B by Joan, who treated me to a satisfying meal and some lively conversation. She was keen to know my plans for the remainder of my walk, but I was forced to admit that they were hazy for the forthcoming section to Tongue, that lies on the north coast. I told her of my desire to see Kylesku Bridge with its impressive view over Loch Cairnbawn before heading across country, weather permitting, towards Loch More. Eventually I hoped to reach Strath More, which, I said, would lead me to the north coast. She suggested that before finalising my route I should wait until morning to see what the weather held in store. If it looked promising she would telephone some friends who lived by Loch More to ask if I could stay with them the following night. Her suggestion seemed sound and I thanked her for the offer to find accommodation. My anxieties eased, until I heard the weather forecast a little later. It was not good news.

DAY TWENTY-SEVEN: KYLESKU - DURNESS

The first thought that hit me as I woke was that a decision was needed. I leapt out of bed and tore open the curtains, in what was becoming a morning ritual, to discover how my fickle friend, the weather, was behaving. It was a nondescript kind of morning; not fair nor foul, merely dull and lack-lustre. This made my choice of route more difficult as I did not know what lay in store. Unbeknown to me, at that moment, the decision was being made for me.

I received the bad news as I sat down for breakfast. Joan had just telephoned her friends at Loch More. They apparently could not see a hand in front of them. A thick mist had just rolled over the loch and appeared to be inconsiderately heading in the direction of Kylesku. No point in anyone venturing there in such conditions, was their advice. Rubbing salt into the wound they added that there was no accommodation either. Apparently there were only estate cottages in the area. That ruled out the cross-country route. I had no option but to keep to the road.

Joan touchingly apologised for being the bearer of bad news, but I pointed out that it was not her fault that the mist was on its way. I told her not to worry as the A894 and I had become bosom pals and it would be a wrench to abandon it. That made her smile, but it soon faded as she asked where I would make for that day. It was a good question, to which I had no immediate answer. I told her that I would consult my map after breakfast. In my mind I pictured Durness as an exciting objective, which unfortunately seemed a great distance away.

The enjoyment ebbed away from breakfast, which I usually relished, for just as predicted, a pea-souper blotted out the view from the window. No photographs today, I thought, and not much to see either. The road was definitely the wise choice.

Back in my room I spread out the map and followed the A894 which snakes through tracts of rock and gigantic puddles to Laxford

Bridge. Here the A838 takes over for the journey to Rhiconich and eventually Durness. The teaser was where to find accommodation along this sprightly band of tarmac. I took the easy option and did nothing, choosing merely to head for Scourie, the first village of any size, that lay roughly ten miles away, and see what developed. When I told Joan of my sketchy plan she suggested that I waited until the mist lifted and whilst I was waiting try and arrange accommodation in Scourie for that night. The call of John O' Groats was too strong for a mere ten- mile day and besides, the mist could hang around for days. I told her of my impatience to reach journey's end, which was now heightened by the enforced circuitous route to Bettyhill that would add extra miles. Seeing my determination to proceed she returned to the kitchen and added extra sandwiches and biscuits to the already substantial packed-lunch that she had prepared. She refused additional payment for her kindness, saying that I should not go hungry.

I left the house and ventured into the grey clamminess of an atrocious morning. A chill breeze wafted over Loch Cairnbawn as I approached the bridge that I had been so anxious to see. It was undetectable until I was almost upon it, merely a black smudge on a steel-grey background. A dampening squall hit me as I stood on its shapely concrete span staring out into nothingness. Visibility was barely thirty yards and the stunning view that I had been eagerly anticipating was non-existent. I mentally chastised Wainwright for enticing me to such an anti-climax when I could have floundered across country, like John Hillaby did from Inchnadamph, and saved myself many miles of road-walking. To be fair to Wainwright, had I not come to Kylesku I could easily have become marooned by a desolate sea of gneiss and water in a vain attempt to reach Strathnaver.

Before crossing the bridge I back-tracked to a concrete column standing by a nearby deserted car park that would provide a fine viewpoint in decent weather. Two plaques on the column indicate that Her Majesty the Queen opened the bridge in 1984 and that it replaced the ferry which had existed since the early nineteenth century.

The rain persisted as I finally crossed the bridge and passed Kylesku's near-neighbour Kylestrome. This larger village straddles a short minor road that terminates abruptly on a shapely headland that intrudes into Loch Cairnbawn. In good visibility I could imagine that terminal point providing a superb view of the mountains of Glendhu Forest that encircle the slender finger of Loch Glendhu.

North of the loch I entered Reay country, uninhabited apart from its coastline, which is indented by two sea-lochs, Laxford and Inchard, each four miles long. It portrays a wildly dissipated appearance on the map, as though shredded by a giant harrow to form a colander. Through its innumerable holes water has intruded, resulting in a fearsome-looking terrain. I felt comforted that I had solid tarmac under my feet. The architect of the forerunner of the modern A894 road was the most hated man in Scotland. When Duke of Sutherland he built the first road to connect Loch Assynt with Durness in the early nineteenth century, at a cost of £40,000. Prior to his dukedom, as plain George Levenson-Gower, he had been responsible for the Sutherland clearances of 1810 to 1820. He evicted 15,000 people to make way for sheep, which were more profitable on his extensive estates, burning their homes and forcing them to the sea. Therefore my lifeline was initiated by a tyrant and quite a task it must have been to find a suitable course through north-west Sutherland. The road swings and lurches in all directions as it negotiates a tricky path between coastal inlets and frolics amidst countless water-filled holes that pock-mark Reay.

A short distance from Kylestrome I became enclosed by the conifers of Duartmore Forest, quite a rarity in that rocky desert. When this retreated I was confronted by dark, heather moorland interspersed with leathery outcrops of gneiss. The only sign of life was forlorn, newly-shorn sheep that frequently appeared from the misty morass. They sported brightly-painted numbers on their backs, looking accusingly at me as though I was responsible for purloining their warm coats.

Eventually I dropped down a hill into the hamlet of Lower Badcall that lies about three miles south of Scourie and overlooks Badcall Bay, normally one of the most attractive on the north-west coast. As I gazed over the rocky inlet all that was visible were black mounds lying in an expanse of tar. These represented the first of the numerous islands that adorn the bay, a great place for lobster fishing.

A further hour of twists and turns brought me into the coastal village of Scourie, which, compared to Kylesku was a metropolis, boasting a store and a post-office. It was Sunday and consequently the place was quiet. Perhaps it was always quiet. I tried the store and thankfully found it open, seizing the opportunity to obtain even more supplies in case I became stranded overnight. As I scanned the shelves the proprietor approached and said unapologetically that the shop was closed. This seemed strange as the door was clearly open. Sunday was closing day, I was informed, and they were only open for stock-taking. This I found even more difficult to grasp. I explained my predicament and asked if an exception could be made in my case. The man was adamant, suggesting that I try the nearest shop. My heart lifted. 'How far is that?' I enquired. Twenty-four miles, was the astonishing reply. My jaw dropped and I left, disconsolate and lost for words.

Despite this set-back I was still determined to cover as much ground as possible that day even if it meant going hungry. Laxford Bridge seemed the next outpost to aim for and I made a hasty exit from unco-operative Scourie, making a mental note to cross it off my list of holiday destinations.

The energetic road swung to the east, heading inland once more as it crosses the lonely peninsula that houses the outlying settlements of Tarbet, Fanagmore and Foindle. I had seen a most impressive postcard view of Fanagmore which featured the ubiquitous white-walled cottage perched on a rock above the glistening blue waters of Loch Laxford. It portrayed a scene of sheer delight that seemed to capture the unique beauty of the area.

I was unable to enjoy such breathtaking scenery, hemmed in as I was by constricting fog. Nearby Handa Island, normally visible beyond Scourie Bay, had gone undetected. This mecca for ornithologists, is uninhabited by humans and home to a large population of seabirds. A wicked thought occurred to me. The miserable store proprietor should be plucked from Scourie and incarcerated on that lonely bastion of rock with only the incessant squawking of millions of birds for company. That would teach him to be kind to walkers.

The road merrily bounced over ripples of gneiss and lurched around innumerable curves as though unsure of its ultimate direction. Two long hours passed on this roller-coaster of a highway before Laxford Bridge materialised from the murk. It stands at an important road junction, but you do have the distinct feeling of being in the middle of nowhere, for the place itself is so tiny. Blink and you have missed it. Strategically placed on the south-east tip of Loch Laxford, it marks the end of the line, as it were, for the A894 road. Here it meets the A838 road that connects Lairg, which lies a

testing thirty-seven mile drive away, to Durness. It is only a change
of number, I reasoned. As long as the road led me in the right
direction, I would happily follow it, despite admitting a certain
affinity with the loyal A894.

There was no sign of accommodation in the vicinity.
Consequently I set full steam ahead for Rhiconich, the next pocket
of habitation, five miles to the north. The feeling of isolation
returned as I followed the differently numbered, but equally
contorted, road. No walkers had been encountered. None were
really expected in the wild conditions that only an idiot would
tolerate. I could imagine them sensibly holed-up in comfortable
surroundings; feet up, glass in hand, waiting serenely for the weather
to break. Why was I so driven? Surely I could have taken Joan's
advice and emulated them. Then I recalled Wainwright's
recommendation to always have an objective to aim for. Mine was
to reach John O'Groats post-haste before my battery ran flat. I was
convinced that, had I hung around, my determination would have
evaporated.

Battered by such conflicting thoughts I strode towards
Rhiconich, blissfully unaware of the distinctive Cambrian quartzite
mountains that rise from Reay Forest, which lies to the east. Eight
miles inland, they are the former hunting grounds of the chiefs of
clan MacKay; the titled Lords of Reay, whose seats were at Tongue
and Dounreay on the north coast. Nearest to hand is Foinaven,
linked by a four-mile ridge running north to Arkle. To anyone over
the age of forty-five these should be familiar names, for they were
given to two famous racehorses of the nineteen-sixties.

The only visible relief from the dull monotony were occasional
clusters of roadside flowers. Flashes of flag irises and bog myrtle were
nectar to a man figuratively dying of thirst. The best that can be said
for walking 'blind' is that it heightens the other senses. Sutherland
had developed a distinctive smell and I could have detected a pin
dropping twenty yards away. I certainly heard a car approaching that
seemed to take minutes to appear. With a screech of brakes it pulled
up a short distance ahead of me. Its occupants were Japanese who
spoke perfect English and the driver politely enquired if I would like
a lift. Wouldn't I just! Then Douglas Bader took control and I heard
myself refusing his most generous offer. This caused a stir amongst
the passengers of the large Volvo Estate, who gabbled animatedly in
Japanese, throwing disbelieving glances in my direction. They

obviously could not comprehend this crazy Englishman who chose to walk through the middle of nowhere in such conditions. With a shrug of his shoulders the driver pulled away, bent on discovering more of Scotland under an impenetrable mist. As the sound of the engine drifted away, the door of my murky prison slammed once more. I began to doubt my purism. A golden opportunity to reach civilisation in comfort had just been exchanged for the uncertainty of finding a bed for the night. The prospect of sleeping under the stars was far from appealing; if indeed they showed themselves at all.

As I followed the road around a series of particularly tortuous bends, the stillness became greatly accentuated. My equilibrium had been disturbed by the recent turn of events. Just like that equally misty day in the hills above Strath Kanaird, I suddenly found myself confronted by water on all sides, but this time my lifeline fortunately did not disappear into it. I had the road to guide me as it squeezed between two of the larger holes in the giant colander of Reay. Eventually the water receded and as I rounded a distinctly vicious bend I came across a welcome landmark. To my left a minor road branched off to nearby Skerricha, indicating that I was only two miles from Rhiconich. This boosted my morale and my pace instinctively quickened as I headed for this outpost that lies at the head of Loch Inchard.

Once again denied the beauty of a superb lochside location, I approached the Rhiconich Hotel, its obligatory white walls beckoning through the gloom. Apart from a few houses strung out along the lochside, it stood in splendid isolation beneath a rocky buttress that loomed angrily above the sheltered bay. I removed my boots before entering as I had no wish to be turned away from this sanctuary. The bar was doing brisk business, courtesy of the weather, and I took my drink to one of the few unoccupied tables. I had a serious decision to make and it had to be done quickly. As I gratefully sat down, the strident tones of a man, who I quickly summed up as a poser, rose above the general buzz of conversation. He was leaning on the bar holding court with a group who clustered around him, hanging on his every word. Not only was he addressing a team of admirers, he was bragging to anyone within earshot about his Munro-bagging prowess. Dressed in designer walking gear that looked too immaculate to be well-used, he sported the indispensable motif on each item. Familiar names such as Suilven, Cansip and Ben More Assynt tripped off his tongue, indicating that they had been easily conquered. He seemed blissfully unaware that the first two were not high enough to be Munros and the paunch that he displayed beneath his open fleece jacket convinced me that he had never been near a Munro. His captive audience however seemed unaware that he would not recognise a Munro if he fell over one.

I would have enjoyed listening to his entertaining rubbish had I not to decide whether to seek accommodation at the hotel or move on. Move on to where? That was the burning question. There was no apparent habitation until Durness, which lay fourteen miles away. A quick check of my watch revealed that it was only three-fifteen, despite the fact that I had already covered twenty miles. My early start and brisk pace along the road had put me in an awkward situation. It was possible to reach Durness by late evening, with the alternative of killing time for the rest of the day at Rhiconich. Reach Durness that evening? I must be mad, I reckoned. Thirty-four miles in one day was a tall order. On the other hand the remaining distance would be straightforward road-walking and I didn't relish the task of completing those fourteen miles on the following day, particularly as it would probably add another day to my walk. My impatience got the better of me and I impetuously decided to make for Durness, despite the fact that I would leave myself very little time to find accommodation. I must have been in a tearing hurry, because in hindsight I could have rung ahead in order to check its availability.

I did not linger over my drink and hastily took to the road once more. Several lorries thundered past me, almost doubling the amount of traffic that I had encountered that day. It soon became apparent from whence they came. A short distance from the hotel a road branches off the A838 and runs along the shore of Loch Inchard to Kinlochbervie, which is a hive of industry compared to its surroundings. It is the most important fishing port in the north-west Highlands, by courtesy of its splendidly sheltered harbour, situated near the mouth of Loch Inchard. The heavy lorries were transporting fish to various markets around the country.

It is a steady climb from Rhiconich through Achriesgill Glen to a watershed that lies 600 feet above sea level. Here stands the remote Gualin House, once a hotel, now a shooting lodge; its gaunt features etched eerily on a blank canvas. Thankfully it marked the end of the final climb of the day. My map indicated that from thereon it was a gradual and straight descent to the Kyle of Durness. Gone were the twists and turns that I had grown accustomed to. It was as though a prodigious iron had removed the wrinkles from the A838 road.

The protracted and ultimately boring descent was almost a blur, for there was nothing to see but mile upon mile of resilient mist. My automatic pilot took over as the landscape, what little I could see of it, took on a different character. No longer was I bouncing over ripples of gneiss; the ground was flatter with a good coating of grass. The road also appeared to be tiring as it led me, straight as an arrow, across the neck of Cape Wrath's majestic headland, that is bounded by Loch Inchard and the Kyle of Durness.

The time had come to pay for my over-eagerness as I struggled to maintain a decent pace. My long-suffering feet were beginning to rebel. Had I taken on too great a challenge? The awful thought that I could grind to a halt at any time had to be kept at bay. I reluctantly stopped before I seized up completely. Feeling too exhausted to search for a rock to sit on, there were so few in evidence, I slumped onto the roadside verge and searched my rucksack for sustenance. The only nourishment I found were a few biscuits and some lukewarm dregs of coffee in my flask. These were soon disposed of. I grimaced as foul-tasting liquid was forced down my throat, and whilst I was doing so, a car suddenly floated past, its engine barely audible. The occupants stared in amazement at the pathetic creature reclining at the roadside pulling disgusting faces.

Hauling myself to my feet I trudged wearily towards Durness, unsettled by the nagging prospect of scouring the village for a night's lodgings; if indeed I got that far. I was compelled to take frequent stops as the interminable miles dragged on. My limbs felt like dead-weights and my tired brain ceased to function. Chafing with every step my abused feet complained bitterly. Time was slipping away and I became vaguely anxious about accommodation as I struggled along the shore of the cheerless Kyle of Durness. It was past seven o'clock before the Kyle retreated into the mist and I began the final two-mile stretch of my journey, that eventually seemed like six. On the stroke of eight o'clock I staggered into Durness, my tired eyes searching for welcoming B and B signs.

My day's struggle ended fortuitously for I soon discovered a small hotel, tottered in and found that they had a spare room. Relief engulfed me, and I realised that I still had time to change and refresh myself before having a meal. I rushed to my room with as much strength as I could muster, but dared not throw myself on the bed for fear of falling straight to sleep and going without food until morning. It was impossible to throw myself around that cramped room at all, but I was past caring. There was a bed and somewhere to hang my clothes, which was all I needed.

Feeling a little more human after a shower and a change of clothes I entered the dining room, now almost deserted. I ate a lonely meal, comforted by the luxurious feeling of reaching Durness against all the odds. Even my smarting feet had admitted defeat and stopped hurting. Contentment washed over me as I demolished the last vestiges of the satisfying meal and retired to my garret. I quickly fell asleep with the consoling thought that the most worrying section of my journey was over.

CHAPTER FIVE

The North Coast

DAY TWENTY-EIGHT: DURNESS - TONGUE

I was jerked from a deep sleep by the fall-out from a battle-royal being waged in an adjoining bedroom. The thin dividing wall reverberated with the blast of angry voices. A humdinger of an argument seemed well underway between what I assumed were husband and wife. They were going at it hammer and tongue as I tried to clear my befogged brain. Still drowsy, I checked my watch; seven forty-five. That cleared my head. I was late. Normally I was up and doing by this time. I must have been more tired than I realised. As the insults rose to a crescendo in the next room I rushed to the window for a weather check. The heartening sight of blue sky greeted me. There was some fibrous cloud, but the sun was working hard to demolish that. The mist had conveniently vanished.

Whilst I was dressing the warring couple ran out of steam. Strangled tones finally lapsed into silence. Then I heard a door slam, which meant that they were probably heading for the dining room.

Having covered so much ground the previous day, I found it hard to motivate myself. The forthcoming day's walk would be no pushover, for my intention was to reach Tongue. I had no time to mess around.

When I entered the dining room it was nearly full. I surveyed the array of faces, intrigued as to which was the fighting couple from the adjoining bedroom. It was impossible to identify them. Everyone seemed to be chatting amicably, apart from a man sitting alone at a corner table. I noticed that he was wearing walking gear so I approached his table and asked if I could join him. He introduced himself as Jamie from Edinburgh, who often came to visit the Cape Wrath peninsula, a firm favourite of his. A place of wild, unfettered charm was his glowing description. Especially Sandwood Bay, a glorious expanse of gilded sand tucked away on its rugged west coast. I told him that a visit to the cape itself would be great if only I had more time.

Jamie had made several trips there, which involve crossing the Kyle of Durness by ferry from Keoldale and following the straggling unfenced road that runs for ten miles across the moor of Parph to the lighthouse. From there, he told me, you have to walk to the tip of the cape. Roads are scarce on the peninsula and Sandwood Bay is five miles from the nearest one. Jamie insisted that I visit the bay at sometime, if only to see the remarkable pillar of rock that stands at its south end. Known as Am Buachaille - The Herdsman - it rises to a height of 200 feet, its craggy features resisting all but the extremely brave and skillful. Jamie recalled a familiar name when he mentioned the first climbers to conquer the pinnacle in 1967. They included Ian Clough, who lived in my home village of Baildon and was tragically killed by an avalanche whilst descending Annapurna a short time later. After his death the Ian Clough Hall was built in the village to commemorate his momentous climbing achievements.

My sketchy knowledge of Cape Wrath, I admitted to Jamie, was gleaned from books that put considerable emphasis on the birds which populate the great cliffs that surround it. I had been amused to discover that migrating gannets use the cape as a landmark and staging post. I could imagine their leader calling 'Right hand down for the Orkneys', or 'Left hand down for St Kilda'. In more serious vein I have always been intrigued by the navigational skills of migrating birds that cover many thousands of miles with uncanny accuracy.

Jamie smilingly admitted that he owned a triangulation point on the peninsula; the most northerly one in Scotland over 1000 feet, to be precise. He had apparently acquired it under the 'Adopt a Trig. Point' scheme, which enables enthusiasts to own and maintain their own ordnance column. Jamie had experienced great difficulty in finding his adoptive piece of concrete, for on the first visit it was obscured by deep snow.

I could have happily talked with Jamie for much longer, but another demanding schedule loomed if I was to reach Tongue by nightfall. The unknown factor was once again the availability of a ferry, this time across Loch Eriboll, a long sea-loch that intrudes deep into the coastline. A pier was indicated on the map at Portnancon, that lies roughly at the mid-point of the loch. If I could get a boat across to Ard Neackie on the east bank I would save twelve miles. If not, thirty daunting miles lay ahead, courtesy of the long journey around Loch Eriboll.

I said goodbye to Jamie as we left the hotel. He was bound for the moor of Parph to do some bird-watching. There was always plenty of activity he assured me. He loved to see gannets diving off-shore and fulmars raking the cliffs and moorland. Often confused with gulls because of their similar plumage, the latter were unmistakable in Jamie's eyes. He reckoned that even I could pick out these graceful birds as they effortlessly skim rolling waves or tracts of heather, their long, narrow wings a marvel of aero-dynamics.

A party of overnight guests were boarding a coach to continue their Highland tour. Their next port of call was to be Portree on the Isle of Skye and there was an air of excitement about them as they began a perfect day for sightseeing. A wave of nostalgia wafted over me, for I realised that they would be covering much of the route that I had taken, albeit in much greater comfort. Many of them gave a friendly wave and shouted their good wishes to Jamie and myself. As we parted company he told me that he had another duty to perform that day. He intended to visit his trig point and ensure that it was still standing.

It was wonderful to have clear views once more and enjoy surroundings vibrantly coated in sunshine. Durness is set on a limestone headland overlooking expanses of silver sand that circle the bays of Sango and Balnakeil. Rarely had I seen a more enticing beach as I walked above Sango Bay, but it was completely deserted. I was to encounter many such tempting beaches, washed by the

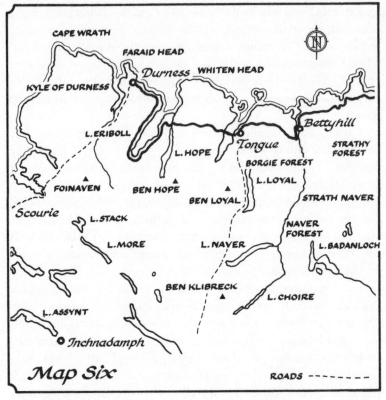

Map Six

ROADS -- -- -- -- --

remarkably blue waters of the Atlantic, but equally devoid of people. The keen winds that sweep in from the sea must be the culprit.

My plan for the journey to John O'Groats was to remain as close to the coast as possible, keeping to the road in the absence of convenient footpaths. Navigation should be easy. Provided that I kept the sea on the requisite side, I couldn't get lost. Unenterprising, but effective. The downside of this strategy is the intrusion of sea-lochs and inlets; Loch Eriboll for example, that had a cloud of uncertainty hanging over it.

My limbs seemed in remarkably good shape after their battering of the previous day. Initial stiffness abated as I got into my rhythm, much to my relief. No protests were forthcoming from my feet, to which I had given a rare treat the previous night in recognition of their outstanding service. They had almost purred when I smothered them in soothing cream.

The premier attraction of Durness is Smoo cave that lies at the head of a narrow cove that slices into the coastline beyond Sango

DUNNET HEAD STROMA DUNCANSBY HEAD John o' Groats Dounreay Thurso Melvich L. CALDER L. WATTEN NOSS HEAD Forsinard L. MORE Wick Lybster MORVEN STRATH OF KILDONAN Helmsdale ROADS - - - - - - - Map Seven

Bay. As I gazed into this deep gash in the limestone cliffs it appeared an ideal haunt for smugglers. Every ingredient required for covert activity was evident; convenient shelter from the open sea, concealment and an enormous cave in which to store loot. I eagerly descended to the cave which lay snugly surrounded by folded cliffs that resembled the pleats of a skirt. An enormous dark opening overlooking its tiny beach revealed the magnitude of this impressive cavity, the result of centuries of water erosion. A slender river still flows in to it through a hole in the roof. The cavern lies conveniently above the water line and unless the river is in spate, you can explore it without fear of a drenching. Unfortunately I was unable to reach the eighty-foot waterfall that tumbles into its innermost depths. Despite this disappointment it proved to be a place of awesome character and I could only wonder at nature's handiwork.

I emerged from the cave concerned that time was once more slipping away. A sense of urgency quickened my pace as I rejoined the road. Beyond the tiny settlement of Leirinmore, that overlooks an inviting bay, I joined a track that climbed into the hills. This was principally to escape from the A838 for a few miles, but also to take a short cut to Portnancon that would hopefully save time. Rather than trace a broad loop around the entrance to Loch Eriboll I reckoned that by cutting off the corner, so to speak, I would save at least a mile. It turned out to be not as straightforward as I hoped because part of my cross-country route was pathless. Things are rarely as easy as they seem.

As I climbed the hillside, heading for the gap between two craggy fells, I could clearly make out the characteristics of my new environment. On slopes exposed to the searching north-west winds healthy vegetation lay in wave-like formation. Small shrubs of heather, barberry and crowberry, their branches nearly horizontal, leaned away from the wind and in the shelter that they provided, mosses and lichens flourished. How different the landscape appeared to the expanses of inhospitable rock that had characterised my journey through north-west Sutherland. The vegetation was even more colourful when, with the pass behind me, I was able to look down on the sheltered banks of Loch Eriboll. Yellow splashes of late-spring gorse peppered the hillsides below me, a perfect foil to the underlying greenness of the limestone's covering. Heather spread its tentacles over hillocks that lined the banks of the loch. Shattered rock fragments littered the landscape; a more typical characteristic of the Sutherland countryside. The long blue band of Loch Eriboll stretched into the distance like a giant tongue that had licked its way into the interior.

The path that I had been following petered out and I carefully picked my way down a tussocky slope to rejoin the A838 road. Only a short distance remained to Portnancon, where I found an immaculate, recently extended house standing impressively by the lochside. In the tiny front garden tables and chairs were conveniently arranged, indicating the likelihood of refreshment. A smart dinghy stood on a trolley by the house. That looked promising, but the nearby pier, what remained of it, was a disaster. Most of it had disappeared and the feeble wooden structure that remained appeared on the verge of collapse.

Whilst I stood staring in disbelief the owner of the house emerged and introduced himself. Apparently he had recently acquired the 200 year-old building and had immediately begun to knock things into shape. In addition to providing refreshments he also offered bed and breakfast accommodation. I ordered tea and sandwiches and sat at one of the tables, trying to pluck up the courage to ask about a boat. When he reappeared I blurted out my burning question. Could he take me across the loch? Disappointingly he replied that his dinghy was not ready for such a trip. Downcast, I glanced again in its direction and it seemed perfectly sound. He must have read my thoughts for he hurriedly explained that he was still in the process of renovating it. Pointing to a tiny one-man boat bobbing by the jetty, he said that this was his only craft for the time being. Apparently he used it for fishing in the loch and visiting a small lighthouse that he looked after. The latter task would soon be unnecessary, he pointed out, for solar panels were to be fitted and the light would no longer require regular maintenance.

The extra twelve miles were now a reality. Before reluctantly leaving I enquired about the rotting pier which, he said, had been disused since the Second World War. I could see from the piles of concrete blocks stored nearby that he intended to repair the jetty, but I did not ask about his intentions for the pier; that would be superfluous.

A frustrating trek around the head of Loch Eriboll faced me, made doubly annoying because from Portnancon I could see the A838 road across the loch. It was returning along the opposite bank and passing Ard Neackie, bound for Tongue. I felt a ridiculous urge to swim across to it. Time was now an enemy. It was nearly lunchtime and only seven miles were completed. I would just have to knuckle down and get around the loch as quickly as I could. Dismissing the thought of two consecutive days of punishment and its possible effects, I strode along the road gritting my teeth in concentration. Numerous cars hurtled past and I tried to ignore the fact that they would reach Tongue hours before I did.

So intent was I on eating up the miles that I paid the loch little heed. If I had I may have caught sight of playful seals frisking about its waters. Jamie had told me that they are particularly noticeable in their breeding season, which runs from September to November. During this period they go onto the beaches to breed. Monitoring of the seal colonies is carried out each year at that time, he said, by means of aerial reconnaissance and physical counts. Unfortunately this information was forgotten in my determination to reach Tongue by early evening. Thud, thud, went my boots on the tarmac. Drip, drip, went the sweat from my brow that scorching afternoon.

Ignoring the heat and passing vehicles I walked like a man possessed. I was convinced that the man had been lying about his dinghy, thereby sentencing me to a route-march. Fortunately, my possibly misplaced anger acted as a spur. Adrenalin was pumping in great spurts and driving my limbs to new heights. Things were not all bad.

When I finally reached Ard Neackie I had not let up, despite the fact that I risked becoming dehydrated. I felt quite pleased with myself. Perhaps my body was becoming accustomed to abuse. I checked my watch. It was three o'clock, which showed that I had made good time. Tongue was still eleven miles away, but with a little luck I might reach it by seven o'clock. I forced myself to take a breather and a drink. It would be foolish to push myself even harder.

Feeling refreshed, I pounded the hot tarmac once more, maintaining a steady pace and watching for signs of protest from my baking feet. To cool them down I stopped to bathe them in one of the small lochans that I passed, taking more refreshment as I did so. I realised that my toil was nearly over when I neared another vast stretch of water; the Kyle of Tongue, that slashes into the north coast almost as deeply as Loch Eriboll. Here a ferry is not needed; that was replaced some years ago by a magnificent causeway and bridge that carries the road across the mile-wide inlet.

It was a great feeling to walk across the attractively indented Kyle, lined with purple hills and a patchwork of copses and lush meadows. The finest view was towards its head; a sunlit vista dominated by the shapely outline of Ben Loyal. Despite its modest height of 2506 feet it appears much grander because it rises in splendid isolation from a spread-eagled landscape. Its five pinnacles resemble a line of jagged teeth, similar to those of An Teallach. From my viewpoint their effect was stunning. Wainwright bestows his highest praises upon it. 'Not many mountains can be described as beautiful, but Ben Loyal can, compelling admiring attention by its graceful sculpturing and challenging appearance'. He was absolutely right.

The tide had receded from the boulder-strewn estuary. Rivulets of water eased along its bed and limpid pools glistened in the early-evening sun. I was impressed by the attractive curve and graceful lines of the bridge which balanced delicately on slender stalks. Mustard-coloured gorse surrounds Tongue Lodge that greeted me as I crossed the estuary. It stands sentinel on a headland and beckons visitors towards the village. I found Tongue itself quiet and appealing. The first building to catch my eye was the brightly-painted Kirk, typical of many such well-kept churches in the Highlands. Despite its importance as a staging post in one of the most sparsely populated areas of the country, Tongue remains unspoiled and peaceful. I came across two inns and saw numerous B and B signs at the gates of well-tended gardens. It was pleasing to note the wide choice of accommodation because I still had to find a bed for the night.

I struck gold at my second attempt, being invited into a small, but engaging, cottage. It was the home of an elderly couple who seemed genuinely pleased to see me. They had a free room, but could not provide supper, which was not unreasonable, for it was already past seven o'clock. I apologised for turning up so late, explaining that I had walked from Durness. This caused Monica and Angus, lifelong residents of the village, to raise their eyebrows and look at me with some concern. I assured them that I was fine and hurriedly switched the conversation to their peculiarly lilting accents. 'Aye many visitors find it unusual' said Angus. To me it appeared more Welsh-sounding than Scottish and Angus found this observation quite funny. 'No doubt you are ready for a rest and a cup of tea', he said kindly. Did I look so exhausted? Wiping the remaining sweat from my brow I reluctantly turned down his offer, saying that I was ravenously hungry.

'You will be wanting to freshen up and have some food' said Monica and she whisked me to my room. It was simply, but tastefully furnished and my eyes lit up at the sight of a blissfully comfortable-looking double bed. She suggested that I sought the nearest inn, which provided good food at a reasonable price. 'After I had soaked away my fatigue', she added. I wallowed in a piping-hot bath that soothed away the self-imposed rigours of the day. The giant bed looked highly tempting as I prepared to go out, but I refused to succumb. I knew that if I were to lie on it I would not get up again until the next morning.

Monica's advice proved sound, for I had an enjoyable and inexpensive meal at the inn. When I emerged into the coolness of a lovely late-evening, the sun was still shining; perfect conditions for a walk. What a ridiculous idea, I thought. Hadn't I had enough? Then I recalled noticing a tower perched on a hill not far from the village, overlooking the Kyle. My curiosity whetted, I decided to pay it a visit. If nothing else the view would be worth a walk and I did feel reasonably fit.

I returned to the cottage for a map, to ensure that I found the tower as quickly as possible. There was not much daylight remaining. As I opened the door to leave Monica appeared and enquired if I had enjoyed my meal. She looked worried when I told her where I was going. She warned that the ruin was farther away than it appeared and there would be a dark wood to negotiate. I assured her that I would be alright, but if I was not back by ten o'clock she was to send out a search-party. Monica's frown deepened until she saw my smile and realised that I was merely joking. I was an impetuous man, she observed. If she had seen me that afternoon she would have realised how right she was.

I hurried from the village along a path that leads down to the Rhian Burn, an energetic stream that rushes into the Kyle. As I galloped along I was reminded of a similar rash venture, an evening climb of Harter Fell in the Lake District, that I had undertaken a few years earlier. On that occasion I had arrived at the summit as the sun was setting and was forced to find my way down in darkness. Was I about to repeat my stupidity, I wondered?

A narrow footbridge took me across the burn and deposited me on a path that annoyingly meandered along its far bank and away from my objective. Eventually the circuitous path left the valley-floor to climb a punishing slope and enter the wood that Monica had mentioned. I was made to pay for my impetuousness as I tried to avoid impeding foliage and shadowy overhanging branches. Despite my tribulations I had ventured too far to be repelled by such obstacles and I battled with the vicious gradient and semi-darkness until I finally broke cover. I could see the ruined tower tantalisingly poised a further hundred feet above me. The light was rapidly fading as I scrambled towards the former Pictish fort, its ghostly outline silhouetted against a cobalt-tinted sky. A shiver ran through me at this unnerving sight, but I continued to drag myself up the final challenging gradient.

A few strenuous moments later I clung to the gnarled stones at the base of Castle Varrich, as the tower is known, in order to recover my strength. Whilst gulping mouthfuls of air, I realised why it had been built in such an inaccessible spot. Enjoying a commanding view over the Kyle of Tongue, it thus ensured that potential attackers could be spotted before they could do much mischief. By the time they had scaled the abrupt hillside the element of surprise would be long gone and they would be nearly as shattered as I was.

When my breath had returned, I looked expectantly around me, to be rewarded by the sight of Ben Loyal basking in the diminishing evening light. Shadows filled its corries and crevices, accentuating the cragginess of its five steeples. To the north I could see along the Kyle to Tongue Bay that lies at its mouth. A memorable view because the setting sun had cast a sheen of burnished gold over this shapely inlet. My foolhardy venture had been vindicated.

DAY TWENTY-NINE: TONGUE - MELVICH

All was quiet when I awoke, in distinct contrast to the uproar of the previous morning. The idyllic warmth and softness of the great bed made me reluctant to face the day. I lay indolently in its seductive folds, being almost lulled back to sleep. The battery was losing its power. I had to force myself into action with the thought of being late for breakfast.

The customary checks were duly executed. Weather - not good, mist hanging around, with accompanying drizzle. Feet - fine apart from one blackening toe-nail, thankfully painless. Route - straightforward according to map, which indicates road-walking, except for one short footpath. Clean clothes - very few; mental note made to try and get washing done at coming night's stop. Cash situation - dire.

A creature of habit; routines on my walks become paramount. The packing and unpacking of my rucksack becomes almost automatic and follows an identical sequence. Revival normally acquires a familiar pattern - tea on arrival at accommodation, followed by bath or shower, then meal. Walk after meal, if fit enough, followed by drink at hostelry, if lucky. To complete the cycle - go to bed, get up, do daily checks, have breakfast, walk all day. Isn't long-distance walking exciting?

Breakfast was ready and waiting when I got downstairs. Monica bustled attentively to and from the kitchen during the meal. Angus wandered into the dining room, ostensibly to enquire if everything was satisfactory. I surmised that he wanted a chat. As a passing stranger I probably represented the highlight of his day. Conversation blossomed and Angus spoke with an authority born of a lifetime's experience of the locality. The castle that I had visited the previous evening was of tenth- century origin, he told me. It overlooks water and grazing land, as did the brochs, those Pictish defensive towers so familiar to the north of Scotland. The remains of one such tower, he said, stand at the head of the Kyle of Tongue amongst other relics of ancient habitation. Since mesolithic times people had inhabited the estuaries and green straths of that area of Sutherland. He added that the relics around the Kyle's head are typical of their influence. Cairns and stones, engraved with cup and ring markings, litter the nearby hill-slopes where the early hunters and later the Bronze and Iron Age people settled, he said.

The Jacobites somehow entered our conversation and I told Angus how I had followed several of General Wade's roads that were built between the uprisings. At the time of the second Jacobite conflict in 1745, according to Angus, a French sloop with a cargo of gold ran aground on the Rabbit Islands that lie in Tongue Bay. He was unsure if it was Jacobite sympathisers' gold, or what eventually happened to it. Bonnie Prince Charlie would certainly have welcomed it, I said.

Regretfully, life had changed dramatically in the village in recent times, according to Angus. Crofting, the mainstay of the area's economy for centuries, was dying out and the young people were drifting away to work in the oilfields or the industrial cities. Those that remained were virtually reliant on tourism or casual work. Angus said that he and Monica were too old to leave even if they had the inclination and I got the feeling that he would have quite happily talked all day. Time was not at such a premium as during my previous two days, but I had to take my leave after a suitable interval and thank the couple for their kindness.

I felt a pang of regret as I stepped into the chill morning air, pulling the hood of my walking jacket over my head to keep the penetrating drizzle at bay. It was my last day in Sutherland. You will have noticed that I have referred to the old counties of north-west Scotland rather than the modern administrative title of Highland Region that now embraces them. Call me a stick in-the-mud, but the original county names have greater meaning in my view. That said, it appeared that my meagre ration of sunshine in Sutherland was over. The previous day's shaft of sunlight would have to suffice, for the day's forecast was not optimistic.

I began a steady climb out of the village, passing a sombre memorial cross that gazed impassively over the forlorn mouth of the Kyle. Tongue was sorry to see me go. About a mile from the village

I encountered a strategic road junction where the A838 road meets the A836 that has travelled north from Lairg. Here I was required to change numbers once again, and join the A836 road, for the remainder of my journey to John O'Groats. Shortly after joining forces we parted company for a couple of miles whilst I threaded my way by track and path around Ben Tongue and Cnoc an Fhreiceadain in order to avoid a pronounced loop in the highway. Visibility was poor, but at least I gained relief from tarmac. As there was very little to see, I occupied myself by studying the map of the area as I walked. Foolish really because I risked tripping on the rough track and spraining my ankle, or worse. Clearly identified were the traces of ancient settlements around the Kyle of Tongue that Angus had told me about. A chambered cairn, a broch and various stones were shown, littering the hills. A symbol stone drew my attention. What purpose had it served, I wondered? Several such stones can be found on the crags that form the northern fringe of Ilkley Moor, near my home. They mark a section of a Bronze Age trade route, the M62 of its era, that linked Ireland with the continent. One of these, known as the Swastika Stone, displays an ornately-carved symbol representing eternal life. I had never fathomed its true meaning, merely assuming that it signifies safe passage to the traveller. With such thoughts of ancient carvings in my mind, into my mental store-cupboard went the reminder to check the symbol on the stone overlooking the Kyle if the opportunity arose to visit the locality again.

Engrossed with my thoughts I mechanically followed the winding track through the gloom until it inconsiderately deteriorated into a path. At this point I had to abandon my reverie and concentrate on my route. A tiny lochan suddenly appeared out of the mist. I had developed an aversion to confrontations with murky stretches of water, but on this occasion there was no problem. The path guided me safely round it before swinging north, not my intended direction, towards Coldbackie. Now there's a name to conjure with. It has the ring of the Klondike about it. My apologies to that tiny settlement nestling in the shrouded hills above Tongue Bay, for I gave it a miss, preferring a short-cut that quickly reunited me with the metalled A836 road. We headed east together, bound for Bettyhill which stands at the mouth of Strathnaver. The cotton wool blanket that obscured the Sutherland landscape ensured that we stuck together like glue.

Flint-like morose lochans flecked the next few miles of encompassing moorland until I passed the fringe of Borgie Forest, a sprawling mass of conifers that stretches many miles to the south. A sign denotes a nature trail within the tall avenues of Sitka Spruce which dominate this first plantation to be established in northern Scotland by the Forestry Commission in 1920. Emerging from the shackles of the forest the pleasant River Borgie wriggled towards a charming stone bridge, whose shapely twin arches straddled its lively waters. On a fine day I could imagine no nicer spot.

A little farther along the road I was overtaken by a farmer on a tractor who shouted to enquire if I needed a rest. I was pleasantly surprised when he invited me to his nearby farm for a drink. His offer was gladly accepted and I followed him through a gateway and along a farm track. He was soon ushering me into a snug kitchen with a stone-flagged floor and white-washed walls. Its coolness was refreshing and I gathered that this old farmhouse had thick walls. My head nearly touched the gnarled beams of the low ceiling as the farmer, Calum, shouted for his wife to come and put the kettle on. A stout, ruddy-faced woman bustled in. Her mouth was opening as if about to tell her husband that she had more urgent things to do than wait on him. When she saw me her manner softened and she uttered a surprised 'Good morning'. Calum introduced us and suggested a welcoming cup of tea. His wife, May, busied herself as Calum asked where I was making for. She produced a mouth-watering fruit cake as I launched into a short resume of my walk. Calum's eyebrows leapt in surprise and May, obviously taking pity on me, handed over an enormous slice of cake, adding that I needed to keep up my strength. My heart warmed to the sympathetic and hospitable couple who refrained from the frequent response that I was barking mad. Consequently I expanded my story and told them about Angus and his mention of the ancient remains around the Kyle of Tongue. As May poured boiling water into an enormous teapot she explained that there was a wealth of history in their locality, particularly Strathnaver. When she learned that Bettyhill lay on my route she gave a satisfied chuckle as she handed a steaming mug of tea to me. The village, she said, lies at the mouth of the River Naver which flows into Torrisdale Bay. I was recommended to take a short detour on my approach to Bettyhill and visit the tiny hamlet of Invernaver. A mere half a mile from this collection of farms, that huddles at the foot of Strathnaver, I would find the remains of a broch and a Bronze Age colony standing on the fringe of the bay. She suggested that if I had the time, a climb to the top of the cliffs overlooking that part of the bay would allow a close scrutiny of the broch and give a bird's eye view of four ruined hut circles.

The cake was sumptuous and I sipped scalding tea as I listened intently to Mary's eager outpourings. I was impressed with her knowledge and particularly interested in her account of the infamous clearance of Strathnaver, which, she indicated, lay only three miles away. According to her description it is now a beautiful, but relatively lonely, valley with numerous cairns and brochs lining the banks of the Naver. The village of Bettyhill, she said, was named after the wife of the hated Duke of Sutherland, who was responsible for burning the crofts in the valley and driving their inhabitants to the coast. His personal fortune leapt when the land was converted to grazing for sheep, she added. I did not dare mention that he was also responsible for pioneering the road that links Loch Assynt with Durness.

I remarked on her store of knowledge and Calum explained that whenever time permitted May indulged her passion for reading. She smilingly added that they were usually books on history, her favourite subject at school. Declining the kind offer to refill my mug, I explained that I still had many miles to cover that day. I thanked them for their hospitality and left with their good wishes ringing in my ear. Once again the kindness that was the hallmark of this remote corner of Scotland, Scourie excepted, had been aptly demonstrated.

After an hour's purposeful walking I entered evocative Strathnaver, where a minor road branches south into the depths of the historic valley, linking the isolated crofts that still remain. As I gazed up the overcast strath I could not rid my mind of the infamy that had made it famous. When I left the main road at the mouth of the river and entered Invernaver I was anxious for a glimpse of the settlement that May had described. Unfortunately a depressing haze hung over the bay and no path to the site was evident. As I gazed disappointedly from the gate that barred further access I was joined by a farmer, who, I discovered, conveniently owned the land that I wished to cross. He proved to be very amenable, indicating that he had no objection to my visiting the ancient site. Pointing out the direction I should take he advised care in skirting the tidal water in the bay.

I followed his instructions and found that I only had to cross two shallow rivulets of water that lay across my path. The dark, brooding cliffs soon appeared and I began a steep ascent of a cleft that the obliging farmer had indicated would lead me to the broch. Five minutes of vigorous exercise brought the remains of the Pictish tower into view and I was soon clambering over its circular base. Three feet of stone wall, with a gap denoting the entrance, were all that remained of the once-proud structure that occupied a fine vantage point overlooking the bay. I peered through the gloom at the dunes below the cliff, searching for the hut circles, which annoyingly proved elusive in the poor visibility. Fortunately, the cliff on which I was perched was not sheer and it was possible to clamber part-way down for a closer view. This revealed two rings of stones, several feet in diameter, that I found, upon reaching ground level, were arranged on the top of mounds whose centres were slightly hollowed out. I wandered amongst the dunes and discovered a simple stone cairn and eventually, the remaining hut circles, their arrangement of small, loose stones forming the rings that I had seen from above.

My curiosity satisfied I returned to the gate where I found the farmer waiting for me. Touched by his concern I told him how I had fared and he seemed genuinely pleased, which prompted him to venture the following information about Strathnaver and its clearance. At the time of the torching of the crofts a blanket of smoke obliterated the valley, extending right down to Torrisdale Bay that lies beyond the mouth of the river. Near to the modern bridge, which carries the A836 over the Naver, lies a gap in the vegetation that formed a demarcation line across the valley immediately after the clearance. The evicted crofters, many of whom had lost most of their possessions in the fires, were not allowed to venture further up the valley than this point. I listened to his words with great interest, once again impressed with such awareness of the area's history. As I departed the farmer proudly informed me that the settlement which I had just explored had been designated a Site of Special Interest.

Time had stolen by during my detour and as I returned to the main road I stepped up my pace. I was well behind schedule. Consequently I ploughed past Bettyhill's extensive scattering of buildings. The village must have taken umbrage, for I even ignored its Museum of Strathnaver that beckoned from the roadside. An incessant drizzle attacked me as I followed the road into open country. It led me past a small wood at Fiscary and onwards to a small stretch of placid water around which circled a flock of gulls. Their raucous cries haunted me for a considerable distance as I walked amidst bleak and undulating moorland.

The afternoon wore on as I progressed east along the contorted road that squirmed at every opportunity. In order to maintain a passing interest in the surrounding countryside, of which very little was visible, I closely studied my map, searching for any distinctive features. Walking in the lee of the Strathy headland that lay to the north I could see that it protrudes from the jagged coastline to terminate at the rocky finger of Strathy Point. Here stands a modern lighthouse, completed as recently as 1958, to keep wayward ships at bay. Great cliffs line the east shore of this rocky peninsula, providing shelter to Strathy Bay that huddles at its south-east corner. The bay is ringed by the straggling village of Strathy where the A836 road almost touches the golden sands of its splendid beach as it crosses the mouth of the River Strathy. A grey pall hung over the village but I was rewarded by a glimpse of those silken sands, so typical of the cruelly exposed north coast.

Further evidence of ancient settlements lie near the village and I was intrigued by one particular stone which was identified on the map as Cross Slab. I also noticed that a track runs south from Strathy for twelve miles into the wild interior of east Sutherland. It follows the course of the River Strathy almost to its source, the lonely and sequested Loch Strathy. On the way it passes the extensive plantation of Strathy Forest before entering an intimidating landscape; the quivering mass known as Strathy Bog. To me it represented a desolate no-mans land, intriguing but frightening. Botanists, however, would be in their element exploring its terrain that resembles a Persian carpet. They would be quick to reveal that sphagnum moss, the basis of bog cover, produces this wonderful springy effect when walked on. I prefer terra-firma myself, knowing only too well that bogs consist of ninety-eight percent water. Nevertheless, botanical enthusiasts will wax lyrical over such colourful tracts of moss, cotton sedge and heather. Dig down in a bog, they will tell you, and every foot represents about 300 years' growth of organic material. According to them there are centuries of history to be found in bogs. Personal experience tells me that they can easily swallow you and should be avoided like the plague. It is fortunate that a coward like myself was not born into an earlier age, for when thick, impenetrable forests covered much of our country it was difficult to avoid them. They disturbingly formed the forerunners of our motorways.

The tarmac seemed comforting beneath my feet amidst the disturbing thoughts of desolate bogs. Road-walking did have its compensations. More practical considerations took over as I tackled the remaining three miles to Melvich. The prospect of finding accommodation loomed large and I hoped that I would not have to spend a great deal of time in searching. I checked my watch and found that I had made good time up to that point so there should be no need to rush. Another scan of the map revealed that I would not have to wander far from the road when I reached Melvich for its buildings were clustered conveniently alongside.

My legs were just beginning to send disconcerting messages as I reached my destination. A metropolis consisting of a hotel, a monument and public conveniences signified my arrival at Melvich. The remainder of the dwellings were strung out on either side of the main road, much as Bettyhill had been. Here was yet another of the settlements that cluster around the foot of the great straths that intrude from the north coast. Melvich shelters at the entrance to the extensive Strath Halladale. A main road runs to the head of the glen and onwards to reach the east coast at Helmsdale. This road effectively divides the north-east corner of Scotland from the remainder of the country.

I spotted a gratifying B and B sign in the garden of an attractive modern bungalow and hurried up the path to enquire if a room was available. Luck was with me. The door was opened by a pleasant lady who introduced herself as Janet and told me that she had a single room available. The interior of the bungalow was very impressive. Janet obviously liked Laura Ashley wall coverings and fabrics, which adorned every room. They were complemented by chintzy, but tasteful, furniture and a wonderful array of ornaments and trinkets. I was asked the usual familiar questions. How far had I come? Where was I heading? As I answered I waited for the normal response of incredulity and disbelief. Janet, however, took it in her stride, remarking that many of her guests were walkers. That was a cue to enquire if I could have some clothes washed, for she would be used to catering for tired and sweaty travellers. You may have observed that I have not mentioned the delicate subject of laundry for some time. This does not mean that I had been wearing the same garments for two weeks. It is merely that I do not wish to bore you with details of my personal hygiene. You do believe me, don't you?

Janet happily agreed to do any laundering that I required, as she showed me my room. It was just as delightful as the living quarters. Tastefully decorated and packed with bric-a-brac. As I took a bath in the adjoining bathroom I was surrounded by a multitude of perfumes, toiletries and knick-knacks. Only the rubber duck was missing.

When I entered the dining room for supper I was greeted rather reservedly by four fellow-guests. Not the four doctors of Camusnagaul, but two married couples who were touring Scotland by car. Janet had obviously told them about me, for I received the usual probing questions relating to my lone journey. I steered the conversation away from my endeavours and asked them about their holiday. The two men, I discovered, were teachers who liked to tour with their wives each year. They elaborated about all the countries that they had visited, adding as an afterthought that it was their first time in the north of Scotland. By the end of the meal I knew all about their world travels and felt quite mundane amongst people so clearly out to impress.

I spent the rest of the evening in their company and found the two wives very pleasant and retiring. Their husbands monopolised the conversation and we were treated to a diatribe concerning the extensive ills of the teaching profession and what was required to put education and the government to rights. All the issues appeared crystal clear to their minds and the remedies, according to them, were remarkably simple. Such arrogance must stem from never having to reason with anyone above the age of sixteen.

It was quite a relief when I was finally able to escape to my room. The thought that my exploits had been completely ignored by the overwhelming pair raised a wry smile. It was the poor wives that I felt sorry for. They must have suffered in silence for years.

In the short time it took me to fall asleep, I lay contemplating the remainder of my journey, which wasn't extensive. It was both comforting and disconcerting to realise that only two more days of struggle remained. After eagerly wishing to put the previous seventy miles behind me, the realisation struck that I would soon have no more to cover. What would I do then? The thorny prospect of returning to normal life loomed. How would I react to not having to hitch on my rucksack and walk each day? According to some pundits you are a changed person after a long expedition. I didn't want to change, I just wanted to remain the same old me.

Wainwright understands that, basically, all long-distance walkers are masochists. This observation, taken from his *Pennine Way Companion* precisely encapsulates why we subject ourselves to hardship and purgatory. 'The final sense of achievement is, as you stagger over the finishing line, but the bliss you feel is the bliss you feel when you stop banging your head against a wall'.

DAY THIRTY: MELVICH - THURSO

The first thought that entered my head as I dragged myself sleepily out of bed was a comforting one. I had a comparatively short distance to cover that day; a mere seventeen miles. After the marathons of the previous three days it should pose no serious problems. I sincerely hoped that despite my conjecture about what happened when my walk was completed, I could maintain an active interest in places along the remainder of my route to the magnet of John O'Groats.

I had the dining room to myself at breakfast. My fellow-guests were evidently not early risers. I took the opportunity to chat to Janet about my previous day's walk, expressing disappointment that I had been unable to make the five-mile detour to Strathy Point. Most of the land in that area is owned by the Ministry of Agriculture and Fisheries, she informed me. The local residents, mainly part-time crofters were actively considering ownership of their properties. Despite their current amicable sharing of common grazing and peat-cutting rights, disagreements had apparently arisen over such a far-reaching proposal. The wind of change, I gathered, was obviously unsettling a proportion of these resourceful people, many of whom supplemented their inadequate earnings by working at the Nuclear Power Establishment at Dounreay. I was also surprised to learn from my host that peat was still burned on such a large scale.

Janet said that had I walked to the point and its attendant lighthouse I would have seen the nets hanging out to dry at the Salmon Station situated part-way along the headland. They are suspended on long poles that overlook the cliffs which drop sharply down to Strathy Bay. So steep are they that the nets have to be raised from the shore by winch. The fishing boat, Janet said, had to be taken to Melvich for launching each spring, the cliffs being too sheer for hauling it up to, and lowering it down from, the station.

I also learned that Strathy Point abounds with wild flowers, some of which are relatively rare. Amongst the plants that she mentioned were field gentian, fragrant orchid and early purple orchid. The most outstanding from Janet's viewpoint is the tiny, distinctively violet-coloured Primula Scotia, or Scottish Primrose. I told her that I would keep watch for such plants and try to capture them on film. Unfortunately I was not astute enough to find any.

Noises from the direction of the bedrooms indicated the imminent arrival of the self-satisfied teachers. Not wishing to endure another one-way conversation I beat a hasty retreat, thanking Janet for her cordiality.

The invigorating freshness of a cloudy morning met me as I left the bungalow and struck out for the Caithness border that lay temptingly four miles to the east. I was thankful for respite from the drizzle of the previous day and visibility, though not brilliant, had also improved. A greater extent of the tracts of featureless moorland was visible, which only induced a yearning for a few shapely mountains.

There seemed little relief from my diet of heather and grey sky until I rounded a sharp bend in the road at Drum Holliston and several miles of rugged coastline suddenly presented itself. The centrepiece of this unexpected view was the great white sphere of the nuclear reactor at Dounreay that John Hillaby had described, when passing it, as 'a golf ball about to be driven into the North Atlantic'. This seemed a perfect description and I reckoned that many objectors to its presence would have gladly wielded the necessary club. Controversy has surrounded this distinctive globe, and the sprawl of buildings that encompass it, since its erection in the 1950's. It looked menacing, even from a distance. At odds with its admirable backdrop of indented coastline, it appeared vulnerable to attack from the breakers that scour the adjacent shore. The Dounreay Nuclear Power Development Establishment, to use its full title, probably represents a necessary evil to the inhabitants of the northern fringe of Scotland. Despite its activities being decreased in recent years, it still provides a major source of employment over a large area. If it ceased to function the redundant employees would have to revert to the indigenous industries of fishing, oil and tourism, which may not offer many opportunities.

Beyond this questionable site lay the leaden waters of the Pentland Firth. A dark smudge on the far horizon was all that was visible through the distant haze, of Hoy, the most westerly of the Orkney Islands. Closer to hand I could trace the next two miles of my journey to the village of Reay which clustered around the band of tarmac that snaked across the ever-present heathland.

My entry into Caithness would have gone undetected but for two prominent signs by the roadside. The first welcomed me to the final county on my route; a fact which induced a stab of excitement. This was tempered by the second sign that invited the traveller to visit the Caithness Glassworks at Wick. Considering that this town is the most easterly one in Caithness, it did not augur well for what lay in between. Surely the county must have other delights. If it had, I reckoned, it was not letting on. I was soon to discover, however, that there was far more to Caithness than the glassworks.

Golfers would be tempted by the next sign that caught my eye as I approached Reay. It advertised the nearby testing links that overlook Sandside Bay. No good for a rabbit like me, I thought, whose sole game on a full-sized course had been interrupted by darkness. My scything and flailing caused my companions to christen me 'The Grim Reaper'. Progress was so laborious we got no further than the fourteenth hole. I shuddered at the memory of this debacle as I entered the compact village of Reay. It seemed an ideal place for holidaymakers who prefer the freedom of camping or caravanning, as it offers ample facilities for both.

Dounreay loomed ahead of me. Its very name has a ring of doom about it. The giant 'golf ball' grew with each step, threatening in my imagination to escape from its moorings and roll down the road crushing everything in its path, including me. My unease was compounded by the straps of my rucksack developing a disquieting creak which accompanied my every step. The strain of supporting my essentials for a month was beginning to tell on them.

I took a breather at the entrance to the complex, trying to imagine what took place behind its grim facade. If I had been more observant I would have discovered an exhibition in the nearby control tower that formerly served the Establishment's own airstrip. Here, I later discovered, a video outlining Dounreay's activities is on display, together with scale models and 'hands on' gadgetry. As I studied a sign which identifies the names of various companies operating within the Establishment, there appeared to be no shortage of traffic using the service road to its gates. Dounreay was a place of considerable activity.

Lunchtime was approaching but I decided to walk on. I had nearly reached the halfway point on my day's walk and I wanted to allow time for exploration, during the afternoon, if the opportunity arose. An hour later found me within reach of the next landmark; Bridge of Forss. Postponing lunch for a little longer, I hurried towards it, reckoning that a place with such an intriguing name must be of interest.

My expectations were not misplaced, for Bridge of Forss turned out to be a delight. The former Norse settlement, now an engaging hamlet, nestles around the winding Forss Water. This collection of shapely, rustic buildings has as its centrepiece the stately Forss House. An array of tall chimneys point skywards from the roof of this splendid three-storey mansion, protruding from the surrounding trees like watchtowers. Now converted into a tasteful hotel, it is built of the eye-catching stone that characterises the neighbouring cottages and barns.

I found a convenient spot, near a preserved watermill, to eat my belated lunch. The tranquil river tumbled lazily over the nearby waterfall that formerly provided power for the picturesque mill. A three-storey building, like Forss house, it displayed no dramatic chimneys, but the gnarled slopes of its lichen-encrusted roof were adequate compensation. As I studied the features of the now-silent mill, the overhanging branches of a sturdy oak wafted gently above me in the afternoon breeze. Standing impassively amidst a wreath of rowan, ash and beech, the building epitomised an earlier, less frenetic age.

Blissfully content, I blessed my good fortune in finding such an endearing retreat. The realisation that a mere five miles of my day's journey remained, presented a golden opportunity to abandon tarmac and explore at my leisure. My map revealed an alternative coastal route to Thurso, which although longer than that by road, should prove more scenic. If I was unable to see any mountains in Caithness, what few exist are tucked away in its south-west corner, I could at least sample its coastline by traversing the cliff-tops to Scrabster, a near-neighbour of Thurso.

I took a quiet road that wound seawards, squeezing between thick hedgerows on its pleasant approach to the hamlet of Crosskirk. A sign indicated a field path leading to St Mary's Chapel, that lay slightly off my intended route. Having no time restriction I made a short detour across colourful meadows to the ruins of the twelfth-century chapel, one of the oldest places of worship in Scotland. The views seawards were still impaired by poor visibility, but the features of the extensive hump of Hoy were now more discernable. I could make out ranging sea cliffs on the island, their sandy-coloured expanses rising from the agitated ocean like battlements decapitated by an embracing mist.

Returning to Crosskirk I peered over the rocky amphitheatre of Crosskirk Bay, where the restless sea tore at rocks, distorted and folded by geological upheaval before man was even thought of. A convenient, though faint, path then guided me along clifftops that skirt lush pastures resplendent with buttercup, milkwort and primrose. At Brims Ness, with its adjacent ruined castle and tiny harbour, the predatory ocean swirls around its rocks in a confusion of currents, eager to trap the unwary.

Greatly enjoying my new surroundings I came upon the remnants of a Pictish hill-fort suspended high above the waves on a rocky promontory whose only tenuous link with the nearby cliffs was a slender ridge. The setting provided a further example of the defensive aptitude of those early Scottish inhabitants. A reminder of the great Caithness flagstone industry, appeared in the form of a long-disused quarry, from which massive blocks of the underlying old red sandstone were once hewn. In addition to producing fine flagstone the ground also affords the fertile farmland that borders the coast of north-east Scotland.

I was becoming progressively convinced that I had made the best possible choice of route for the final leg of my journey. An original option had been to miss out the north coast and head diagonally across to John O'Groats by way of Altnaharra and the Flow Country; that inner wilderness of Caithness. However, the disturbing thought of wallowing through a lonely expanse of blanket bog-land had brought about a rapid change of plan. Naturalists, who flock to the Flow Country from all over the world, will sing its praises, with great justification, but for a chicken like me it presented a formidable challenge. The north coast was serving me well, thank you.

Such were my thoughts as I stood on the craggy Spear Head, an intriguing name for a small projection into the North Atlantic. The wind tousled my hair and sweet coastal air tantalised my nostrils as I scanned the ocean for, as yet, unseen shipping. I knew that Scrabster lay around the larger headland of Holborn Head just to the east and that a ferry operates from there to Stromness on Orkney. Numerous fishing boats were visible, some probably carrying sea-anglers hunting the famous giant halibut that inhabits the Pentland Firth. Larger craft had so far remained elusive.

I followed the cliff-tops around Holborn Head, that guards the entrance to Thurso Bay, and acquired my first view of the urban sprawl of Thurso that surrounds the bay's south shore. Stately Holborn Head lighthouse heralded my arrival at the fishing port of Scrabster that lay a hundred feet below me in the lee of the ranging cliffs. Its harbour basks in the natural shelter provided by a towering wall of rock that encircles it.

A careful descent brought me to the busy road that serves the port and the fearsome draught from passing juggernauts nearly flung me to the ground. Massive container-loads of fish were being whisked away to far-flung markets. Oil tankers scurried to and fro, quenching their thirst at the austere tanks of a storage depot. Hustle and bustle were everywhere. Despite activity in the thriving fish market being past its day's zenith, vehicles were still busily swallowing the catches and scurrying from the docks. Upon reaching the road they tangled with traffic leaving the ferry terminal.

I walked amidst the buzz and excitement of the energetic port, passing a variety of sheds which housed everything from ships' chandlers and riggers to an enticing 'Wee Shop'. Craft of all sizes were gently bobbing at their moorings. Tiny launches vied for dockside space alongside tall-masted yachts and fishing boats. The most eye-catching of all was the brightly-painted RNLB lifeboat, the 'Queen Mother'. Its orange superstructure gleamed, providing a colourful reminder that the real Queen Mother often resides at the Castle of Mey that lies not far from John O'Groats.

As I sought out the Seamens' Mission which advertised refreshments, I passed the harbour office. On the cluttered noticeboard at its entrance a disquieting notice caught my attention. It indicated gale warnings for the area, a salutary hint of the danger always lurking in open waters. The next notice I saw urged forgetful drivers to drive on the left as they leave the ferry terminal. Amidst assorted groups of seamen, anglers and visitors I enjoyed a welcome break in the Seamens' Mission, sipping hot tea and listening to contrasting tales of woe and elation concerning the day's haul.

The remaining distance to Thurso was accomplished by means of a convenient path that skirted the bay and permitted elevated views of the jagged rocks and firm sands below. Amongst the rolling breakers expending themselves on the shore skimmed several surfers, a surprising sight on Scotland's north coast. I was later to learn that the sport is more common to the area than I had realised. Several of these northern bays are utilised and major surfing championships take place amongst the mighty swells that pound their beaches. Apparently autumn is the best time of the year for surfing when high rollers sweep in from the Atlantic.

My approach to Thurso coincided with a rapid deterioration in the weather and I entered a town annoyingly shrouded in a veil of sea-mist. Its buildings and streets had a dispirited look as I made my way to its heart. Greyness was all-pervading in Thurso, concealing its landmarks such as the statues that inhabit St John's Square. The handsome figures of a soldier atop the War Memorial and Sir John Sinclair, Baronet of Lybster, standing proudly on a nearby pedestal, were reduced to nondescript, shadowy forms. The impressive parish church that overlooks them fared little better, its tall tower, with shapely Gothic windows, a disappointing blur. I felt apologetic for having caught Thurso on such a bad day.

Searching for my accommodation, I combed the symmetrical network of cheerless streets in a process of elimination which was rewarded when I met June and Raymond, the lively and affable proprietors. June asked what I thought of their town. Diplomatically I replied that I had been unable to see much of it, but I was particularly anxious to explore the castle and Harold's Tower, the burial place of the Sinclairs of Lybster. Sir John Sinclair, who's misty form had caught my eye, was apparently a notable member of the family, being the architect of the herring industry in Thurso and a pioneer of the Agrarian Revolution. Raymond enquired if I had seen Princess Street, the town's main thoroughfare. When I nodded, he explained that it was named after its counterpart in Edinburgh. Thurso, he said, was designed on a similar grid pattern to that great city.

When I had scrubbed and changed I was obliged to go back into the town centre for a meal and June pointed out the best place to eat. I followed her recommendation and was not disappointed. The mist was still lurking as I left the restaurant and walked towards the river. Thurso Bridge was a dark hump spanning its inky waters. Photographs were impossible. Having time to kill I went in search of the castle which lies out of the town, overlooking Thurso Bay.

A long walk was necessary along roads, and finally a riverside path, to its lonely remains. The hollow shell and its once-proud towers presided over a gloomy bay, as though shunned by the town and condemned to rot in solitude. I could visualise the small but elegant castle in its prime when it commanded the entrance to Thurso harbour. Visitors are now prohibited from entry as the building is deemed unsafe. I was, however, able to examine its exterior and discovered within the sturdy seaward-facing wall the protruding barrels of cannons that had not been fired in anger for many centuries.

My enthusiasm for further investigation waned in the murky evening light. I decided to give Harold's Tower, which stands farther afield on the flanks of Clardon Hill, a miss. Fanned by a stiff offshore breeze I retraced my steps alongside Thurso Bay which funnels into the narrow harbour at the mouth of the River Thurso. In this sheltered inlet bounced the odd pleasure craft, a reminder that fishing activity is now the preserve of busy Scrabster. I imagine that this has not always been the case, particularly in the time of the Norsemen who created a settlement here and gave it the name of Thurso (Thors River). It is easy to imagine Viking long-boats skimming across the bay and diving for the haven of the well-protected river.

I decided to try a different route and crossed a footbridge that spanned the restless waters of the dark river. My surroundings appeared lack-lustre in the bleary evening light until a splash of brightness caught my eye. The sparkling-white hats and webbing of a group of sea cadets, drilling on a riverside wharf, shone like beacons. They were being put through their paces by a businesslike Petty Officer, whose raucous instructions carried on the air for all to hear. The years rolled away as the memory of square-bashing days in the RAF came flooding back. Those youngsters were doing it by choice, we National Servicemen had no say in the matter.

As I approached the town centre I passed Robert Dick's house, once the home of one of the outstanding naturalists of the nineteenth century. Unaware of their proximity to greatness, a posse of starlings gossiped on nearby telephone wires. In towns and cities these gregarious birds can be a problem when they leave their trademark on buildings and pavements and deafen the populace with their raucous clamour. They do, however, possess more endearing qualities, like the friendly group that extract worms and anything else that they can find, from my lawn. Twice a day they totter through the grass, their yellow beaks drilling for tasty morsels. You can set your watch by these creatures of habit who turn up at precisely the same time each day for their breakfast and teatime rituals. I have often wondered where they call for lunch.

Returning to my lodgings, the sound of my footsteps reverberated through the silent emptiness of the streets. Where had all the people gone? Thurso resembled a ghost-town.

DAY THIRTY-ONE: THURSO - JOHN O'GROATS

The big day had dawned. Absurdity ruled as I lay semi-conscious, reluctant to stir. I was in Billy Liar-cum-Walter Mitty mode; my imagination running riot. Convinced that news of my imminent arrival would have set John O'Groats aflame, I pictured my triumphal entry that coming afternoon. Flags fluttered, the hurriedly assembled brass band played with gusto and the village was packed with ecstatically cheering crowds. I was barely able to reach journey's end at the famous signpost that points the way to Lands End. Battered by back-slapping, hands aching from continuous pumping, I pushed through the milling throng of admirers to be greeted by Wainwright. He was normally averse to personal appearances, but had made an exception in my case. Shaking me by the hand he was about to congratulate me when my reverie was abruptly curtailed. A call for breakfast rang out.

The final daily ritual of dressing, packing and preening was completed in double-quick time, for I was eager to be on my way. I joined two young men at breakfast who were working in the area for several days. When they learned what I was about, their jaws dropped. They appeared incredulous at the idea of walking more than 500 miles for enjoyment. I waited for the customary query as to why I did it. Thankfully it never came. They were mercifully short of time and had to hurry away, but not before subjecting me to a few pitying glances.

Stepping into the cool morning air I gratefully noted that the sea mist had retreated. Thanks to my earlier day-dreaming, my usual weather-check had been overlooked. It was tempting to linger and see Thurso in more agreeable conditions but I was impatient to see journey's end. My route that day would be the shortest and most direct possible. No meandering diversions would be entertained. The battle with hostile terrain and wicked rocks that trip the unsuspecting boot lay far behind. A tarmac trail beckoned, ever ready to nurture blisters, but allowing the maximum rate of knots.

I re-crossed Thurso Bridge and said farewell to the town that I had unfortunately not seen at its best. On the outskirts I cast a farewell look over Thurso Bay and the spreadeagled township that had developed from such small beginnings many centuries ago. A distinctive castellated archway framed my view. I wondered if it had been a former entrance to Thurso castle, which was visible over the adjoining fields. A prominent notice warned that access was prohibited. Even when viewed from a distance, the castle looked far more impressive than it had on the previous dank evening.

The A 836 road proved ideal for my purpose. It aimed in a dead-straight line for the only village of any significant size between Thurso and John O'Groats. This is Castletown, that straddles the road as it prepares to sweep around the broad curve of Dunnet Bay. The intervening four miles were covered at a rapid pace and I was soon marching past the shops and inviting café that stand on Castletown's mile-long main street. I was stopped in my tracks by a sign indicating a unique quarry at nearby Castle Hill. Forcing myself to stop my reckless race to the finish, I went to investigate.

There I discovered the noted Flagstone Trail of Castle Hill, set in the cradle of the flagstone industry on the shore of Dunnet Bay. Amongst the sand dunes runs a path leading to the derelict remains of the quarry buildings, and eventually, the sandstone quarry itself. The decaying shells of a windmill and quarrymens' cottages huddle in the dunes near Castle Hill House that was partially destroyed by fire thirty years ago. These structures are potent reminders of the once-thriving industry that blossomed here in the early nineteenth century. To illustrate this fact, elegant Devonian sandstone flags border the path leading to the site. From the quarry, Caithness flags were transported worldwide and paved the greater part of the nineteenth-century areas of Edinburgh, Sydney, London and other major cities.

As it skirts Dunnet Bay the road is flanked by mountainous dunes that guard the golden sands. Dunnet Forest creeps remorselessly to the fringe of the bay, enveloping the road as it approaches the hamlet of Dunnet. I clambered over intimidating, grass-cloaked dunes to scan the great sweep of the bay. Energetic waves licked the luxurious expanse of sand. A group of predatory gulls, undaunted by my presence, stalked the beach, bathed in sparkling rivulets, or teetered ponderously on mossy boulders. A few families dotted the bay and a handful of hardy, vociferous children splashed in the chilly-looking ocean. Their excited cries reverberated around the great inlet that is protected on its north side by the massive bulk of Dunnet Head.

At Dunnet a minor road branches north to traverse Dunnet Head and terminate at the lighthouse and viewpoint that mark the most northerly point of mainland Britain. A prominent sign invites motorists to undertake a journey across this significant landmark that juts like a giant nose from the splintered coastline that borders the Pentland Firth. This notorious stretch of water is a place of turbulent and dangerous channels.

The A836 road straightens once more between Dunnet and the intriguing hamlet of Mey, whose main attraction, apart from the nearby Castle, is the Castle Arms, a prominent roadside inn. I pressed my nose inquisitively to its windows, hoping to catch sight of the collection of photographs of the Royal Family that supposedly hang within. Luckily the place looked empty, so my intrusive face was unlikely to put any drinkers off their beer. Of the photographs there was annoyingly no sign.

Since noticing the conspicuous stacks on the roof of Forss House I had been conscious of an abundance of tall chimneys in the area. Mey proved no exception. A glance along its main street revealed clusters of them on the roofs of the surrounding houses. I wondered if they were a pre-requisite for the burning of peat. One thing was certain, Caithness chimney sweeps would never want for work. Accommodation signs also sprouted everywhere, as they had done frequently since entering the county. Caithness would do well to transplant some of its signs in the more remote parts of Wester Ross and Sutherland, where they are sorely needed.

Less than a mile from the village I passed the entrance to the Castle of Mey, the residence loved by the Queen Mother. Sadly the castle is not open to the public, but on certain days in summer its gardens are made available to visitors. I had to be content with a long-range view of the castle from a minor road that zigzags towards the coast near East Mey.

The cry of inquisitive gulls accompanied my steps towards the furrowed contour of Gills Bay. Here there is an exciting view across the Pentland Firth to the island of Stroma that lies a mere two miles from the mainland. A small pier intrudes into the bay and I ventured along it for a closer view of the waves tearing at the jagged folds of rock that line the shore. Ragged cliffs loomed menacingly above me. The rocks beneath them suggested that a colossal force had torn away the edge of the land leaving a frenzy of tormented strata in its wake. A ruptured swirl of coastline encircles the bay which is battered by the fastest sea current in Britain. The Atlantic Ocean and the North Sea meet head on in the narrow confines of the Pentland Firth, creating a notorious tide-race known as the Merry Men of Mey. Far from merry, it induces a maelstrom of wicked inshore currents that threaten to drag unsuspecting ships onto the treacherous rocks.

Evocative Canisbay Kirk overlooks the eastern flank of Gills Bay, from the tiny hamlet of Kirkstyle. Its adjoining churchyard displays an infinite assortment of elegant memorials. Proud headstones and graceful pillars sprout from the earth like an ornate forest. Marble complements skillfully carved stone, within this tangible illustration of the area's history. The kirk has its origins in mediaeval times and the most notable inhabitant of its graveyard is Jan de Groot, whose uniquely inscribed tombstone dates back to 1568. He gained immortality by giving his name to the village of John O'Groats. The story runs thus. In the late fifteenth century Orkney came under Scottish rule and James IV of Scotland instigated a ferry to the mainland in order to embrace the islands into his kingdom. He enlisted three young Dutch brothers by the name of de Groot to run the ferry. They were granted land, by the Earl of Caithness, where John O'Groats now stands. The family multiplied as the years passed and by the mid-sixteenth century there were eight different proprietors with the name of de Groot, including Jan. They held an annual feast to celebrate their landing in Scotland and unfortunately at one of these functions a dispute arose over precedence in the family. This manifested itself in an argument over who should sit at the head of the table. Jan, older and wiser than his counterparts, foresaw a bitter feud erupting. He called a truce for a year, and assured his family that by the next anniversary celebration he would have found a solution. During the intervening year Jan built a symmetrical eight-sided house, with eight doors and an eight-sided table inside. At the next anniversary he and the other seven could enter by their own door and sit at their own side of the table. As there was now no head to the table, further argument was eliminated. This unusual house became known as Jan de Groot's House and the name was soon applied to the whole village. The ferry service was run by the de Groot family for 250 years and the name of the village eventually evolved into John O'Groats.

I tried to decipher the oddly-shaped inscriptions on Jan de Groot's tombstone. It stood defensively with its back to the wall of the church where the Queen Mother worships when residing at the Castle of Mey. The prolific letters almost tumbled into each other, so closely-packed were they. A more conventional inscription on the base revealed that the tombstone had been removed from its original position, which was under the church floor. Its present site was probably chosen to protect it from the worst of the ferocious squalls of the Pentland Firth. Before leaving the historic place I enjoyed an admirable view across the bay to rock-strewn St John's Point, where those rocky bastions, the Men of May reside.

Throughout the final leg of my journey I could not avoid noticing the significant number of hollow, deserted crofts and here was no exception. These sad harbingers of change reflect the transition affecting much of Scotland's north coast. Old industries are receding and many young people are leaving to find regular employment elsewhere, as Angus had highlighted at Tongue. I tried to push such sobering thoughts aside for celebration was imminent.

My excitement growing by the minute, I strode past the huddle of crofts at Huna, acutely aware that there were only two miles remaining. The suspense was agonising for I imagined that John O'Groats would appear around each subsequent bend in the road. At last it lay before me, a scattering of farms and whitewashed cottages with a cluster of houses at its centre. Rolling, fertile farmland stretched from the ocean to the distant moorland, where civilisation yielded to sombre vastness. Sheep and cattle flecked rich pastures which mingled with fields of waving wheat and barley.

Why was I surprised by a vista that is so typical of the north-east corner of Britain? Had I been expecting something unique of this last outpost? Over many miles I had carried a mental picture of John O'Groats that had not materialised at my moment of triumph. How often is the actual different from the imagined.

Dismissing this idle reflection, I ticked off the remaining few hundred yards as I approached the hub of the village. Only the sound of the wind greeted my arrival. Where were the imagined crowds? Waving flags and blaring music were conspicuous by their absence. Life went quietly on around the Post Office and village store. No-one gave me a second glance and I felt a tremendous urge to kick a nearby pile of peat in my frustration. Then I saw the sign indicating the John O'Groats House Hotel, craft shops and museum that lie half a mile away by the harbour. What a fool I was. I had not reached the finishing point. That was where I would receive my tumultuous welcome.

I galloped down to the shore to find the crowd that I was seeking. However, the throng of visitors had commercial interests in mind rather than welcoming exultant walkers. They flitted around a swathe of tarmac and disappeared into the John O'Groats craft workshop or the nearby souvenir shops. The inanimate figure of Eric the Viking welcomed them to the workshop complex. Had he been alive, poor Eric would have reeled at the startling transformation of his surroundings since the arrival of his ancestors many centuries ago. The workshops and adjoining shops offered unlimited goods ranging from glassware and knitwear to satin-craft and furniture.

I was disconcerted by the worshippers of Mammon who should have been féting my arrival instead of pursuing earthly goods. Did no-one care that I had covered 550 miles to reach here? Only Wainwright might have cared and he was nowhere to be seen. Sic Transit Gloria, as the saying goes.

The sight of a traditional whitewashed fisherman's cottage on the periphery of the swarm raised my dented spirits. A prominent sign at its door broadcast that the building was the famous Last House and that it contained a folk museum. More faithfully portraying the original character of the village, it brought home to me that I had reached the end of the road. Wishing to share my achievement I realised that there was no Maurice to slap me on the back and pump my hand as he had done at Robin Hood's Bay on our completion of Wainwright's Coast to Coast Walk.

I hurried to an adjacent hill upon which perches the celebrated signpost, overlooking the harbour and the Pentland Firth. It was a thrill to touch the post where countless completions of the 874 mile cross-country marathons have been recorded. No-one paid any heed to me. Local inhabitants are all too familiar with the regular stream of arrivals from, or departures to, Lands End and visitors were busy taking photographs for the family album. I basked alone in the thrill of my achievement at the spot where hopefuls depart for the tip of Cornwall, some in every conceivable mode of conveyance from rickshaws to bathtubs.

My eyes eventually lit upon the John O'Groats House Hotel, which some believe is the true emblem of the village. It has dominated the grassy cliff-top since its opening by the Prince of Wales in 1874. Little changed over the years it still boasts an octagonal tower built on the style of Jan de Groot's House. An oasis of permanence amidst a desert of change, it caused a public outcry when the first of its recent purchasers, Peter de Savary, unveiled an abortive scheme to demolish it and rebuild it as the flagship hotel of the northern Highlands.

The present owner, Kevin Leach, appreciates its olde-worlde charm, but also recognises its potential. He puts the dilemma of John O'Groats in a nutshell when he says that people are moving out of the area through lack of employment at a time when tourism is a growing area of work creation. This opportunity, he feels, should be harnessed by carrying through long-dormant plans for attracting visitors. Whatever the future holds, I hope it benefits John O'Groats.

My story is almost complete, but a final tribute to my companions, real and in spirit, should be paid. To Maurice, who's humour and friendship made the section from Inversnaid to Shiel Bridge so enjoyable. To John Hillaby, whose *Journey Through Britain* captured my imagination. Finally to Wainwright, the prime-mover in my tackling the walk. He accompanied me through the medium of his splendid *Wainwright in Scotland*. I was able to re-live the journeys he so lovingly described and see at first hand many of the book's delightful illustrations.

Let me conclude with an amusing episode that took place at the farmhouse where I stayed on the final evening. It seemed a fitting climax to my journey. After supper I joined the Gill family and their dog in the cosy sitting room. I was asked if I minded listening to a tape of Pavarotti, because it was a great favourite with the dog. Eyebrows raised, I told them to carry on. As the strains of the great tenor filled the room, they were accompanied by the enthusiastic howls of the dog who sang along with his idol. Amazed by an opera-loving dog, I was tickled to see that the Gills were alive with the sound of music.